JONAH IN THE SHADOWS OF EDEN

INDIANA STUDIES IN BIBLICAL LITERATURE
Herbert Marks, editor

JONAH

in the

SHADOWS OF EDEN

YITZHAK BERGER

INDIANA UNIVERSITY PRESS

Bloomington & Indianapolis

This book is a publication of

Indiana University Press
Office of Scholarly Publishing
Herman B Wells Library 350
1320 East 10th Street
Bloomington, Indiana 47405 USA

iupress.indiana.edu

∞ The paper used in this publication meets
the minimum requirements of the
American National Standard for Informa-
tion Sciences — Permanence of Paper for
Printed Library Materials, ANSI
Z39.48-1992.

Manufactured in the United States of
America

Library of Congress Cataloging-in-
Publication Data

Names: Berger, Yitzhak, author.
Title: Jonah in the shadows of Eden /
    Yitzhak Berger.
Description: Bloomington ; Indianapolis :
    Indiana University Press, [2016] | ?2016 |
    Series: Indiana studies in biblical
    literature | Includes bibliographical
    references and index.
Identifiers: LCCN 2015047498 | ISBN
    9780253021298 (cloth : alk. paper)
Subjects: LCSH: Bible. Jonah—
    Criticism, interpretation, etc. |
    Bible. Jonah—Theology. |
    Paradise—Judaism.
Classification: LCC BS1605.52 .B47 2016 |
    DDC 224/.9206—dc23 LC record
    available at http://lccn.loc.
    gov/2015047498

1 2 3 4 5   21 20 19 18 17 16

To our children
Racheli, Sara, Tehilla, Baruch Meir, Breindy, Tova, and Batsheva

עץ חיים היא למחזיקים בה

You cast me into the deep waters in the heart of the seas,
A river surrounding me.

Jonah 2:4

This refers to the famous river that goes forth from Eden
from beneath the Tree of Life.
It surrounded me and gave me life.

Rabbi Moses Alshekh, sixteenth century

CONTENTS

ACKNOWLEDGMENTS

I AM DEEPLY grateful to Professor Benjamin Sommer, whose comments helped me improve the book's presentation significantly. I also thank the many individuals at Indiana University Press and elsewhere who helped guide the book through the publication process, enhancing it along the way.

As I completed my last substantial revision, I learned of the passing of my mentor and teacher Rabbi Aharon Lichtenstein, head of Yeshivat Har Etzion, where my interest in biblical studies grew in a pivotal way. An advocate of the literary study of the Bible already in the early 1960s (see his essay cited in the bibliography), Rabbi Lichtenstein devoted his life to studying and teaching the rabbinic tradition, his legendary brilliance matched only by the wholesomeness of his character. His legacy and inspiration will endure.

When other topics beckoned, my study partner Menachem Leff tolerated my seemingly endless musings on Jonah. I thank him for his patience and encouragement.

Above all, I am indebted to my family. My parents, Pearl and Professor David Berger, and my parents-in-law, Pearl and Carmi Schwartz, continue to assist me in ways that cannot be measured. My father also offered many helpful comments at various stages of the work. My children, to whom I dedicate the book, showed remarkable patience while I worked on the project, and are a source of boundless joy. I pray that the final product will enhance their appreciation of the Bible and its richness.

As for my wife Ditza, her devotion to me and to the family transcends description. If that were not enough, she also made a crucial observation on the text of Jonah that sparked this entire project. If the book contains other worthy insights, I regard them to be, much like Ditza herself, a gift from heaven.

ABBREVIATIONS

<table>
<tr><td>AB</td><td>Anchor Bible</td></tr>
<tr><td>AJBI</td><td>Annual of the Japanese Biblical Institute</td></tr>
<tr><td>AOTC</td><td>Abingdon Old Testament Commentaries</td></tr>
<tr><td>ASOR</td><td>American Schools of Oriental Research</td></tr>
<tr><td>ATD</td><td>Alte Testament Deutsch</td></tr>
<tr><td>ATSAT</td><td>Arbeiten zu Text und Sprache im Alten Testament</td></tr>
<tr><td>BBET</td><td>Beiträge zur biblischen Exegese und Theologie</td></tr>
<tr><td>BDB</td><td>Brown–Driver–Briggs Hebrew and English Lexicon of the Old Testament</td></tr>
<tr><td>BEATAJ</td><td>Beiträge zur Erforschung des Alten Testaments und des antiken Judentum</td></tr>
<tr><td>Bib</td><td>Biblica</td></tr>
<tr><td>BibInt</td><td>Biblical Interpretation</td></tr>
<tr><td>BINS</td><td>Biblical Interpretation Series</td></tr>
<tr><td>BJS</td><td>Brown Judaic Studies</td></tr>
<tr><td>BN</td><td>Biblische Notizen</td></tr>
<tr><td>BT</td><td>Bible Translator</td></tr>
<tr><td>BTCB</td><td>Brazos Theological Commentary on the Bible</td></tr>
<tr><td>BTB</td><td>Biblical Theology Bulletin</td></tr>
<tr><td>BZAW</td><td>Beihefte zur Zeitschrift für die alttestamentliche Wissenschaft</td></tr>
<tr><td>CAT</td><td>Commentaire de l'Ancien Testament</td></tr>
<tr><td>CBQ</td><td>Catholic Biblical Quarterly</td></tr>
<tr><td>CBQMS</td><td>Catholic Biblical Quarterly Monograph Series</td></tr>
<tr><td>CBR</td><td>Currents in Biblical Research</td></tr>
</table>

CC	Continental Commentary
CHANE	Culture and History of the Ancient Near East
CTJ	*Calvin Theological Journal*
CurBS	*Currents in Research: Biblical Studies*
EOS	Editions Sankt Ottilien
FAT	Forschungen zum Alten Testament
FRLANT	Forschungen zur Religion und Literatur des Alten Testament
GBS	Guides to Biblical Scholarship
HALOT	*Hebrew and Aramaic Lexicon of the Old Testament*
HAR	*Hebrew Annual Review*
HSM	Harvard Semitic Monographs
ICC	International Critical Commentary
IDB	*Interpreter's Dictionary of the Bible*
Int	*Interpretation*
ISBE	*International Standard Bible Encyclopedia*
ISBL	Indiana Studies in Biblical Literature
JAJSup	Journal of Ancient Judaism Supplement Series
JANER	*Journal of Ancient Near Eastern Religions*
JBL	*Journal of Biblical Literature*
JETS	*Journal of the Evangelical Theological Society*
JHS	*Journal of Hebrew Scriptures*
JPS	Jewish Publication Society
JQR	*Jewish Quarterly Review*
JNSL	*Journal of Northwest Semitic Languages*
JSOT	*Journal for the Study of the Old Testament*
JSOTSup	Journal for the Study of the Old Testament Supplement Series
KAT	Kommentar zum Alten Testament
LHBOTS	Library of Hebrew Bible / Old Testament Studies
NAC	New American Commentary
NICOT	New International Commentary on the Old Testament
NJPS	New Jewish Publication Society Translation
OTE	*Old Testament Essays*
OTG	Old Testament Guides
OTL	Old Testament Library

OTS	Oudtestamentische Studiën
RB	*Revue Biblique*
SBL	Society of Biblical Literature
SBLSymS	Society of Biblical Literature Symposium Series
SBS	Stuttgarter Bibelstudien
SHBC	Smyth & Helwys Bible Commentary
SJOT	*Scandinavian Journal of the Old Testament*
SPOT	Studies on Personalities of the Old Testament
SSU	Studia Semitica Upsaliensia
StudBib	Studia Biblica
TOTC	Tyndale Old Testament Commentaries
TynBul	*Tyndale Bulletin*
VT	*Vetus Testamentum*
VTSup	Vetus Testamentum Supplement Series
WBC	Word Biblical Commentary
ZAW	*Zeitschrift für die Alttestamentliche Wissenschaft*

A NOTE TO THE READER

THIS STUDY OFFERS a new reading of the book of Jonah that draws on cumulative, often interlocking evidence. To keep the presentation clear and simple, I allow the argument to unfold gradually. As a result, many observations do not show their full force immediately. A similar point obtains regarding method: my appeals to certain subtle literary devices – such as allusion by way of phonetic analogy – gain increasing cogency as suggestive examples accumulate. It will be helpful, therefore, for the reader to bear this in mind when encountering such literary devices early on.

To make the study more accessible, I have chosen not to provide an expansive introduction on methodology. Because I invoke a wide variety of literary techniques – including inner-biblical allusion, multiplicity of meaning, and several types of wordplay – a detailed discussion of method, especially at the beginning, would have presented an obstacle for many readers. It would also have begged the real question: does the author of Jonah, when all is said and done, employ these techniques in the ambitious way that I claim? The true test of this lies in my analysis itself, which yields mutually confirming conclusions that best substantiate the validity of the method. I anticipate, accordingly, that the reader's assent will depend not on detached methodological argument, but on the suggestive convergence of the study's results.

In the first chapter, therefore, I provide just a brief account of my broader methodological premises, with a measure of elaboration in some lengthy endnotes. This decision, I hope, has facilitated a more succinct, concrete, and lucid presentation, one that will contribute meaningfully to the interpretation of this widely cherished book of the Bible.

JONAH IN THE SHADOWS OF EDEN

Escape to Eden

THESIS: JONAH'S PURSUIT OF EDEN

This study advances one core thesis. In the book that bears his name, the prophet Jonah, profoundly troubled by God's response to the sins of humanity, persists in an escapist quest for an idyllic, Eden-like existence. Repeatedly, however, just when Jonah thinks he has attained such an existence, he finds himself banished from it. Eventually, therefore, he must confront the stark realities that provoke his moral indignation.

Crucially, the story gives rise to two opposite understandings of the prophet's defiant stance. In one reading, a moralistic Jonah resists providing an opportunity for salvation to the sinful population of Nineveh and instead seeks out an Edenic realm that tolerates no imperfection. By contrast, according to a second intended meaning, a pacifist Jonah shrinks from pronouncing doom on the Assyrian city and undertakes an escape toward a blissful world that contains no suffering. Taken together, these two readings yield a single, encompassing message: the Lord, by denying the prophet's quest for Eden, shuns the escapism born of either extreme reaction to sin and its consequences. Rather, the flawed conduct of human beings is inevitable, and both forgiveness and the threat of punishment play necessary roles in the divine response to human iniquity.[1]

Methodological Premises

This thesis draws on two oft-noted features of the work: allusion to other biblical texts and multiplicity of meaning. The text of Jonah, I argue, generates a remarkable array of inner-biblical connections, especially to Eden-related material.[2] These connections, in turn, provide the foundation for a sustained multivalent reading of the story.

My analysis of the book rests on several assumptions:

- The author of Jonah crafted the story with meticulous care, targeting an audience capable of nuanced literary analysis.[3]
- Biblical texts may feature a complex web of meaningful allusions to earlier material.[4]
- Thematic, lexical, and even phonetic parallels may help produce such allusions.[5]
- In works of this kind, the broader story – not just individual motifs and formulations – may give rise to multiple meanings.[6]

All these assumptions draw on legitimate precedent. More important, as a basis for examining the text of Jonah, they yield an expansive set of striking, mutually confirming results, solutions to numerous long-standing problems in the text, and explanations for nearly all of the book's distinctive formulations. Indeed, both my argument and the premises that sustain it find increasing confirmation as the discussion progresses; and we encounter consistent, highly suggestive indications of the author's methods for producing meaning. This collective evidence, I contend, provides ample support for the thesis that I advocate.[7]

Structure of the Book's Presentation

This study takes the following form. In this chapter, I endorse the proposal that Jonah pursues, or gratefully inhabits, a variety of Edenic sanctuaries.[8] Significantly, I offer a fundamentally new and much expanded version of that proposal, whereby the prophet's quest for a paradisiacal existence occupies a central place in the story. In chapter 2, I provide evidence of Jonah's moral perfectionism, including some new important observations, and I advance a reading of Jonah 3–4 that fits this standard conception of the prophet's attitude. This part of the presentation, moreover, features some additional noteworthy evidence that Jonah is seeking

Eden. In chapter 3, the most innovative part of the study, I make the case for a pacifist Jonah who resists proclaiming destruction on Nineveh – an interpretation that complements the more common, moralistic understanding of his motives. In chapter 4, I provide an original analysis of Jonah's prayer inside the fish, one that accords with the book's Eden theme and fits both readings of the story. Finally, in chapter 5, I present some supplementary proposals that emerge from my interpretation of the book, including a novel, comprehensive explanation of the text's deployment of divine names.

A TARSHISH-BOUND SHIP
AND THE GARDEN OF GOD

Eden, Tarshish, and the Divine Mountain

In the story of Jonah, the prophet seeks out and/or occupies numerous locations that, in one way or another, provide refuge. All these locations, moreover, evoke suggestive associations with a divine abode reminiscent of Eden.

In the book's opening scene, Jonah flees in the direction of Tarshish. The word "Tarshish," in addition to serving as a place-name, denotes one of several precious stones that, according to the prophet Ezekiel, endow the Garden of Eden with its majestic splendor (Ezek 28:13).[9] As a literary motif, in fact, Tarshish is aptly characterized as a "distant paradise" containing an abundance of riches – its legendary wealth comparable to that Edenic grandeur described by Ezekiel.[10] When Jonah heads toward Tarshish, the possibility thus immediately arises that he seeks to inhabit this type of realm.

Subsequently, when a storm threatens the Tarshish-bound ship, the fleeing prophet descends to the *yarkĕtê hassĕpînâ*; that is, the "nethermost part of the vessel" (Jonah 1:5). Elsewhere in this passage, the text consistently refers to the ship by the standard term *'ŏniyyâ* (1:3–5). By contrast, *sĕpînâ* occurs just this one time in the entire Bible. The distinctive phrase *yarkĕtê hassĕpînâ*, in turn, evokes an association with the more familiar expression *yarkĕtê ṣāpôn*, "the uppermost reaches of Zaphon."[11]

Zaphon, a mountain to the north of Israel, represented a divine abode in the ancient period.[12] Accordingly, Zaphon in the Bible signifies either a heavenly divine location ("I will rise up to the heavens. . . . I will sit on the mountain of [divine] assembly, in the *yarkĕtê ṣāpôn*"; Isa 14:13) or the sacred mountain in Jerusalem ("Mount Zion, *yarkĕtê ṣāpôn*"; Ps 48:3).[13] The divine mountain, for its part, constitutes a "secure, paradisiacal" location, one that Ezekiel, in that same context, likens to "the garden of God" (Ezek 28:13–14).[14] Indeed, based on biblical and comparative evidence, scholars characterize the Garden of Eden as "an archetypal sanctuary, a place where God dwells and where man should worship him." Correspondingly, the Israelite temple on Mount Zion "is identified with the primeval hill, paradise, the cosmic mountain."[15] In conjunction, then, with Jonah's quest to reach Tarshish, his boarding of a Zaphon-like ship and entry into its deepest part (*yarkĕtê hassĕpînâ*) begin to generate meaningful evidence that our protagonist yearns for an Eden-like existence.

The Edenic Kingdom of Tyre and Imperiled Ships of Tarshish

Ezekiel invokes imagery of the Edenic divine mountain in order to depict the magnificence of the coastal city of Tyre. That wider prophecy on Tyre, in fact, concludes a lengthy series of speeches that acknowledge its glory, only to proclaim impending doom on the city and its arrogant leadership (Ezek 26:1–28:19). Crucially, this sequence features striking parallels to the story of Jonah, which bear significance that remains vastly underappreciated.[16]

Ezekiel 27 begins with a description of the resplendence of Tyre. The chapter reaches a turning point when ships of Tarshish, which enabled Tyre to amass riches "in the heart of the seas" (*bĕlēb yammîm*; Ezek 27:25), are broken apart (*šbr*) by an east wind (*rûaḥ qādîm*; 27:26). As a result, the city's wealth descends into the sea along with many of its people, including sailors (*mallāḥayik*) and ship pilots (*ḥōbĕlāyik*; 27:27). Other seafarers then cry out (*wĕyizʿāqû*), roll in ashes (*ʾēper*), and don sackcloth (*śaqqîm*; 27:28–31), among other expressions of grief. These behaviors resemble a reaction foreseen by the prophet in the previous chapter, where coastal rulers, witnessing the destruction of Tyre, descend from their thrones (*kisʾôtām*), remove their royal robes, "clothe themselves in trembling," and sit on the ground (26:16). In that context, Ezekiel envisions the city engulfed by the Deep (*tĕhôm*) and submerged in mounting waters (26:19).

Parallel motifs in Jonah immediately come to mind. A ship carrying our prophet toward Tarshish threatens to break apart (*šbr*) during a storm (Jonah 1:3–4) – although an east wind (*rûaḥ qādîm*) appears only later in the story (4:8). The ship's sailors (*mallāḥîm*) then cry out (*wayyizʿăqû*; 1:5), the chief pilot (*ḥōbēl*) challenges Jonah (1:6), and eventually the prophet descends into "the heart of the seas" (*lĕbab yammîm*; 2:4) where the waters and the Deep (*tĕhôm*; 2:6) engulf him. When Jonah at last carries out his mission, the Ninevites, among other demonstrations of repentance, don sackcloth (*śaqqîm*; 3:5, 8). And their king, reminiscent of the coastal rulers who react to the fall of Tyre, rises from his throne (*kisʾô*), removes his royal cloak, dons sackcloth (*śaq*), and sits on ashes (*ʾēper*; 3:6). Several expressions cited here that recall terminology used in Ezekiel, including *lēb/lĕbab yammîm*, the root *zʿq*, and the nouns *mallāḥ* and *ḥōbēl*, stand out in at least one of the two texts by appearing multiple times. Notably, *mallāḥ* and *ḥōbēl* occur nowhere in the Bible except in Jonah and Ezekiel 27.[17]

Significantly, the resemblance between the actions of the king of Nineveh and those of the coastal rulers in Ezekiel – which in both cases entail rising from a throne/thrones, removing royal garb, donning sackcloth/trembling, and sitting on ashes/the ground – points strongly toward the purposefulness of the broader set of parallels.[18] The relevant verse in Ezekiel, after all, appears in a speech that stands apart from the prophet's later depiction of a sea storm, and this reaction of coastal rulers to the destruction of Tyre bears no intrinsic connection to any such tempest. Likewise, the actions of the king of Nineveh do not take place in the context of a sea storm. It seems hardly plausible, therefore, that the motifs common to our passage and Ezekiel's prophecies merely represent typical features of sea-storm texts. Almost certainly, the author of Jonah was working off this material in Ezekiel.

Recall, then, that in this sequence of prophecies, Ezekiel compares the glamorous Tyre – a kingdom supplied/signified by ships of Tarshish – to the divine mountain and the Garden of Eden.[19] If, accordingly, Jonah occupies a Tarshish-bound vessel that stands in parallel to those ships, this yields additional evidence that our protagonist seeks an Eden-like realm of the kind that Ezekiel describes.

Indeed, other features of the passage in Jonah confirm this connection and its proposed significance. After our prophet receives his instructions, we are told that he "arose to flee toward Tarshish away from the Lord, went down to Joppa (*yāpô*), found a ship going to Tarshish, provided its fare (*śĕkārāh*), and went down into it to go with them toward Tarshish away from the Lord" (Jonah 1:3). In this notably long-winded verse, two matters have defied easy explanation: the choice and specification of the port city of *yāpô*, and the presence of the clause "he provided its fare" (*wayyittēn śĕkārāh*).[20]

Consider, then, that when describing the beauty of Tyre and its leaders, Ezekiel employs the related roots *yph* and *ypʿ* a total of eight times, a concentration found nowhere else in Scripture.[21] Tyre declared itself "perfect in beauty (*yōpî*)" (Ezek 27:3), because its builders had "perfected [its] beauty (*yopyēk*)" (27:4) and its protectors succeeded in maintaining that "beauty" (*yopyēk*; 27:11). Nevertheless, the prophet affirms that foreigners will unleash their weapons on the "beauty" (*yĕpî*) of its ruler's wisdom and defile his "splendor" (*yipʿātekā*; 28:7). The doomed king of Tyre, moreover, was "perfect in beauty (*yōpî*)" (28:12), until his "beauty" (*yopyekā*) gave rise to arrogance and his "splendor" (*yipʿātekā*) corrupted his wisdom (28:17). Accordingly, Jonah's descent to *yāpô*, considered together with the parallels already seen, calls to mind this key terminology, suggesting that the prophet seeks to attain the idyllic beauty – of a kind facilitated/signified by ships of Tarshish – that characterizes the exquisitely Eden-like kingdom of Tyre.

As for Jonah having provided the *śākar* of the vessel ("*its* fare") – a formulation that, to many readers, has suggested a value beyond the cost of the prophet's own voyage – consider the familiar motif of *treasure-laden* ships of Tarshish, whose implications for our story have been almost entirely overlooked to date.[22] Of critical importance, *every* biblical reference to ships of Tarshish signals this luxuriant motif, none more emphatically than the one in Ezekiel 27.[23] In turn, the clause in Jonah "he provided its fare" (*wayyittēn śĕkārāh*), much like the place-name *yāpô*, gives rise to a highly consequential secondary meaning: in "stocking/providing [the vessel's] *śākar*," a fleeing Jonah, pursuing the idyllic realm that ships of Tarshish supply/signify, hastily stowed on the ship the *fortune* that it is designated to carry. The text therefore suggests that the prophet, seeking to escape toward the paradisiacal domain of Tarshish, started out in pursuit of that "beautiful" location (*yāpô*). Then, having found a vessel that was not simply "setting out/going to (*yōṣē't/hōleket*) Tarshish" but was "approaching (*bā'â*) Tarshish" – arguably, by implication, a vessel poised to *attain the status* of a "ship of Tarshish" – he eagerly invested it with that standing by placing on it the necessary riches (*śākār*) and then descended into it to enter (*lābō'*) the Eden-like realm that he craved.[24]

Furthermore, the word *śākār* bears a phonetic resemblance to *shr* ("trade/do business"), which likewise stands as a key term in Ezekiel 27.[25] The root *shr* appears six times in that chapter in connection with the wealth supplied to Tyre, most prominently by Tarshish, and once more to denote foreign merchants foreseen reacting to the city's collapse (Ezek 27:12, 15–16, 18, 21, 36). This resonance helps confirm that Jonah, in providing the *śākār* of the vessel, was not merely paying his fare or even commissioning the whole voyage. Rather, the prophet endeavored to load the ship with resplendent treasures, of a kind worthy of the Eden-like city of Tyre and designated to be borne by ships of Tarshish.

Isaiah, Ships of Tarshish, and the Fall of Tyre

The association between *shr* and the opulence of Tyre finds confirmation in a prophecy on that kingdom found in Isaiah 23. As in the Ezekiel text, *shr* stands out as a keyword in Isaiah 23, appearing five times in connection with the bounty of Tyre (Isa 23:2–3, 8, 18) – a kingdom on the sea for which ships of Tarshish again stand as a prominent metaphor (23:1, 14). The association between the root *shr* and the Tarshish-supplied wealth of Tyre is thus not confined to just one prophetic speech. It becomes all the more likely, therefore, that the *śākār* stowed by Jonah on a Tarshish-bound ship is meant to evoke the phonetically similar *shr*.

More important, two additional connections to Isaiah 23 prove essential to a proper understanding of the passage in Jonah. Like the analogous prophecies in Ezekiel, the Isaiah text refers to prideful individuals in Tyre who will be humbled by the fall of the city. After all, the prophet affirms, it shall be God's design to "dishonor (*lĕhāqēl*) all the honored ones of the land" (Isa 23:9). It hardly seems coincidental that, in our own Tyre-recalling ship-of-Tarshish passage, we encounter the only other occurrence in the Bible of the word *lĕhāqēl*: "The sailors feared and cried out, each man to his god, and they hurled the items that were on the ship into the sea in order to get the weight off them (*lĕhāqēl mē'ălêhem*); but Jonah went down to the nethermost part of the vessel (*yarkĕtê hassĕpînâ*), and he lay down and went to sleep" (Jonah 1:5).

In this rather verbose account of the sailors' reaction to the storm, note first the long-winded phrase, "the items that were on the ship." Even if, to highlight the contrast with Jonah's conduct, the author deemed it necessary to recount not only the sailors' supplications but also their physical efforts to save the vessel, could the text not have stated merely that they hurled "items" (*kēlîm*) into the sea to lighten the load? Why instead does it say "*the* items" (*'et-hakkēlîm*), and why the explicit reference to the vessel? And in the next clause, do not the sailors wish to get the weight off the *ship*, not off "them"?

The explanation for this problematic wording, I submit, lies with the contents of this paradigmatic ship of Tarshish. The vessel's precious cargo, which promised to supply the God-defying, Tarshish-bound prophet with an Eden-like existence, instead helps instigate a tempest that threatens to take him down along with the crew. Consequently, seeking to avoid the fate of the Tyrian aristocrats whose honor, according to the passage in Isaiah, will be tragically negated (*lĕhāqēl*), the sailors prayerfully humble themselves before the divine, casting off *all* of the boat's extravagant contents ("*the* items that were on the ship"). In this way, they divest the *ship* of its luxuriant, Tarshish-like quality and renounce any involvement in their passenger's audacious quest for a paradisiacal domain ("to get the weight/honor off *them*").[26] Jonah, by contrast, dreamily pursues his utopian existence by proceeding to the *yarkĕtê hassĕpînâ*, a location that indeed symbolizes the Edenic *yarkĕtê ṣāpôn*.

In the ensuing dialogue between the sailors and Jonah, still another key term in Isaiah 23 helps resolve a challenging set of cruxes. The root *'br* ("cross over") occurs four times in the Isaiah passage, including three instances where the prophet directs an ironic, futile exhortation to the population of a crumbling Tyre: "Cross over (*'ibrû*) to Tarshish" (Isa 23:6); "Cross over (*'ibrî*) your land as the Nile" (23:10); "Arise, cross over (*'ibrî*) to Cyprus" (23:12).[27] The other instance of the root appears in the phrase *'ōbēr yām mil'ûk* (23:2), an opaque formulation that, according to numerous interpreters, in one way or another denotes seafarers setting out on a "mission" (*mĕlā'kâ*).[28] In part, this interpretation draws on a sea-storm text in Psalms (107:24–32) that describes sailors setting out on the waters to perform a "mission" (*mĕlā'kâ*), only to find themselves in mortal danger spawned by a violent tempest. Indeed, that passage in Psalms almost certainly bears a connection, direct or otherwise, to our Jonah text: among other shared terms, both accounts use the rare verb *štq* to denote the eventual "quieting" of the storm (Ps 107:30; Jonah 1:11–12).[29]

Observe, then, that when the lottery ominously falls on Jonah, the crew asks him a series of questions: "Tell us, please, you on account of whom this disaster has befallen us! What is your mission (*mĕla'ktĕkā*), and from where are you coming? What is your land, and of what people are you?" (Jonah 1:8). In the prophet's response, however, only one clause, "I am a Hebrew (*'ibrî*)" (1:9), seems to address these questions: it identifies his people and perhaps conveys, if only by implication, that his land and the origin of his journey are both Israel.[30] Yet the sailors' first question – "What is your mission?" – seems to go entirely unanswered. Furthermore, the remainder of Jonah's reply, in which he affirms his fear of the Israelite deity, bears no apparent relevance to the queries presented to him.

Once we recognize, however, that this chapter alludes to Isaiah 23, then Jonah's affirmation "I am an *'ibrî*" takes on a new, secondary sense. The word *'ibrî*, which looks and sounds identical to two of the four occurrences of *'br* in the Isaiah text, may now denote "one who crosses over" – specifically a seeker of a paradisiacal domain such as Tyre who, in the face of the Lord's punitive wrath, fruitlessly attempts to attain/retain a coveted idyllic environment.[31] The prophet, then, does respond to the sailors' first inquiry, however subtly: my mission (*mĕlā'kâ*), he states, is to cross over (*'br*) to Tarshish and arrive at an Edenic, Tyre-like realm, because I am frightened by the designs of the prodigious God of Israel.[32]

In support of this interpretation, consider the serious difficulty generated by the next verse. The sailors, we are informed, continued to confront Jonah "because they knew that he was fleeing from the Lord, for he had told them" (Jonah 1:9). This awkward affirmation, which appears to suggest that the prophet – at some unspecified point – had apprised the sailors of his objective, has long presented a problem.[33] The reading set forth here, however, offers an elegant solution: in the brief exchange recounted in the text, Jonah indeed "told them," however obliquely, that he was fearfully running away from the Israelite God by crossing over toward Tarshish. The narrator thus provides a charitable hint that, beneath the surface, we ought to look hard for that information in the multivalent reply uttered by the Eden-seeking prophet.[34]

What is more, the crew's recognition that Jonah is pursuing Eden both validates and helps explain still another proposed correlation. Reacting to the prophet's remarks, the sailors exclaim *mah-zō't 'āśîtā* ("What have you done?"; Jonah 1:10), the same question that God poses to Eve after she partakes of the forbidden tree (*mah-zō't 'āśît*; Gen 3:13).[35] Indeed, only in these two instances does this expression – regardless of the form taken by the verb – end abruptly, amounting to the entire challenge posed by the questioner. Consider, then, that according to our approach, Jonah's initiative, much like that of Eve, provokes an apparently lethal divine response that will deny him the idyllic existence that he craves. It is fitting, therefore, that the prophet's panicked shipmates, fearing the consequences of his unauthorized quest for Eden, confront him with the ominous words *mah-zō't 'āśîtā*. After all, in the biblical Eden story, it is this very fateful expression that God utters shortly before banishing Eve from the paradisiacal garden.

Nineveh and the Edenic Kingdom of Tyre

Finally, we return briefly to the prophecies on Tyre in the book of Ezekiel. Ezekiel's portrait of the devastation of Tyre, we have seen, parallels the account of Jonah's ill-fated journey. Recall, however, that the reaction of coastal rulers to Tyre's fall corresponds to something else entirely: the humble conduct of the king of Nineveh, which triggers the *redemption* of the Assyrian city. Might it be, then, that the salvation of Nineveh stands in pointed contrast to the collapse of Tyre? And if, in fact, Nineveh shows a correspondence to Tyre, might it bear any relevance to the central question of Jonah's motivations?

The opening prophecy in Ezekiel 28 supports this apparent connection between Nineveh and Tyre. The prophet affirms that the ruler of Tyre became arrogant, seeing himself as occupying "the seat of God in the heart of the seas" (Ezek 28:2). Indeed, Ezekiel repeatedly states that this leader considers himself a god and that he perceives his heart to be like "the heart of God" (28:2, 6, 9). Foreign invaders, therefore, will humble him and bring about his demise (28:7–10).[36]

This ruler, because of his vanity and divine pretensions, bears a similarity to the sinning Ninevites and their king. Consider that our story features a recurring motif whereby ostensibly "great" forces are subject to the control of the biblical God.[37] Thus, it is the Lord who sends a "great wind" that generates a "great storm" (Jonah 1:4) and who directs the actions of a "great fish" (2:1). By the same token, the text consistently refers to Nineveh as a "great city" (1:2; 3:2–3; 4:11), only to underscore that its population, including its "great/powerful" citizens, must humble themselves before the divine to escape destruction (3:5, 7).

Observe, then, that right before Jonah relays his prophecy, the text calls the self-important Nineveh not merely a "great city" (*'îr-gĕdôlâ*) but "a city of God-like greatness/magnitude" (*'îr-gĕdôlâ lē'lōhîm*; Jonah 3:3). This expanded formulation suggests that, at this crucial juncture, the haughtiness of the Ninevites has borne the presumption that they have attained divine stature.[38] Taken in light of our story's many references to Ezekiel's prophecies on Tyre, the phrase thereby places Nineveh in parallel to that extravagant kingdom, which Ezekiel condemns precisely because of the godlike pretenses of its leadership. At this very point, accordingly, the analogy between the two arrogant cities underscores how Nineveh manages to elude disaster by humbling itself (3:5–10). Whereas coastal rulers, in the wake of the fall of Tyre, display grief by descending from their thrones and shedding their royal garb, the king of Nineveh, by taking similar action, shows a capitulation to God that forestalls the liquidation of his city. Consequently, Jonah's affirmation that Nineveh will be "upended" (*nehpâket*; 3:4) becomes realized not by the city's annihilation, but by a sharp reversal of its character and fate.[39]

If Nineveh thus bears an analogy to Tyre, it warrants asking if the Assyrian city likewise possesses an Eden-like quality. Might Jonah, in other words, run away from one idyllic location toward the direction of another? More specifically, might our prophet's quest for a prototypically Edenic realm arise, in some way, from his reluctance to engage a paradisiacal yet sinful Nineveh? Crucially, our story's inner-biblical allusions – to Ezekiel and beyond – point toward a decidedly affirmative answer to these questions. The Eden-like character of Nineveh, in fact, finds immediate confirmation as we move past Jonah's voyage on a Tarshish-bound ship and extend our inquiry to the rest of his paradisiacal sanctuaries.

A PLANT, A FISH, AND THE GARDEN OF EDEN

Nineveh, the Qîqāyôn, and the Trees of Eden

Shortly after the presentation of Ezekiel's oracles on Tyre, we encounter his vision of the downfall of Egypt. That nation, the prophet affirms, will ultimately descend to Sheol, much like the kingdom of Assyria before it (Ezek 31:18). In fact, the vast majority of that prophecy depicts the collapse of Assyria. Invoking Eden on four occasions (31:8, 9, 16, 18), Ezekiel states that, initially, Assyria resembled a cedar of Lebanon that towered above the trees of the Garden of God. The arrogance of the empire, however, brought about its fall into oblivion.

As in the case of Tyre, Ezekiel employs the root *yph* numerous times to underscore Assyria's Eden-like beauty. The metaphorical cedar, he declares, which displayed "beautiful branches" (*yĕpê 'ānāp*; Ezek 31:3), was "beautiful (*wayyîp*) in its greatness" (31:7), and the other trees of Eden failed to approach the cedar's "beauty" (*yopyô*; 31:8) and could only envy how God had made it so "beautiful" (*yāpê*; 31:9).[40] The prophet, furthermore, employs the root *gdl* four times to underscore the haughtiness epitomized by Assyria (31:2, 4, 7, 18), reminiscent of our text's repeated use of *gdl* ("great") to signal the arrogance of Nineveh.

This grandiose, Eden-like depiction of Assyria, taken together with Nineveh's similarities to the paradisiacal Tyre, supports the proposed analogy between Nineveh and the divine garden. Of critical importance, moreover, consider a striking, recently discovered correlation between the cedar that symbolizes Assyria and the *qîqāyôn*-plant that provides shade to Jonah as he gazes toward Nineveh (Jonah 4:6).[41] Much like the *qîqāyôn*, this magnificent cedar, which provides shade to its surroundings (Ezek 31:6, 12, 17), is eventually attacked and destroyed (31:10–12). Consequently, like our prophet who, by means of the rare verb *'lp* (עלף), is said to feel faint (*wayyit'allāp*; ויתעלף) after the plant shrivels (Jonah 4:8), the leaves on the trees shielded by the cedar proceed to wither (*'ulpê*; עלפה) in the wake of the great tree's downfall (Ezek 31:15).

Indeed, the passage in Jonah reinforces this correlation by referencing Ezekiel 17, which recounts the fate of a young plant derived from a branch of a cedar of Lebanon. In that context, Ezekiel describes how an east wind (*rûaḥ qādîm*) causes the shriveling (*ybš*) of the plant, with the root *ybš* appearing five times in the space of two verses (Ezek 17:9–10). Likewise, then, the plant in our story, itself bearing an equivalence to a cedar of Lebanon, leaves Jonah exposed to the elements when it, too, proceeds to shrivel (*ybš*). And subsequently, it is none other than an east wind (*rûaḥ qādîm*) that causes the prophet to grow weak.[42]

Thus, our author, in invoking the motif of Nineveh, was almost certainly working with Ezekiel's Edenic depiction of the cedar that represents Assyria. Simultaneously, the plant that brings delight to Jonah, because of its correlation with that paradisiacal tree, itself suggests a correspondence to the divine garden.[43] It appears, therefore, that our prophet indeed shuns an Eden-like Nineveh in favor of a comparably paradisiacal domain. As we continue, then, to identify evidence of Jonah's quest for an Edenic existence – and, ultimately, to evaluate the significance of that quest – we should bear in mind our story's multifaceted deployment of this central Eden motif.

Jonah, Cain, and the Pursuit of Eden

The text of Jonah, just before it recounts the rise of the plant, generates parallels to the story of Cain that merit far greater attention than they have drawn.[44] After Jonah fulfills his mission, he experiences anger (*wayyiḥar*; Jonah 4:1), much as Cain does when God refuses his offering (*wayyiḥar*; Gen 4:5). Subsequently, the Lord contests Jonah's indignation ("Are you really that angry?" [*hahêṭēb* (ההיטב) *ḥārâ lāk*;]; Jonah 4:4), recalling a similar divine challenge presented to Cain ("Why are you angry? . . . After all, if you improve . . ." [*lāmâ ḥārâ lāk . . . hălō' 'im-têṭîb* (תיטיב) . . .]; Gen 4:6–7).[45] Then, we learn that Jonah "went forth . . . and stationed himself east of the city" (Jonah 4:5), just as Cain "went forth . . . and stationed himself . . . east of Eden" (Gen 4:16).[46]

This sequence of parallels gives expression to a highly significant thematic correlation: both Jonah and Cain decline – each in his own way – to embrace the prospects offered by repentance. In turn, both men seek out a paradisiacal existence free of moral vicissitudes and calls for self-improvement, only to find this goal impossible to attain. Cain, for one, can move no closer to Eden than the location to its east, where the entrance to the garden stands hopelessly obstructed (Gen 3:24).[47] Jonah, for his part, who sits to the east of Nineveh, is denied his Edenic aspirations when the *qîqāyôn* – which, like the towering cedar in Ezekiel, bestows the Eden-like comforts of Assyria – shrivels to the point of inefficacy. Indeed, although the term *qîqāyôn* (קיקיון) is rightly said to play on the root *qy'* (קיא; "vomit") and the name *yônâ* (יונה; "Jonah"),[48] the second occurrence of the letter *qôp* (ק) helps generate a simultaneous resonance with the name *qayin* (קין; "Cain"): the plant, by effectively vomiting Jonah out of its blissful shade, recalls Cain's exclusion from the Garden of Eden.

Earlier in the story when Jonah flees toward Tarshish, moreover, we encounter key terminology that contributes to this analogy to Cain. The expression "away from/from the face of the Lord," which is invoked three times to describe Jonah's flight (Jonah 1:3, 10), appears likewise in Genesis (4:16), where we are told that Cain "went forth *away from the Lord* and stationed himself . . . east of Eden."[49] Now the verse in Jonah 4 ("Jonah went forth . . . and stationed himself east of the city") that parallels the line in Genesis could not incorporate the phrase "away from the Lord," because of the constraints of its context. Our author, employing a long-recognized technique in Jonah, thus divides the phraseology of the source-text and distributes it in disparate passages.[50] For example, whereas typically it is an east wind that breaks apart ships of Tarshish, our story uses other terminology to describe the storm that threatens the Tarshish-bound vessel (1:4). An east wind, by contrast, appears only in the final chapter of Jonah and in an entirely different context (4:8).

Similarly, then, the expression "away from the Lord" appears not in Jonah 4 where the prophet exits Nineveh toward a location to its east, but earlier in chapter 1 where our protagonist first moves in a direction away from that city. For no sooner does Jonah receive his initial instructions than, much like Cain, he defies the call of the God who encourages repentance and proceeds to seek, however fruitlessly, a blissful divine presence free of moral inadequacies and their disquieting ramifications.[51]

The Sukkâ, the Plant, and the Divine Garden

When Jonah arrives east of Nineveh and constructs a *sukkâ* ("shelter," of the root *skk*; Jonah 4:5), his action immediately bespeaks his longing for Eden. In numerous contexts, after all, this kind of structure stands as a symbol of divinely bestowed sanctuary. The Psalmist, for example, yearns for the Lord to shelter him in a *sukkâ*, so that he might eventually gain the upper hand on his advancing enemies (Ps 27:5). Moreover, when Ezekiel compares Tyre to an Edenic divine abode, he twice describes how its king – himself bedecked (*swk*) with precious stones – shielded (*skk*) the city like a cherub before being purged from its midst (Ezek 28:13–16). In keeping, then, with our book's technique of alluding to key terminology found in its source-texts – including this very sequence in Ezekiel – Jonah's *sukkâ* quite probably alludes to this key root *swk/skk*, which helps portray the overtly paradisiacal character of Tyre in Ezekiel's prophecy.

As for the *qîqāyôn*, two more proposed connections to Eden warrant mention. First, only when reporting the growth of the plant does our story use the exact phrase "the Lord God," with the word "God" (*'ĕlōhîm*) taking no special grammatical form. Consider, then, that this expression dominates in just one selection in the Bible: the account of Adam and Eve in the Garden of Eden (Gen 2–3).[52] Consequently, when our text affirms that "the Lord God appointed a *qîqāyôn* and raised it above Jonah," it brings to mind that account, in particular the assertion that "the Lord God planted a garden in the east of Eden" where he placed the first human being (Gen 2:8).

Second, Ancient Near Eastern iconography features multiple illustrations of a serpent or other symbol of Chaos attacking the Tree of Life. Indeed, when the biblical Eden story depicts a serpent instigating the expulsion from Eden, it employs a variation of that motif to impart its unique message. Observe, then, that likewise in our own text, a slithering creature attacks Jonah's plant and triggers the loss of his blissful shade. This scene thus not only evokes that standard image but also, together with other evidence, helps generate a specific analogy to the banishment of Adam and Eve from the paradisiacal garden.[53]

The Plant, the Fish, and Manna from Heaven

Next, we turn to a recently discovered correlation between the *qîqāyôn* and the manna in the wilderness. I shall demonstrate that this correlation yields immense significance for the meaning of Jonah 4. Significantly, moreover, it provides an important foundation for the Edenic symbolism of the fish that consumes our prophet.

In several ways, the episode of the *qîqāyôn* recalls the chapter immediately following the Song of the Sea, in which the Israelites leave portions of the manna (*mān*) uneaten or uncollected (Exod 16:20–21). First, our text features three occurrences of *wayĕman* (וימן ["he appointed"]; Jonah 4:6–8), a verb that resonates with the word *mān* (מן). Second, a worm and hot weather conditions assail Jonah's blissful comfort, the same elements that, each in the appropriate circumstance, spoil the manna that remains unconsumed.[54] Third, the word *wayyîbāš* ("and it dried up"; 4:7), which depicts the worm's effect on the plant, recalls the phonetically similar *wayyib'aš* ("and it became putrid") used to describe the worm-infested manna.[55]

This analogy between the *qîqāyôn* and the manna, considered in light of Jonah's pursuit of Eden, helps explain God's remark about the plant near the end of the book (Jonah 4:10). The plant, the Lord affirms, much like the manna, arrived on the scene without any human effort and did not last for more than one day. He implies, accordingly, that *enduring value cannot be attained by way of unearned gifts amassed in a day*.[56] The relentlessly bliss-seeking prophet, therefore, had no justification for lamenting the abrupt death of the *qîqāyôn*, the last one of his unmerited Edenic sanctuaries.

With this in mind, consider the one other occurrence of *wayĕman* in the story. At the beginning of chapter 2, when Jonah is drowning in the sea, we are told that the Lord "appointed" (*wayĕman*) a fish to swallow the prophet (Jonah 2:1). Now if the other three occurrences of this verb recall the manna, the possibility immediately arises that this occurrence does so as well. Might it be, then, that the fish, like the blissful plant, embodies a short-lived paradisiacal haven that Jonah wished to occupy indefinitely? Remarkably, the text yields highly suggestive evidence in favor of this unexpected conclusion. To appreciate this properly, however, it will be helpful to shift our attention briefly and consider a broader, widely acknowledged relationship between the story of Jonah and the early travails of Israel.

Jonah and the Exodus from Egypt

Whereas the *qîqāyôn* episode recalls the story of the manna, Jonah's rescue from the water corresponds to the preceding account of the Israelites' salvation at sea. His prayer of thanks, accordingly, invites an analogy to the Song of the Sea. Indeed, expressions in Jonah's poem such as *mĕṣûlâ* ("the deep waters"; Jonah 2:4), *lĕbab yammîm* ("the heart of the seas"; 2:4), *tĕhôm* ("the Deep"; 2:6), and *sûp* ("reeds"; 2:6) have drawn suitable comparisons to terminology in that earlier song (Exod 15:4–5, 8).[57] We might have expected, therefore, that the fleeing prophet would exhibit a consistent equivalence to the departing people of Israel. The text, however, with pointed irony, generates another set of parallels, whereby the Gentiles in the story bear an analogy to the Israelites and the recalcitrant Jonah corresponds to the God-defying Egyptians.

When the Israelites reach the Sea of Reeds, they fear (*wayyîrĕ'û*) and cry out (*wayyiṣ'ăqû*) to the Lord (Exod 14:10). In our book, by contrast, it is the imperiled sailors who fear (*wayyîrĕ'û*) and cry out (*wayyiz'ăqû*) to their gods, whereas the Israelite prophet descends to the *yarkĕtê hassĕpînâ* and goes to sleep (Jonah 1:5). Like the Israelites, moreover, who achieve salvation when the Egyptians are hurled into the sea (Exod 14:26–28; cf. 15:1), the crew in Jonah survives after the prophet is thrown overboard (Jonah 1:15). As a result, both the rescued Israelites and the sailors stand in awe of the Lord (*wayyîrĕ'û*) (Jonah 1:16; cf. 1:10; Exod 14:31) – unlike Jonah whose claim to be God-fearing (Jonah 1:9) stands at odds with his conduct. In addition, the text affirms that the Ninevites believed (*wayya'ămînû*) in God (3:5), whereas elsewhere in Scripture, the word *wayya'ămînû* occurs only where the Israelites react to their salvation at sea (Exod 14:31; Ps 106:12).[58]

Further, when the sailors challenge Jonah, a would-be analogy between the prophet and the Israelites ironically underscores his similarity to the Egyptians. The sailors, we are informed, said to the prophet, "What have you done?" (*mah-zō't 'āśîtā*), because they "knew (*yd'*) that he was escaping (*brḥ*) from the Lord, for he had told (*ngd*) them" (Jonah 1:10). Observe, then, that after the departure of the Israelites, "it was told (*ngd*) to the king of Egypt that the people had escaped (*brḥ*) . . . and [Pharaoh and his servants] said, 'What have we done?' (*mah-zō't 'aśînû*)" (Exod 14:5). That verse, moreover, follows God's affirmation that the Egyptians "will know (*yd'*) that I am the Lord" (14:4).

On the surface, this correlation does equate Jonah with the departing Israelites (*brḥ*), while the sailors seem to parallel the leaders of Egypt (*ngd*, *yd'*) who, using language much like that of the Tarshish-bound crew, ruefully exclaim, "What have we done?" (*mah-zō't 'aśînû*). Crucially, however, the sailors' similar-sounding cry of *mah-zō't 'āśîtā* features a pivotal difference: far from signifying any defiance of the Lord on *their* part, this exclamation, which places the verb in second-person form ("What have *you* done?"), suggests that it is Jonah who bears the equivalence to the fatefully intransigent Egyptian leadership. The sailors, by contrast, appropriately terrified of the God of Israel, will in the end transform their terror into inspiration, as their newly acquired "fear of the Lord," like that of the Israelites, yields a grateful expression of devotion to their divine savior (Jonah 1:16).

Yet, our prophet does show one genuine similarity to the people of Israel in that episode. Predictably, however, it does not relate to the Israelites' cries to God, fear of him, or belief in him. It concerns, instead, their defiant affirmation that they would rather have remained in Egypt than to follow the direction of the Lord.

When Jonah finally explains why he fled, he begins his remarks with the expression, "Was this not my word" (*hălô'-zê dĕbārî*; Jonah 4:2). Notably, the only similar biblical phrase appears in the first part of the Israelites' reaction when they reach the Sea of Reeds: "Was this not the word (*hălô'-zê haddābār*) that we spoke: 'Leave us alone and let us serve Egypt'?" (Exod 14:12). In the next verse, moreover, the prophet declares, "My dying would be better than my living" (*ṭôb môtî mēḥayyāy*; Jonah 4:3; cf. 4:8), thereby recalling the latter half of the Israelites' remarks: "because serving the Egyptians would be better for us than our dying in the wilderness" (*kî ṭôb lānû 'ăbōd 'et-miṣrayim mimmutēnû bammidbār*).[59] Thus, Jonah affirms that, much like the Israelites who wished to return to Egypt, he ran in the direction of Tarshish in pursuit of a better alternative.

Recall, then, that in a prophecy invoked by our story, Ezekiel draws a prominent comparison between the land of Egypt and the Eden-like kingdom of Assyria (Ezek 31:2, 18). Indeed, the book of Genesis likewise draws an analogy between Egypt and Eden (13:10): these two locations stand as prototypes for the bountiful Plain of the Jordan, which encompasses the affluent city of Sodom. Might we suggest, therefore, that Jonah, by comparing himself to the Israelites who sought to return to Egypt, expresses his idealization of the *Eden-like environment* that Egypt exemplifies? Furthermore, might the broader association between Jonah and the Egyptians underscore not just the prophet's defiance of God but also the *Edenic aspirations* that motivate his conduct?

The possibility that Jonah is invoking Eden when he alludes to the Israelites' remarks might initially seem remote. After all, when the Israelites express their preference to have remained in Egypt, they make no mention of its idyllic character. Crucially, however, there remains one ingeniously subtle inner-biblical allusion that casts this entire Egypt connection in a substantially new light. That allusion suggests that our prophet, after being hurled into the sea like the Egyptians, in fact perceives the fish that rescues him – much like Egypt itself – to embody a paradisiacal domain.

The Great Fish and the Garden of Eden

In the book of Numbers (11:9), we are told that the manna (מָן; *mān*) fell each morning on a layer of dew (טַל; *ṭal*). With this in mind, note that our book's four instances of *wayĕman* (וַיְמַן) – a word that displays just two root-letters, which spell out the word *mān* – follow four occurrences of the uncommon biconsonantal root *ṭl* (טל; *hiphil* "hurl"). First, the Lord hurls (*hēṭîl*) a great wind on the sea (Jonah 1:4). Then, the sailors hurl (*wayyāṭilû*) the items on the ship overboard (1:5). Jonah, for his part, advises his shipmates to hurl *him* (*hăṭîlunî*) overboard (1:12), after which the crew carries out the prophet's bold recommendation (*wayeṭiluhû*; 1:15).[60] This sequence of terms raises the immediate possibility that, just as *wayĕman* brings to mind the *mān*, the recurring verb *ṭl* is designed to recall the word *ṭal*. For much as the *ṭal* precedes the *mān*, the events marked by the verb *ṭl* presage a corresponding number of actions introduced by *wayĕman*.[61]

Further, observe that the second chapter of Jonah contains four references to a great fish that, after ingesting the prophet, ultimately grants him a rebirth.[62] In three of these instances, the text refers to this sea creature by the standard term *dāg*. By contrast, just before Jonah's prayer of gratitude we encounter the alternative form *dāgâ* (Jonah 2:2), which denotes an individual fish just this one time in the Bible. Some interpreters, accordingly, propose that *dāgâ*, as a feminine noun, serves to signify the transformation of the fish's belly from tomb into womb.[63] Whatever the merits of this explanation, however, a serious difficulty remains: if that is the case, should not the description of the prophet's three-day gestation period (2:1), and certainly of his "birth" at the end of the chapter (2:11), similarly employ this feminine form of the word?

Instead, the primary significance of the term *dāgâ* lies elsewhere. In the passage that describes the *mān* falling on the *ṭal*, the Israelites are complaining about the manna's inadequacies (Num 11:5–6). Fancying a return to the putative luxuries of Egypt, the people thus declare, "We remember the *dāgâ* that we would eat in Egypt for free." Working off this text, then, our story, in the one instance where Jonah offers his own hopeful perspective on the prospects offered by the fish, refers to it by the same word *dāgâ*. For in the prophet's mind, the fish provides not a means to an end but an enduring, blissful escape analogous to the idyllic environs of Egypt. In actual fact, however, the sanctuary offered by the creature – much like the shade of the *qîqāyôn* – resembles the short-lasting manna, which the Israelites see fit to *contrast* to the heavenly Egyptian fish. It is purely for the sake of irony, then, that the text, after four allusions to the *ṭal*, mentions the sea creature an equal number of times. More significant are the four corresponding allusions to the heaven-sent *mān*, which exemplifies the inexorable transience of unmerited divine favor.

Considerable evidence, moreover, suggests that Jonah, when expressing his thanks for the fish, perceives it not merely as a source of bliss but also as an Eden-like abode. First, scholars note a correlation between the creature and the city of Nineveh, whose name and ideogram bear the symbolism of fish.[64] It stands to reason, in turn, that when the ingested prophet utters a triumphant prayer of gratitude, he does so because the sea animal that encases him – much like the joy-inducing paradisiacal plant – bestows the Edenic comforts that characterize the resplendent kingdom of Assyria.

More important, let us briefly go beyond the narrative portion of the book and steal a glance at an essential allusion generated by a formulation in Jonah's prayer. Near the beginning of the prayer, when depicting his situation, the prophet uses the phrase *wěnāhār yěsōběběnî* ("flowing waters surrounding me"; Jonah 2:4). On a basic level, of course, this expression describes Jonah's predicament when he was struggling in the water. Consider, however, that in only two other instances in the Bible do we find a *nāhār* surrounding (*sbb*) something, and both of them are in Eden-related passages. First, immediately after the planting of the garden in Genesis, we are told of a *nāhār* ("river") that flows out of Eden, yielding one stream that surrounds (*sbb*) a land filled with riches and another that surrounds (*sbb*) a different location (Gen 2:10–13). Second, when Ezekiel compares Assyria to Eden, he describes how that kingdom drew sustenance from the waters and the Deep, its *nĕhārôt* ("rivers") still surrounding (*sbb*) the site on which it initially flourished (Ezek 31:4). Taken together with the parallels to the divine garden already encountered, the analogous phrase in Jonah thus strongly suggests that our prophet – according to a more profound layer of meaning – is actually describing his condition inside the fish, which offers him a paradisiacal environment surrounded by prototypically Edenic waters.[65]

Finally, we proceed to the concluding verse of Jonah 2: "The Lord said/spoke (*wayyō'mer*) to the fish, and it vomited (*wayyāqē'*) Jonah onto dry land." By disgorging the prophet from its belly, the great sea creature grants him a rebirth. Simultaneously, however, according to our approach, the regurgitation of Jonah back into the real world frustrates his aspirations again, expelling him from his latest Edenic escape and forcing him to confront the realities of an imperfect existence. Indeed, in all probability, this rare deployment of the word *wayyō'mer* without reference to what was "said" generates a subtle connection to the Cain story, where a similarly unfinished clause prefaces the murder of Abel: "Cain said/spoke (*wayyō'mer*) to his brother Abel; and when they were in the field, Cain rose up against his brother Abel and killed him" (Gen 4:8). The defiant Cain, who shares Jonah's resistance to the path of repentance, condemns himself to perpetual banishment by killing his brother. Correspondingly, our self-deceiving prophet, who thinks he has attained a lasting Edenic existence, ironically becomes the *object* of aggression when the giant creature ejects him from its paradisiacal belly.

Only our reading, furthermore, seems to account for the verb "to vomit" (*qy'*); after all, it seems highly unlikely that the text would have used such a term to describe an act that is fundamentally restorative.[66] In addition, recall that the word *qîqāyôn* suggests a combination of the root *qy'* and the name *yônâ*, implying that Jonah will effectively be vomited out of the plant's blissful shade. Our verse too, then, fittingly uses the verb *qy'* to depict the prophet's expulsion from an Edenic enclosure.

The sailors, moreover, having cast Jonah overboard, implore God not to "place on [them] innocent blood (*dām nāqî'*; Jonah 1:14)." The notable inclusion of the letter *'ālep* in the spelling of *nāqî'* (נקיא) has prompted the suggestion that this word likewise plays on the root *qy'*;[67] and here also, only our interpretation accounts for this wordplay in a genuinely satisfying way. For now it emerges that *each* time Jonah attains an idyllic environment, the location in question "vomits" him out. The Eden-like *qîqāyôn* lives up to its name "vomits-Jonah" when, on its drying up, it exposes the prophet to the scorching weather. After the sailors expel Jonah from the Zaphon-like ship, they describe him as a *nāqî'*; that is, a "vomited one." And being "vomited" out of the sea creature doubtless brings only devastation to our protagonist, who, far from seeking salvation in the flawed province of humanity, had actually placed all his chips on the blissfully paradisiacal fish.

Wrathful Moralist

Why, then, does Jonah defy the will of God? What motivates him to resist his mandate and instead to seek out a paradisiacal existence? To begin answering these questions, it helps to consider the initial command that the Lord directs to the prophet.

In the book's opening scene, God tells Jonah, "Arise, go to the great city of Nineveh, *ûqrā' 'ālêhā* ("and call out on/to it") *kî* ("because/that") their evil has risen up before me" (Jonah 1:2). This verse yields two distinct readings, which give rise to fundamentally different conceptions of the prophet's resistance. According to the standard interpretation, Jonah must warn the Ninevites about the dire threat to their city so that they might repent and forestall its destruction. This explanation best suits the rendering, "and call out *to it that* their evil has risen up before me," which suggests that the prophet must communicate the urgent necessity of repentance.[1] When Jonah refuses to comply with this divine command, we may reason that, inspired by perfectionist zeal, he cannot tolerate a world that grants a sinful city like Nineveh a chance to preserve its Eden-like majesty. The moralistic prophet, therefore, spurns his restorative mission, and instead pursues a more genuine Edenic realm from which God banishes sinners and whose moral wholesomeness justifies its aesthetic grandeur.

Alternatively, Jonah's mandate, at least as he understands it, calls for *pronouncing doom* on the wicked Assyrian city. Indeed, the more common translation of the verse's final clause – "*because* their evil has risen up before me" – suggests that the prior, now rather curt phrase *ûqrā' 'ālêhā* might well bear the meaning, "and proclaim on it [destruction]."[2] The defiant prophet, however, maintains an uncompromising, radically pacifist stance, which prompts him to avert his eyes from evil and the attendant need for moral accountability. Consequently, he runs from fulfilling his ostensibly destructive mission, and in keeping with his dreamy idealism, he seeks out a paradisiacal world precisely of the sort represented by a glamorous and enduring Nineveh.

Ultimately, I am convinced that the text is designed to yield *both* of these readings. First, however, we focus our attention on the standard, moralistic conception of Jonah's motives. Indeed, in the book's opening passage, we encounter allusions that point strongly toward this widely accepted reading of the story.

A RAGING TEMPEST AND A WRATHFUL PROPHET

Jonah, Jeremiah, and a Great Storm

The text of Jonah has spawned numerous associations with the book of Jeremiah.[3] In ch. 36, for example, Jeremiah relays a prophecy of doom intended to inspire "each man to repent his evil ways." Yet despite the receptiveness displayed by a fearful, fasting population, the Judean king and his officers fatefully reject Jeremiah's message. Our own story, by contrast, employing notably similar language (Jonah 3:8–10), recounts how the leaders of Nineveh, including its king, humble themselves and call a fast in response to Jonah's warning. Hence, unlike the Judean leaders, they succeed in rescuing their city from destruction.

In Jeremiah 26, moreover, the prophet admonishes his audience in language even more reminiscent of the repentance of the Ninevites: "Perhaps they will give heed and repent, each man of his evil ways, so that I will revoke the dire decree that I am planning to mete out on them" (Jer 26:3; cf. Jonah 3:8–10).[4] Further, when Jeremiah faces execution as punishment for the audacity of his words, he warns that should the people kill him they would "place on" themselves "innocent blood" (Jer 26:15). In Jonah, by contrast, the protagonist is thrown overboard for having *failed* to relay his prophecy, and it is ironically the God-fearing sailors who plead to the Lord not to "place on [them] innocent blood" (Jonah 1:14).[5]

In multiple instances, then, our story alludes to passages in Jeremiah to generate meaningful contrasts. With this in mind, observe that the Lord, having resolved to threaten Jonah's vessel, dispatches not an "east wind" (*rûaḥ qādîm*) – the kind typically designated to break apart ships of Tarshish – but rather a "great wind" of unspecified provenance, which in turn engenders a *saʿar-gādôl* ("great storm"; Jonah 1:4). Significantly, the phrase *saʿar gādôl* occurs only one other time in the Bible, where Jeremiah, in the passage immediately preceding ch. 26, describes the devastation visited on a group of sinful nations (Jer 25:32). This *saʿar gādôl*, in fact, is triggered by none other than the *ḥărôn hayyônâ* ("rage of the oppressor"; 25:38) – the only instance outside of Jonah where the root *ḥrh* appears together with the word *yônâ*.[6] In that same verse, moreover, Jeremiah compares the unleashing of God's rage to a lion bursting forth from its *sukkâ* ("lair"), reminiscent of the *sukkâ* inhabited by our prophet precisely when he experiences his own *ḥărôn* ("rage"; Jonah 4:1–5). Finally, Jeremiah employs the uncommon root *qyʾ* ("vomit"; Jer 25:27) when depicting the effects of Lord's anger, the same verb that our text invokes – explicitly or otherwise – each time God orchestrates the expulsion of Jonah from an Edenic sanctuary. Taken together, these parallels generate a striking relationship between our story and the latter part of Jeremiah 25, strongly suggesting that the *saʿar gādôl* that threatens Jonah's vessel indeed draws on that passage.

Consider, then, the implications of these parallels for our prophet's motives. If the term *yônâ* in Jeremiah denotes an oppressor, one that pours out its rage on sinful nations, it follows that *yônâ* ("Jonah") in our story, who likewise exhibits rage, wishes to ensure the annihilation of Nineveh. Yet in another instructive contrast to the prophecies of Jeremiah, in our story a *saʿar gādôl* does not help *yônâ* accomplish his objective, but thwarts his efforts. Unlike the raging *yônâ* that destroys nations in the wake of the Lord's vomit-inducing anger, our *yônâ* fails to bring about the devastation that he advocates. Instead the zealous prophet repeatedly finds *himself* "vomited" out of Eden-like enclosures, which represent the idyllic, faultless world that he relentlessly seeks to inhabit.

Jonah, Elijah, and a Great Wind

The "great wind" (*rûaḥ-gĕdôlâ*) in Jonah derives from a story about a different moralistic prophet. Our text generates a set of oft-noted parallels between Jonah and the zealous Elijah who, after fleeing the Northern Kingdom of Israel, is compelled by God to turn back and resume his prophetic duties.[7] Much as our prophet does – if in disparate contexts – Elijah undertakes a one-day walk (*hlk . . . yôm*), finds refuge under a tree, and lies down (*wayyiškāb*) and goes to sleep (1 Kgs 19:4–6, 9; cf. Jonah 3:4; 1:5; 4:6). While still under the tree, Elijah dejectedly asks to die (*wayyiš'al 'et-napšô lāmût*), saying, "Now, O Lord, take my life," and adding that he is no "better than" (*ṭôb mê-*) his predecessors (1 Kgs 19:4; cf. Jonah 4:3, 8). Later, an angel must approach Elijah "a second time" to prod him to fulfill his responsibilities (1 Kg 19:7; cf. Jonah 3:1). While resting again, the reluctant prophet is disrupted by "the word of the Lord," who asks him, "What are you doing (*mah-lĕkā*) here, Elijah?" (1 Kgs 19:9; cf. 19:13; Jonah 1:1; 1:6; 3:1). The prophet, then, is compelled to stand "before the Lord" (1 Kgs 19:11; cf. Jonah 1:3, 10). And then God, spurning Elijah's fiery zeal in favor of a quieter, softer posture, imparts a theological lesson that begins with none other than a *rûaḥ gĕdôlâ* ("great wind"; 1 Kgs 19:11–12).[8]

These similarities between Jonah and Elijah confirm that our prophet, too, is motivated by zealotry.[9] In a notably apt way, moreover, the matter finds expression in the corresponding *rûaḥ-gĕdôlâ* that assails Jonah's ship. Much like the powerful gust in the Elijah passage, the ferocious wind in our own story helps teach the moralistic prophet an ironic lesson: the Lord, far from seeking to unleash his ferocity on transgressors, embraces the kinder, gentler path of compassion and forbearance, granting a sinful population like the Ninevites every opportunity to rectify its conduct and salvage its future.

A RELUCTANT PROPHET AND A DUTIFUL DOVE

With a zealous *yônâ* bestriding us, we thus embark on a sustained reading of the second half of the book, joining our freshly regurgitated protagonist on the shore of the Mediterranean. We will find that this latter part of Jonah, particularly the final chapter, contains the most straightforward evidence of the prophet's moralistic stance. It also offers yet more indications that he longs for an Eden-like existence.

Jonah, we have seen, finds himself vomited out of three Edenic sanctuaries: the ship, the fish, and the plant. This sequence of three banishments sharpens a correspondence that has captured the attention of many readers: the prophet's name (*yônâ*), considered together with his experiences, suggests a connection to the dove (*yônâ*) dispatched from the ark in the flood story in Genesis (8:8–12).[10] For just as Noah sends the bird off the boat on three occasions, Jonah is driven out of a protective haven this same number of times. This similarity, moreover, suggests that our *yônâ*, who dreads the prospect of accomplishing his mission, stands in stark opposition to the dutiful *yônâ* in the story of Noah.

The obedient dove in the flood narrative, when sent out for the first time, finds no hint of receding waters and returns to the ark empty-handed (Gen 8:8–9). In our story, by contrast, it is the God-fearing sailors who fail to gain access to dry land (*yabbāšâ*; Jonah 1:13), whereas a recalcitrant *yônâ* is the source of all the trouble. Then on its next try, the compliant bird achieves partial success when it retrieves a nonsubmerged olive leaf (Gen 8:10–11). Jonah, by contrast, after being forcibly cast onto dry land (*yabbāšâ*; Jonah 2:11), performs his duty only partially because of his continued *reluctance* to carry out his task. Finally, whereas on the third occasion the liberated dove faithfully signals the disappearance of the lethal floodwaters (Gen 8:12), the moralistic prophet – both before and after the plant dries up (*wayyîbāš*; Jonah 4:7) – stubbornly seeks to escape the reality of Nineveh's rescue from extinction. Furthermore, two verbs used in connection with the bird's efforts – *ybš* ("dry up" Gen 8:7, 14) and *qll* ("lighten" 8:8, 11) – play a role in highlighting Jonah's resistance: in addition to employing *ybš* in each of these three instances, our text makes use of *qll* where the sailors – in sharp contrast to the prophet – try valiantly to fend off the violent surge of the tempest (Jonah 1:5).[11]

What in our text suggests that, on that second occasion when Jonah finally makes his way into Nineveh, he still hesitates to encourage the people to repent? The relevant passage, especially when examined with the flood narrative in mind, actually provides several indications of the prophet's abiding reluctance.[12] First, all Jonah does is curtly declare that "in another forty days Nineveh will be upended" (Jonah 3:4). With this formulation, moreover, he calls to mind the irrepressible waters that destroy the earth after forty days of rain (Gen 7:12).[13] Further, after his own three-day process of rebirth (Jonah 2:1), the prophet neglects to complete the three-day trek through Nineveh, making his lone pronouncement on the city after completing just one day of the journey (3:4).[14]

What is more, consider the distinctive word *wayyāḥel* ("he began"; of the root *ḥll*) used by our passage when recounting Jonah's truncated walk through the city. At first glance, this verb seems notably extraneous: the text, instead of leading with *wayyāḥel*, could easily have just read, "Jonah proceeded (*wayyābōʾ*) into the city the distance of one day's walk." Significantly, though, *wayyāḥel* appears twice in the story of Noah. By using the same term here, our author quite probably meant to invoke *both* of those instances to underscore the inadequacy of the prophet's efforts.

First, when recounting that Noah waited before sending out the *yônâ* a second time, the text uses the verb *wayyāḥel* (of the root *yḥl*) to express this delay (Gen 8:10).[15] In our passage, correspondingly, the homonymous *wayyāḥel* intimates that, by journeying for just one day, Jonah delayed the completion of his mission.[16] More important, after his salvation from the flood, we learn that Noah "profaned himself" (*wayyāḥel*; of the root *ḥll*) by planting a vineyard and drinking to the point of inebriation (9:20–21). Our text, accordingly, by using this same distinctive verb, hints that the recently saved prophet likewise profanes himself by failing yet again to follow the Lord's instructions properly. In fact, unlike Noah who, when reaching dry land, at least takes the trouble to build an altar (*mizbēaḥ*) and offer sacrifices (8:20), the disillusioned Jonah, having been vomited out of the Edenic belly of the fish, provides no indication of honoring his pledge to offer sacrifices of his own (*ʾezbĕḥâ*; Jonah 2:10).[17]

Finally, the text underscores the prophet's failure by generating a widely noted, if often misunderstood, comparison to the first scene of the book.[18] The first time God directs Jonah to arise (*qûm*), go (*lēk*), and call out (*ûqrāʾ*) to Nineveh (Jonah 1:2), the prophet actually arises (*wayyāqom*) to flee (1:3). In chapter 3, by contrast, when confronted with an analogous divine command, Jonah finally does arise (*wayyāqom*) and go (*wayyēlek*) "in accordance with the word of (*dĕbar*) the Lord" (3:3). In addition to "arise" and "go," however, our passage contains multiple occurrences of

two other verb roots. On three occasions, it employs *dbr* ("speak") to refer
to the word of God (3:1, 2, 3). And it uses *qr'* three times to denote "calling
out": first God tells Jonah to "call out" (*ûqrā'*) to Nineveh the "calling
(*qĕrî'â*) that I am relating (*dōbēr*) to you" (3:2), and shortly thereafter, we
are informed that Jonah "called out" (*wayyiqrā'*) his prophecy to the city
(3:4).[19]

Much as in chapter 1, then, where the directive "call out" follows "arise
and go," our passage contains precisely these three imperatives. But crucially,
it is the command to "call out" that receives the most emphasis: the relevant root appears twice in the expression "call out to it the calling," and by
adding the phrase "that I (*'ānōkî*) am relating (*dōbēr*) to you," God pointedly
affirms that his *dābār* ("word") specified what Jonah was expected to proclaim. This latter clause, moreover, recalls another biblical passage – the
only earlier text containing a similar line – to stress that the prophet *must*
carry out this particular directive. The passage is found in the beginning
of the exodus story, where the Lord instructs a decidedly reluctant Moses
to impart to Pharaoh everything "that I am relating (*dōbēr*) to you" (Exod
6:29).[20] In Jonah, likewise, it is the transmitting of the Lord's *dābār*, rather
than the mere imperative to "arise and go," whose fulfillment will prove
to be of utmost concern. Finally, our text's notable use of *'ānōkî* instead
of *'ănî* to indicate the first-person singular – one of only two such instances
in the book – adds to the formality and, in turn, the urgency of God's in-
sistence that the prophet satisfy this particular aspect of the divine
command.[21]

With this in mind, we return to the ensuing affirmation that Jonah
"arose and went to Nineveh in accordance with the word (*dābār*) of the
Lord." It is, of course, true that the prophet dutifully heeds these two parts
of God's orders. As for "calling out" to Nineveh, however, our passage first
indicates that Nineveh was "a city of divinely great proportions spanning
the distance of a three-day walk" and emphasizes Jonah's starting/delay-
ing/self-profaning (*wayyāḥel*) in connection with his trek through just
a fraction of the city (Jonah 3:3–4). Only then does the text, *omitting* any
mention of adherence to "the word of the Lord," recount the prophet's curt
pronouncement (*wayyiqrā'*) that in forty days Nineveh will be destroyed.
For although Jonah, in this instance, finally obeys God's command not
only to "arise" but also to "go," he falls well short of fulfilling his mandate

"to call out to it the calling" that God related to him. That calling, after all, consisted not just of a declaration of impending doom but also of an appeal for repentance toward the goal of saving the city.

Jonah's failure to "call out" in the way God intended also draws support from a notable variation in terminology.[22] Recall that the phrase *ûqrā' 'ālêhā* in chapter 1 yields two possible meanings: Jonah must call out *to* the Ninevites and urge them to repent, or in line with the usual sense of *'al*, he must proclaim *on* the city a terrible fate. In 3:2, by contrast, *ûqrā'* allows only one meaning: Jonah must call out the Lord's message *to* Nineveh (*'ēlêhā*). My approach, accordingly, offers an explanation for the change. Now that the moralistic prophet can no longer dodge his mission, there remains reason to worry that, instead of encouraging repentance, he will opt for the more zealous reading of God's initial directive and simply pronounce destruction on the city. The Lord, consequently, seeks to make perfectly clear that, of the two ways of reading his command, only one carries validity. He therefore engages Jonah a second time, instructing him to arise, go to Nineveh, and – so that there is no room for misunderstanding – "call out *to* it (*'ēlêhā*) the calling that *I* (*'ānōkî*) am relating to you!" For if the prophet does not try to inspire the city, then any definitive pronouncement *on* it (*'ālêhā*) remains unwarranted. Instead, it is Jonah's unequivocal task to convey *to* the Ninevites (*'ēlêhā*) that, in line with God's true intentions, there remains a genuine opportunity for repentance and salvation.

And yet, even as he is left with no choice but to follow the Lord's instructions, there is no overestimating the resolve of our zealous protagonist: by proclaiming that in forty days Nineveh will be "upended" (*nehpāket*), the prophet cleverly conceals the divine message of hope in a secondary meaning of that verb, offering only a faint indication that the "upending" of the city could take the form of a *transformation* of its conduct. Taken straightforwardly, after all, Jonah's affirmation hardly suggests the potential for a reversal of Nineveh's ominous fate. The prophet's words affirm far more plainly that, in line with his own wishful reading of the divine command, nothing at all can rescue the sinful city from the impending annihilation decreed by God.

A ZEALOUS PROPHET AND A PARADISIACAL CITY

The Repentance of Nineveh: Opening Observations

Ironically, despite the inadequacy of Jonah's efforts, the Ninevites respond with appropriate urgency to his pronouncement. Like the Gentile sailors encountered in chapter 1, the people of the city cry out to God that they "not perish" (Jonah 3:9; cf. 1:6, 14). In addition, when depicting the Ninevites' penitent response, the text maintains an analogy to groups that, like the Tarshish-bound crew, face the prospect of annihilation by lethal waters.[23] Thus, as in the case of the Israelites at the Sea of Reeds, the reaction of the Ninevites includes "believing" (*wayya'ămînû*) in God (3:5) and "crying out" (*wayyaz'ēq*; 3:7). And in pointed contrast to the population wiped out by the flood, the people of Nineveh abandon their "violence" (*ḥāmās*) and "evil" (*rā'â*; 3:8, 10; cf. Gen 6:11, 13).[24] Consequently, the Lord relents (*nḥm*) from what he intended to do (*'śh*) to them (Jonah 3:10), rather than, as in the case of the sinners obliterated by the deluge, to regret (*nḥm*) that he made (*'śh*) them (Gen 6:6–7).[25]

Crucially, however, this passage also initiates a highly significant set of parallels to Ezekiel 34–36. This correlation equates the salvation of the paradisiacal Nineveh to the restoration of the idyllic land of Israel. Furthermore, it generates a corresponding analogy between the zealous Jonah and the people of Edom, whose joy over the fall of Israel gives way to their own desolation and the revival of the nation of God.

Nineveh and the Edenic Land of Israel

After the king of Nineveh humbly descends from his throne, he begins to rally his subjects, providing instructions that pertain to animals as well as to humans: "And he issued a proclamation, saying, 'In Nineveh, on the authority of the king and his nobles, the people and the animals (*hā'ādām wĕhabbĕhēmâ*), the large cattle and the small cattle – let them not taste anything, let them not graze, and let them not drink water'" (Jonah 3:7).[26] Moreover, he affirms, both the people and the animals (*hā'ādām wĕhabbĕhēmâ*) must cover themselves with sackcloth and call out to God with vigor (3:8). The terms *'ādām* and *bĕhēmâ*, in fact, appear yet a third time in our story, where the Lord – employing forms of *rbh/rbb* ("multiply/be numerous") likewise three times – emphasizes that the great city of Nineveh contains "more (*harbê*) than twelve myriad (*ribbô*) people (*'ādām*) . . . and many animals (*běhēmâ rabbâ*)" (4:11).[27]

Now the combination of *'ādām* and *běhēmâ* in the Bible indeed occurs most distinctly in Ezekiel, albeit chiefly in a speech comparatively early in the book (Ezek 14:12–23). In that context, the prophet stresses that, when a land faces destruction, the presence of even a small number of righteous individuals keeps the Lord from annihilating *'ādām ûbhēmâ* ("people and animals"). The phrase *'ādām ûbhēmâ* appears four times in that prophecy (14:13, 17, 19, 21), and it is quite possible that, when describing the efforts of the Ninevite leaders to encourage repentance, our author sought to invoke the message of that chapter. More important, however, *'ādām ûbhēmâ* also occurs in Ezekiel 36, where together with other terminology it suggests a far more consequential link to the story of Jonah.

In chapter 36, Ezekiel picks up on an earlier, premature assumption by Israel that, merely because of its "large numbers" (*rabbîm*), God would necessarily redeem the nation (Ezek 33:24). Having disabused the Israelites of that conviction, the prophet now affirms that eventually the Lord will indeed restore them, filling their Eden-like land with people, animals, and produce. Thus, God will bestow large amounts (*wěhirbêtî*) of grain and large amounts (*wěhirbêtî*) of fruit (36:29–30). He will cause the people to attain large numbers (*wěhirbêtî . . . 'ādām*; 36:10) and to multiply like flocks of small cattle (*'arbê . . . kěṣō'n 'ādām*; 36:37). He will pack Israel's devastated cities with "flocks of people" (*ṣō'n 'ādām*; 36:38). And he will endow Israel with large numbers of "people and animals," who will in turn multiply even more (*wěhirbêtî 'ălêkem 'ādām ûbhēmâ wěrābû ûpārû*; 36:11). Consequently, by the end, stunned passersby will compare the restored land of Israel to none other than the Garden of Eden (36:35).

Immediately, the possibility arises that the text of Jonah, by using *'ādām*, *běhēmâ*, and *rbh/rbb* as key terms, likens the salvation of the great, populous city of Nineveh to the restoration of the paradisiacal Israel described by Ezekiel. Observe, in fact, that when depicting the multitudes of *'ādām* and *běhēmâ* in Nineveh, our text invokes a rare comparative usage of the *hiphil* form *harbê* ("more") and strikingly presents the number 120,000 as "twelve *ribbô* ('myriad')."[28] It bears serious consideration, in turn, that *harbê* serves to recall the keyword *hirbêtî* in the Ezekiel text, and that *ribbô* (רבו), *'ādām*, and *běhēmâ* stand in parallel, respectively, to the orthographically identical *rābû* (רבו; "will multiply") and the terms *'ādām* (אדם) and *běhēmâ* (בהמה) that, along with *hirbêtî* (הרביתי) itself, punctuate the relevant phrase in Ezekiel 36:11 (והרביתי עליכם אדם ובהמה ורבו ופרו; cf. ובהמה רבה ... הרבה משתים עשרה רבו אדם).

Crucially, moreover, the words *'ādām* and *běhēmâ* at the end of Jonah generate a resonance with the *'ādām* who – along with animals (*běhēmâ*) – populated Eden at the beginning of the Genesis story (Gen 2:8, 20), and who, as the Lord says about the Ninevites in this same concluding line, *did not yet know the difference between good and evil*. If our author, accordingly, sought to evoke the Eden story in the final verse of the book, it becomes far more likely that the verse also alludes to the Eden text in Ezekiel 36.

In the final analysis, then, what may we conclude about this proposed set of parallels? To answer this question, let us turn our attention to some additional motifs in Jonah that, on close inspection, tip the balance decisively in favor of the correlation.

The Humbling of Nineveh and the Arrogance of Israel

We begin with the opening directive issued by the leadership of Nineveh: "let them not taste (*'al-yiṭ'ămû*) anything" (Jonah 3:7). As is widely observed, the root *ṭ'm* also appears earlier in the verse, where it denotes the "authority" (*ṭa'am*) behind the Ninevite leaders' pronouncement.[29] It has gone unremarked, however, that this evident wordplay adds another layer of meaning to the phrase *'al-yiṭ'ămû*: the haughty people of Nineveh must not only refrain from eating but must also show humility by not arrogating to themselves unwarranted supremacy ("let them not impose authority"). This observation, considered in light of the Ezekiel material, helps explain some problematic terminology in the ensuing clauses, including the puzzling directive *'al-yir'û* that – appearing right after *'al-yiṭ'ămû* – oddly seems to say that animals *and people* should not "graze."

In Ezekiel 34, the prophet, not yet up to depicting Israel's redemption, describes the momentous failures of its leadership. In that speech, Ezekiel uses the key root *r'h* more than thirty times, culminating in an assurance that the Israelites will ultimately remain the flock tended by God (*ṣō'n mar'îtî 'ādām*; Ezek 34:31). At the present time, however, the self-indulgent "shepherds/leaders" (*rō'îm*) of Israel, instead of "tending" (*r'h*) the Israelite flock, have chosen to "graze" (*rʿh*) on their own (34:8), "drink clear water" (*ūmišqaʿ-mayim tištû*; 34:18), and oppress the downtrodden "with vigor" (*bĕḥozqâ*; 34:4).

Consider, then, the terminology of our passage, beginning with the expression *'al-yirʾû*. As does the immediately preceding phrase *'al-yiṭʿămû*, *'al-yirʾû* now generates a subtext, one that fittingly relates to the *people* of Nineveh. First, much like *'al-yiṭʿămû*, this phrase addresses the Ninevite citizens' presumptions of authority, implying that they must not act as though they are in charge of what they are not. Additionally, *'al-yirʾû* suggests that, like the arrogant leaders of Israel in Ezekiel, the self-important Ninevites must desist from "grazing" in the sense of *tending to themselves* rather than to the people in need of their care.[30] Furthermore, they must not follow those Israelite leaders' poor example of indulging in water instead of fulfilling their responsibilities (*ūmayim 'al-yištû*). And unlike the aristocrats in Ezekiel who oppressed the needy "with vigor" (*bĕḥozqâ*), the residents of Nineveh must *call out to God* "with vigor" (*bĕḥozqâ*) in an effort to salvage their city. It bears emphasis, in fact, that the closest biblical parallel to the expression *ūmayim 'al-yištû* is unmistakably the analogous formulation in Ezekiel (*mayim tištû*), and that Scripture contains just three appearances of *ḥozqâ* (Judg 4:3; 8:1; 1 Sam 2:16) apart from these occurrences in Ezekiel and Jonah. These parallels provide the clinching evidence in favor of our book's correlation with this sequence in Ezekiel, implying that, indeed, the imperiled, resplendent city of Nineveh bears an analogy to a sinful Israel that, for all its transgressions, will ultimately be restored to a state of paradisiacal grandeur.

Jonah and the Fleeting Joy of Edom

To this point, then, we have identified two broad correspondences between our story and these chapters in Ezekiel: the Ninevites in Jonah 3, by rectifying their conduct, stand in contrast to the corrupt Israelites in Ezekiel 34, and the redeemed Nineveh in Jonah 4:11 recalls the paradisiacal Israel in Ezekiel 36. Significantly, however, this sequence of correspondences encompasses one additional component, which pertains to the intervening prophecy on Seir/Edom in Ezekiel 35.

Ezekiel's speech on Edom appears at that point, rather than with his other prophecies against foreign nations, because of its relevance to the

fate of Israel.[31] In chapter 35 and in the transitional passage that opens
chapter 36, the prophet affirms that Edom will fall because of its oppres-
sion of Israel, and he calls special attention to Edom's joy over Israel's
desolation. Three times Ezekiel makes reference to this "rejoicing" (śmḥ;
Ezek 35:14–15; 36:5), and by doing so, he generates yet another keyword
that provides a source for terminology in the Jonah text.

Before being banished for the last time, our prophet experiences "joy"
(wayyiśmaḥ … śimḥâ) over the paradisiacal qîqāyôn (Jonah 4:6). Now in
the book of Isaiah, we encounter a reference to śimḥâ in a redeemed, Eden-
like Israel (Isa 51:3), and it seems likely that our allusion-minded author,
when using this term in connection with Jonah's plant, had that Isaiah text
in mind.[32] The śimḥâ of Edom in Ezekiel 35, however, presents a far more
significant analogy to this motif in Jonah. According to Ezekiel, a high-
flying Edom experiences śimḥâ over Israel's collapse, but it will eventually
fall, whereas Israel will rise. In similar fashion, then, our prophet, who
wished for his own Edenic escape and for Nineveh's destruction, attains
just a short-lived śimḥâ: after he rejoices over his latest source of divine
protection – one that not only shields him from witnessing the fate of
the city but also might imply that God has acceded to his perfectionist
ideology – Jonah's Eden-like plant proceeds to shrivel.

There emerges, then, a notably instructive analogy between Jonah and
Edom. The joy of the fallen Edomites, for its part, turns into shame (Ezek
36:7) when the people of Israel, inhabiting a land reminiscent of Eden, gain
the upper hand. Likewise, the joy of our zealous prophet can only give way
to dejection when, after being banished yet again from a blissful environment, he must confront the unsettling reality that it is the long-sinning
Ninevites, after submitting to God only in the face of their impending
annihilation, who will succeed in preserving their paradisiacal domain.

NINEVEH, MOUNT SINAI,
AND THE GARDEN OF EDEN

The king of Nineveh, when proclaiming that the 'ādām and běhēmâ
must fast, makes specific reference to the city's "large cattle and small
cattle" (habbāqār wěhaṣṣō'n; Jonah 3:7). On the one hand, this reference

to *ṣō'n* may call to mind the *ṣō'n* in Ezekiel 34 and 36, which stand as a metaphor for the *'ādām* who, after being exploited by a corrupt leadership, eventually populate a restored, Edenic land of Israel. The presence of the word *bāqār*, however, strongly suggests that our author had another objective in mind when constructing this formulation.

Observe also that the phrase *'al-yir'û* ("let them not graze") appears without a conjunctive *wāw* ("and"). According to one astute proposal, the expression thereby *parallels* the preceding clause *'al-yiṭ'ămû mĕ'ûmâ* ("let them not taste anything") instead of adding to it. The two phrases, along with the nouns that appear immediately beforehand, may thus be read distributively: the first and third nouns, *'ādām* ("people") and *bāqār* ("large cattle"), govern *'al-yiṭ'ămû mĕ'ûmâ*, whereas the second and fourth nouns, *bĕhēmâ* ("animals") and *ṣō'n* ("small cattle"), govern *'al-yir'û*.[33] In this way, the formulation in the text – additional layers of interpretation aside – yields a legitimate surface-level meaning, one that does not place "people" among the subjects of the verb "graze." What is more, this explanation accounts for the order of the nouns in the phrase *habbāqār wĕhaṣṣō'n*, which is a reversal of the more common formulation that features *ṣō'n* in the first position. This inverted order, in keeping with more typical usage, enables *ṣō'n* rather than *bāqār* to govern the verb "graze."

At the same time, *'al-yir'û* generates still another inner-biblical parallel. And, as we quickly realize, that parallel almost certainly provides the main motivation for both the omission of a *wāw* in *'al-yir'û* and our verse's inclusion of the phrase *habbāqār wĕhaṣṣō'n*.

As widely acknowledged, the language of our text, from the king's proclamation until after the listing of God's attributes in 4:2, recalls the divine forgiveness that Moses elicits after the Israelites commit the sin of the golden calf (Exod 32–34).[34] The divine-attribute formula itself, a version of which Jonah invokes, appears for the first time in that context in Exodus (34:6–7). What is more, the roots *šwb* (שוב; "turn back"), *nḥm* (נחם; "relent"), *r'* (רעע; "be bad"), *ḥrh* (חרה; "blaze"), and *'śh* (עשה; "do"), which together bring to mind select, pivotal phrases in that story (e.g., שוב מחרון אפך והנחם על הרעה לעמך ["Turn back from your fury and relent from the bad decree directed at your people"]; 32:12), pervade these verses in Jonah. Thus, when the Ninevites "turn back" (שוב) from the "bad" (רעע) that they "did" (עשה), their action prompts the Lord to "turn back" (שוב) from the "bad" (רעע) that he intended to "do" (עשה) to them (Jonah 3:8–10). In this way, the text both invokes God's attributes and appeals to the principle of reciprocity, thereby justifying the efficacy of repentance despite the persistent objections of the prophet. For even now, the alleviation of the Lord's "fury" (חרה) and the rescinding of his "bad" (רעע) decree end up triggering Jonah's own "fury" (חרה) and intensely "bad" (רעע) state of mind (Jonah 3:9–4:1).

Consider, then, that almost immediately before God enumerates his attributes in the Exodus passage, he issues two warnings: not only must nobody approach the mountain along with Moses but "even the small cattle and large cattle (*haṣṣō'n wĕhabbāqār*) may not graze (*'al-yir'û*)" anywhere nearby (Exod 34:3). It follows that our author includes the phrase *habbāqār wĕhaṣṣō'n* – albeit in this inverted manner – to recall that line in Exodus, likewise adopting the exact phrase *'al-yir'û* – with no conjunctive *wāw* – to help generate the parallel.[35] For once our author decided that the text would allude to the "shepherd" (*r'h*) prophecy in Ezekiel 34, refer to both *'ādām* and *bĕhēmâ* in the royal pronouncement, and invoke this particular passage in Exodus, the line *haṣṣō'n wĕhabbāqār 'al-yir'û* offered not only a suitable phrase containing the root *r'h* but also a way to justify a restriction on the Ninevite animals (*bĕhēmâ*). After all, in accordance with the Lord's directive in Exodus, when a group seeks to elicit divine forgiveness it would do well to ensure that even its animals exhibit deference and restraint.

Crucially, moreover, our text's reference to this prohibition illuminates the *entire* correlation with the Exodus passage. Scholars have affirmed, based on several parallels, that the Israelites' encounter at the sacred mountain of Sinai bears a correspondence to the presence of Adam and Eve in the Garden of Eden.[36] Significantly for our analysis, both the Israelites and those primeval humans, when in their respective sacred locations, must exhibit a specific form of restraint lest they die (*môt tāmût/yāmût*; Gen 2:17; Exod 19:12). Indeed, the Israelites must not even "touch" (*ng'*) the mountain (19:12), much as Eve, adding to God's prohibition, affirms that she and Adam must not even "touch" (*ng'*) the forbidden tree (Gen 3:3). When the people of Israel, accordingly, seek divine forgiveness after their transgression, they are attempting to preserve the effects of their *Eden-like experience*.

It follows, then, that the author of Jonah, when recounting the divine absolution elicited by a sinful Edenic city, sought to invoke the *Eden-restoring* compassion that the Lord extended to the worshipers of the golden calf. Thus, in addition to our passage recalling the forgiveness-related terminology of that story, the chastened Ninevite king insists that neither people nor animals may taste anything or "graze" in the environs of the city. For like the rewards of both Mount Sinai and the Garden of Eden, the resplendence of Nineveh will, in the long run, remain available only to a population that shows submission to God by constraining its indulgence in the site's paradisiacal pleasures.

Finally, consider the Lord's injunction to the Israelites, "Let them be (*wĕhāyû*) ready for the third day," as he commands them to sanctify them-selves in advance of the revelation at Sinai (Exod 19:11; cf. 19:15). Jonah's three-day gestation period, like the three-day walk he should have taken in Nineveh, similarly marks a span of time that facilitates the preparation necessary for accessing – or remaining inside – an Eden-like realm.[37] Moreover, the inclusion of the word *wayĕhî* in the line, "Jonah was (*wayĕhî*) in the belly of the fish for three days and three nights" – consistent with other occurrences of the root *hyh* in our book (*yihyê* ["will come to be"], *hāyâ* ["came into being"]; Jonah 4:5, 10) – encourages me to embrace the additional meaning, "Jonah *advanced toward a new state of being*" in the span of those three days.[38] For if the text is merely affirming that the prophet "was" in the fish for that duration, the entire line might have been omitted in favor of a more succinct, adverbial formulation in the ensuing clause ("And Jonah prayed to the Lord his God *on/after the third day* from the belly of the fish"). Instead, in conjunction with the three-day motif itself, *hyh* recalls the expression "Let them be (*wĕhāyû*) ready for the third day" in Exodus, which specifies the preparation time typically required in anticipation of an Edenic experience.[39]

JONAH, JOEL, AND THE GARDEN OF EDEN

Our passage in Jonah generates an oft-noted correlation with one more biblical context: the exhortation of a sinful Israel in the second chapter of Joel.[40] First, consider the distinctive version of the divine-attribute formula uttered by our prophet. Whereas the formula in Exodus contains an affirmation of God's "truthfulness" (*'ĕmet*), Jonah "the truthful one" (*ben-'ămittay*; literally "son of Amittai"; Jonah 1:1) questions the integrity of the Lord's policies on moral accountability. Consequently, he shuns the term "truthfulness" in favor of a different expression: "For I know you are a gracious and compassionate God, slow to anger and abounding in kindness, *who relents from causing harm*" (*wĕniḥām 'al-hārā'â*; 4:2).[41] This version of the formula appears elsewhere only one other time in the Bible – in a speech by Joel, who implores the Israelites, old and young, to return (*šwb*) to God and seek out his mercy (*ḥws*) by means of crying and fasting (*ṣwm*). After all, the Lord is "gracious and compassionate, slow to anger, and abounding in kindness, *and he relents from causing harm* (*wĕniḥām 'al-hārā'â*)." Thus, Joel proceeds to affirm, "Who knows, [God] might turn and relent" (*mî yôdēa' yāšûb wĕniḥām*; Joel 2:12–17).

Joel's exhortation, in fact, exhibits several additional parallels to our passage in Jonah. The Ninevite leadership similarly calls on people of all ages to repent (*šwb*) and fast (*ṣwm*), because "who knows, God might turn and relent" (*mî-yôdēa' yāšûb wĕniḥām hā'ĕlōhîm*; Jonah 3:7–10),[42] and later, the Lord refers to the "mercy" (*ḥws*) that the city eventually merited (4:11; cf. 4:10). Hence, only the direction of influence here is said to remain uncertain, as the order of these books' composition remains a matter of significant dispute.[43]

Consider, however, that among our story's biblical source-texts, we have by now identified every explicit reference to Eden or to the "Garden of God/the Lord" – with only one exception: in that very speech by Joel, the prophet affirms that, whereas Jerusalem presently resembles the Garden of Eden, the city will eventually stand desolate (Joel 2:3).[44] By admonishing the people, then, Joel seeks to rescue a domain reminiscent of that idyllic location. It follows, accordingly, that Joel's prophecy was circulating when the book of Jonah was composed and that our author, by alluding to the Joel text, sought to compare the salvation of the Eden-like Nineveh to the restoration of the similarly paradisiacal Jerusalem. For even without further argument, it seems highly improbable that the overt mention of the garden in Joel owes to the *implicit* references to Eden in our own story.

Moreover, the first two chapters of Joel are dominated by the motif of locusts that threaten to destroy the land of Israel. With this in mind, recall how the worm that destroys Jonah's Eden-like plant, like the snake that tempts Eve to partake of the forbidden tree, conforms to an image in Ancient Near Eastern iconography whereby a serpent attacks the Tree of Life. Might the crawling, Eden-wrecking locusts in Joel likewise accord with that image? And might the author of Jonah, who shortly thereafter recounts the episode of the worm, have intended to include these locusts in a triad of crawling/slithering creatures that devastate the resplendence of Eden?

To answer these questions, observe the following remarkable lexical analogy. When Jonah refers to God's merciful traits, using the same version of the formula found in Joel, he does so to explain why he fled his mission: "Was this not my word when I was still on my land (*hĕyôtî ʿal-ʾadmātî*)? That is why I took preemptive action in escaping toward Tarshish" (Jonah 4:2). Now only one other phrase in the Bible bears a close resemblance to *hĕyôtî ʿal-ʾadmātî*: when Moses warns Pharaoh of an impending plague of locusts, he affirms that the Egyptians – who inhabit, we recall, a paradisiacal domain of their own – have not experienced so severe an infestation from the time "they have been on the land" (*hĕyôtām ʿal-hāʾădāmâ*) until this day (Exod 10:6).

Our text thus indeed generates a meaningful allusion to locusts that devastate Eden-like terrain. First, Jonah intimates that, much like those early Egyptians, during the time he was on his land (*hĕyôtî ʿal-ʾadmātî*) he knew of no instance when God sent locusts to ravage an Edenic region. Then, he proceeds to enumerate divine attributes that, as previously affirmed by Joel, in fact prevent such crawling pests from destroying the Eden-like land of a repentant population. Accordingly, explains our zealous prophet, he escaped to Tarshish in defiance of the Lord's persistent restraint and mercy. For indeed, Jonah had every reason to believe that, if he were to prompt the Ninevites to change their ways, God would spare their paradisiacal city. Hence, the plaintive prophet, having been compelled to bring about precisely the result that he dreaded, finds himself overwhelmed by anguish, unable to confront a world where a population with a long record of wicked behavior continues to bask in its Edenic splendor.

A WRATHFUL PROPHET YEARNS FOR EDEN

Jonah Protests, the Lord Contests

This allusion to Joel initiates a series of references to Eden that occupy a central place in the final chapter of the book of Jonah. We have seen that Jonah's anger (*wayyiḥar lô*), God's response to his objection (*hahêṭēb ḥārâ lāk*), and the prophet's departure to a location east of Nineveh recall a sequence of phrases in the episode that brought Cain to an area east of Eden. To appreciate this fully, let us return to Jonah's words of protest, citing a bit more of his Hebrew phraseology.

"Was this not my word when I was still on my land?" (*hălō'-zê dĕbārî 'ad-hĕyôtî 'al-'admātî*), begins Jonah. "That is why I took preemptive action (*qiddamtî*) in escaping toward Tarshish" (Jonah 4:2). Consider, first, that this usage of *'ad* ("when"), a preposition that usually means "until," is quite rare.[45] Second, the force of the extra verb *qiddamtî* ("I took preemptive action") calls for explanation.[46] Third, by the parsimonious standards of our book, Jonah's reference to his destination ("toward Tarshish") appears extraneous. On the assumption, however, that the prophet has been seeking Eden from the beginning, this verse generates a layer of meaning that not only resolves these difficulties but also consigns added significance to the phrase *hĕyôtî 'al-'admātî*.

If the preposition *'ad*, in line with almost every other occurrence in the Bible, indeed means "until," then Jonah's formulation would most straightforwardly indicate the future tense: "*Will this not be* my word until I am on my *'ădāmâ*?" Now the term *'ădāmâ*, along with *'ādām*, dominates the Eden story in Genesis, where *'ădāmâ* denotes the earth that, at God's prompting, gives rise to the *'ādām* ("human"; Gen 2:7), provides all good things in an Edenic environment (2:9), and withholds its vigor in the wake of humanity's single transgression so that the *'ādām* must labor ceaselessly until returning to the dust of that very *'ădāmâ* ("until [*'ad*] you return to the earth [*'ădāmâ*]"; 3:17–19).[47] According to a more profound layer of meaning, it follows that our indignant protagonist alludes to that story to reaffirm his ideological position: Jonah will adhere to his moralistic convictions ("Will this not be my word") until (*'ad*) he reaches his *'ădāmâ*, meaning an idyllic, morally perfect *'ădāmâ* like the Garden of Eden or, alternatively, the *'ădāmâ* that will reclaim his lifeless body. In fact, the prophet continues, it is precisely this quest for Edenic perfection that prompted his flight "toward Tarshish," that distant paradise whose treasure-laden ships supply/signify an Eden-like domain. By means of the verb *qiddamtî*, moreover, Jonah provides a further indication that, figuratively speaking, he was escaping toward the garden located "in the east (*miqqedem*) of Eden" (Gen 2:8). Finally, in keeping with the sense of the verb *hyh* noted earlier, which this chapter invokes multiple times, the phrase *'ad-hĕyôtî 'al-'admātî* might well suggest that the prophet seeks not only to "be" in that blissful realm but also to attain a new kind of "being" by entering it.

Recognizing, however, that he has failed in his pursuit of Eden, Jonah falls back on his alternative wish for death (Jonah 4:3). The Lord, having none of this, responds by posing a succinct challenge to the prophet: *hahêṭēb ḥārâ lāk* ("Are you really that angry?"). With this reply, God condemns Jonah's attitude toward repentance, a stance that, as in the case of Cain, leads inexorably to the hopeless pursuit of Eden-like perfection. In fact, recall how in that story, after asking Cain *lāmâ ḥārâ lāk* ("Why are you angry?"), the Lord uses a *hiphil* form of *yṭb* to mean "to improve oneself" ("After all, if you improve yourself [*têṭîb*] . . ."). In turn, there is a strong case for embracing a rendering of *hahêṭēb ḥārâ lāk* that, although rightly discredited as a primary translation, yields an instructive added layer of meaning. Employing the infinitive absolute *hêṭēb* – itself a *hiphil* form of *yṭb* – not as an adverb ("really") but as a noun, so that, however atypically, it serves as the subject of *ḥārâ*, God asks Jonah, "Does *self-improvement* make you angry?" That is to say, do you indeed reject a world where sinning people possess an opportunity to enhance their moral standing?[48]

Allusions of Ascent, Illusions of Assent

Much like Cain, however, Jonah silently holds his ground, placing himself east of an Eden-like domain where he longs for an idyllic existence. The prophet accordingly constructs a *sukkâ*, signaling his relentless desire to inhabit a divine abode. And yet, the *sukkâ* cannot by itself satisfy his paradisiacal aspirations: for the structure to provide a genuine divine haven, the Lord would need to show his endorsement of the prophet's ideological stance. Indeed, by sitting confined in a *sukkâ*, powerless to bring about Nineveh's destruction, Jonah presents a striking contrast to the raging *yônâ* in Jeremiah: whereas that *yônâ* releases a lion from its *sukkâ* on the helpless targets of God's fury, our *yônâ* can only wait and see what a compassionate God has in store for Nineveh.[49] Jonah thus remains seated under the shade (*ṣēl*) of his would-be paradisiacal hut, awaiting an indication of Nineveh's fate. Will the Lord persist in his decision to allow the city to survive? Or might he, by some slight chance, at last come around to the prophet's position?

When God then appoints (*wayĕman*) a plant that provides shade (*ṣēl*) to save (*lĕhaṣṣîl*) Jonah from his bad state (*rā'ātô*), the prophet rejoices greatly (Jonah 4:6) – a triumphant reaction that the text initially validates in multiple ways. First, the *rā'â* of Jonah almost certainly refers not only to the effects of the strong sun but also to the prophet's theological angst denoted earlier by the same noun *rā'â* (4:1).[50] The alleviation of this *rā'a*, accordingly, suggests that the Lord has finally acceded to Jonah's wish. Further, the *ṣēl* provided by the *qîqāyôn* evidently corresponds to the *ṣēl* generated by the *sukkâ*, implying that God has responded favorably to the prophet's efforts.

An ingeniously subtle literary device, moreover, adds to this impression of the plant's significance. In numerous instances, our book features an inversion of letters or sounds that serves to underscore a thematic opposition or reversal. Consider the following examples:

- In chapter 1, after the recurring letter-sequence ירד (*yrd*; "go down") traces Jonah's sinking trajectory (Jonah 1:3–5), the phrase וידרו נדרים (*wayyiddĕrû nĕdārîm* ["and they took vows"]; 1:16) reverses the consonants *rd* (ירד ← וידרו), thereby contrasting the inspired crew with the submerged prophet.[51]
- In that same passage, an inversion of letters in the expression להשיב אל היבשה (*lĕhāšîb 'el-hayyabbāšâ* ["to return to dry land"]; 1:13) highlights the sailors' valiant effort to reverse course – the only imperfection involving the position of the vowel/semivowel *yôd*.[52]
- In chapter 3, inversions of similar-sounding consonants in ויכס שק (*wayĕkas śaq*; 3:6) and ויתכסו שקים (*wĕyitkassû śaqqîm*; 3:8), phrases that denote the Ninevites' donning of sackcloth, emphasize the fundamental change in attitude of that arrogant population.[53]

Further, in three of the four verses that feature the word *wayĕman*, a reversal of letters/consonants signifies a transformative development.[54]

- The expression דָּג גָּדוֹל (*dāg gādôl* ["great fish"]; 2:1) hints that the sea creature will spawn a reversal of Jonah's fate.
- The phrase תּוֹלַעַת בַּעֲלוֹת הַשַּׁחַר (*tôla'at ba'ălôt haššaḥar* ["a worm on the rising of the dawn"]; 4:7) marks the worm's fatal attack on the plant.
- A רוּחַ קָדִים חֲרִישִׁית (*rûaḥ qādîm ḥărîšît* ["scorching east wind"]; 4:8) assails Jonah's comfort and prompts his wish for death.[55]

Consider, then, our book's one remaining occurrence of *wayĕman*, which prefaces the growth of the *qîqāyôn*. Notably, here we encounter sequences of consonants that do *not* display any sort of reversal. First, the expression וַיַּעַל מֵעַל לְיוֹנָה (*wayya'al mē'al lĕyônâ*) denotes that the plant "rose above Jonah." Second, the phrase לִהְיוֹת צֵל . . . לְהַצִּיל (*lihyôt ṣēl . . . lĕhaṣṣîl*) affirms that the *qîqāyôn* provided "shade" for Jonah in order to "to save" him from his predicament.[56] Why then, in this lone instance of *wayĕman*, does the text not only shun any inversions but also feature these *straight* consonantal repetitions? The answer lies in the significance of the as yet unmolested *qîqāyôn*. Initially, when the Lord prompts the growth of the plant, he gives the impression of *endorsing* the Edenic aspirations of the *sukkâ*-inhabiting prophet. Only subsequently does God, in order to teach Jonah a harsh lesson, signal his opposition to those aspirations when, abruptly and without warning, he instigates the death of the *qîqāyôn* and exposes the prophet to the scorching elements. Appropriately, therefore, it is those later occurrences – and not the growth of the plant – that the text marks with inversions of letters.[57]

Finally, the favorable symbolism of the *qîqāyôn* emerges from its analogy to the Garden of Eden. This equivalence, we have seen, draws on allusions to the Eden account in Genesis, the Cain narrative, and Ezekiel's depiction of the paradisiacal cedar, complemented by a parallel to the heaven-sent manna in the exodus story. Additionally, the Edenic character of the *qîqāyôn* finds confirmation in the phrase *rûaḥ qādîm ḥărîšît*, which denotes the wind that attacks Jonah after the plant shrivels. Indeed, on close inspection, that entire expression underscores the prophet's expulsion from an Eden-like domain.

Recall that, elsewhere in the Bible, it is a *rûaḥ qādîm* ("east wind") that breaks apart treasure-filled ships of Tarshish. The author of Jonah, however, rather than summoning a *rûaḥ qādîm* to threaten the Tarshish-bound vessel, deploys the motif in our chapter instead, where it joins two other occurrences of the Eden-recalling root *qdm* (*qiddamtî, miqqedem*; Jonah 4:2, 5). This east wind, furthermore, strikes the prophet at the beginning of the day. The phrase *rûaḥ qādîm* thus triggers a resonance with the Eden story in Genesis, where God's presence in the east of Eden "during the *rûaḥ* of the day" (Gen 3:8) presages the banishment and affliction of humanity. If, accordingly, the *qîqāyôn* symbolizes the paradisiacal garden, then the analogy now fittingly extends to the plant's demise. For much as in the case of Adam and Eve, an eastern *rûaḥ* attends our prophet's exclusion from Eden and the onset of his suffering, as his idyllic existence gives way to the gloomy prospect of death.

As for the unique, intractable adjective *ḥărîšît*, most often rendered in the sense of "scorching/cutting," we return to the analogy between the *qîqāyôn* and the Edenic cedar of Lebanon.[58] When Ezekiel first characterizes that tree, he describes it as *yĕpê 'ānāp wĕḥōreš maṣṣēl* ("displaying beautiful branches and shady thickets"; Ezek 31:3). Recall, then, that our story features numerous parallels to that prophecy – including allusions to the root *yph* ("be beautiful") and to the blissful *ṣēl* ("shade") of Eden – to help convey that Jonah is seeking a paradisiacal existence. It follows, in turn, that the word *ḥărîšît* invokes the Eden-like *ḥōreš* in that same phrase in Ezekiel, a noun that typically denotes an area densely populated with trees.[59] In this way, much like the word *qādîm* right before it, the opaque term *ḥărîšît* – whatever its primary meaning – identifies the origin of the *rûaḥ* afflicting Jonah as the tree-lined Garden of Eden, calling to mind the *rûaḥ* that attended God's confrontation of the soon-to-be-expelled primeval humans.[60]

JONAH, THE PLANT, AND THE SALVATION OF NINEVEH

The Fate of Unmerited Bliss

After the withering of the *qîqāyôn*, Jonah again expresses a wish for death, even reiterating this desire when the Lord confronts him about it (Jonah 4:8–9). At that point, God finally provides an outright condemnation of

Jonah's stance, beginning with a notably long-winded assertion regarding the prophet's attitude toward the plant: "You had compassion for/wished to spare (ḥastā ʿal) the qîqāyôn, which you neither toiled for/in (lō'-ʿamaltā bô) nor raised up/made great (wĕlō' giddaltô), and which came into being in one night and perished in one night" (4:10).[61]

Now on the surface, of course, Jonah had no interest in – and certainly no compassion for – the plant in and of itself. According to the simple reading of the passage, the qîqāyôn merely served to provide him with some extra shade, whereas his true frustration over its demise arose only when the hot wind and sun subsequently afflicted him. The Lord's remarks, accordingly, leave the odd impression that, at this climactic moment, he chooses to trump Jonah by deliberately misinterpreting the prophet's intentions.[62]

Once we recognize, however, that the plant embodies an Edenic domain, this problem falls away. First, God asks Jonah, "Are you really that angry concerning the qîqāyôn?" challenging the prophet's anger over the loss of his latest Edenic escape. Indeed, like the similar divine query earlier in the chapter, this line probably bears the added meaning, "Is it self-improvement (hêṭēb) that angers you concerning the qîqāyôn?"[63] For if Jonah's embrace of the paradisiacal plant results from his indignation regarding the efficacy of repentance, then his despair over this latest banishment amounts to an expression of that same moralistic zeal. Predictably, in fact, the prophet responds by reaffirming his position, uttering a line that may be rendered, "Self-improvement (hêṭēb) angers me to the point of [my seeking] death (ʿad-māwet)," or alternatively, "Self-improvement will anger me until [the day I] die."

The Lord, however, rebuffs Jonah's stance, appealing to the crucial analogy between the qîqāyôn and the manna. The manna-hoarding Israelites, after being rescued at sea, illicitly seek to preserve their latest installment of divine largesse. Similarly, our prophet, after his own salvation at sea, renews his audacious quest for a permanent idyllic existence under God's protection. The Lord thus teaches Jonah, much as he showed in the story of the manna, that *unmerited divine gifts bear no enduring value.* Rather, only by persistent, plodding effort can human beings strive for a better world – an opportunity that our perfectionist prophet seeks to deny to the flawed inhabitants of Nineveh.

When God reprimands Jonah for wishing to spare the *qîqāyôn*, his intention is then to impart this message. The phrase *lō'-ʿāmaltā bô*, in fact, yields two simultaneous meanings that underscore the plant's unsustainability: Jonah "did not toil for it," because it arose at God's prompting, and he also "did not toil *inside* it," because it provided him, however briefly, with a blissful, Eden-like existence. Similarly, the ensuing phrase *wĕlō' giddaltô* yields two translations: the prophet neither worked to "grow" the plant, nor did he "make it great"; that is, endow it with any true worth.[64] Inevitably, therefore, much like the manna sent from heaven, Jonah's paradisiacal *qîqāyôn* was gone within a day of its arrival. By contrast, the Lord continues, there was every reason to spare the "great" (*gĕdôlâ*), Edenic city of Nineveh with its multitudes of *'ādām* and *bĕhēmâ* (Jonah 4:11), whose paradisiacal splendor bears real value, he intimates, because it came about by means of genuine effort on the part of its inhabitants.[65]

It is essential, however, that we distinguish two issues here, both of which occupy a place in this concluding dialogue: the necessity of laboring for one's rewards and the more central question of Nineveh's moral worthiness. The manna connection gives emphasis to the necessity of human toil, which stands at odds with our prophet's pursuit of unearned paradisiacal bliss. Jonah's protest, by contrast, chiefly concerns the moral failures of the Ninevites and the second opportunity that God nonetheless grants them. Before addressing this moral dimension, however, let us briefly acknowledge another inner-biblical correlation, which both relates to the book's Eden theme and accounts for some distinctive formulations in this final part of the story.

Jonah, the Plant, and the Falling Star of Dawn

In the book of Isaiah, the prophet draws an analogy between the king of Babylon and the mythological *hêlēl ben-šāḥar*, literally rendered "Day Star son of Dawn" (Isa 14:12).[66] This luminary endeavors to rise up to the *yarkĕtê ṣāpôn*, yet it ultimately falls into the *yarkĕtê bôr* ("nethermost reaches of the Pit"; 14:13–15). Scholars, accordingly, compare this passage to Ezekiel's depiction of the fall of the Edenic cedar into the abyss.[67] Like Ezekiel's prophecy, moreover, this Isaiah text has prompted an association with Jonah's transient divine shelters.[68] For example, much as a worm (*tôla'at*) brings about the demise of the heavenly *qîqāyôn*, in Isaiah we encounter worms (*tôlē'â*) crawling over the site where the arrogant king descended to Sheol (14:11).[69]

Indeed, on close inspection, this passage in Isaiah bears an especially consequential relationship to our own. When recounting the efforts of the *hêlēl ben-šāḥar* to attain great heights, the prophet uses the root *'lh* (עלה; "rise") four times in the space of two verses[70]:

> You said in your heart, "I will rise (*'e'ĕlê*; אעלה) to the heavens;
> Above (*mimma'al*; ממעל) the stars of God I will raise my throne.
> I will sit upon the mountain of [the divine] assembly,
> In the *yarkĕtê ṣāpôn*.
> I will rise up (*'e'ĕlê*; אעלה) upon the heights of the clouds;
> I will be like the Most High (*'elyôn*; עליון).'"   (Isa 14:13–14)

Consider, then, that in our story, the worm attacks the plant *ba'ălôt haššaḥar* ("on the rising [עלות] of the dawn"; Jonah 4:7), the verb deriving from this same root *'lh*. This combination of *'lh* and *šaḥar* suggests that the Eden-like *qîqāyôn*, which signifies the unmerited paradisiacal existence sought by Jonah, stands in analogy not only to the doomed, grandiose cedar of Lebanon but also to the foolhardy morning star whose illusions of transcendence brought it down into the Pit. Thus, our text affirms, right after the rise (*'lh*) of the *šaḥar*-like plant (*ba'ălôt haššaḥar*) God dispatched a worm to kill it, much as the presence of worms punctuates the fall of the similarly Star-of-Dawn-like Mesopotamian king.

Observe, moreover, that when describing the inexorably fleeting nature of the *qîqāyôn*, the Lord employs the striking and problematic formulation *šebbin-laylâ hāyâ ûbin-laylâ 'ābād* (Jonah 4:10). Literally, this phrase appears to mean, "which came into being one night old and perished one night old." Does it make any sense, however, to say that something "came into being one night old"?[71]

The connection to Isaiah 14 offers a compelling solution. Whereas the phrase *ben-šāḥar*, which may be translated "dawn-like," identifies the not-yet-fallen star as one that brightens the morning, the contrasting expression *bin-laylâ*, which may accordingly be translated "night-like," portrays the shade-bestowing *qîqāyôn* as an entity that, literally and figuratively, epitomizes darkness.[72] The Lord means to say, then, that this fundamentally worthless plant – which Jonah did not "make great" (*giddaltô*) – "came into being characterized by darkness (*bin-laylâ*) and perished [no less] characterized by darkness (*bin-laylâ*)." Further, the word *laylâ* (לילה) features the letters of *hêlēl* (הילל) in essentially reverse order, the only imperfection – much as in the case of להשיב אל היבשה (*lĕhāšîb 'el-hayyabbāšâ* ["to return to dry land"]; 1:13) – involving the position of the vowel/semivowel *yôd*. Once again, then, we encounter an inversion of letters that calls attention to a contrast: the Lord, by calling the would-be star-like *qîqāyôn* a *bin-laylâ*, underscores the negation of the heavenly quality that the prophet had hoped it would perpetually retain.

Nineveh, Sodom, and the Garden of Eden

We now return to the book's final verse, where the Lord contrasts the great city of Nineveh to the fleeting and inconsequential *qîqāyôn*. On the basis of the analogy between the plant and the similarly unmerited manna, I have suggested that God, if only by implication, means to ascribe the magnificence of the Assyrian city to the hard work of its inhabitants. The Edenic plant, by contrast, because it arose by divine decree, did not warrant any enduring existence. Still, for the purpose of Jonah's debate with God, the far greater concern remains Nineveh's *moral* worthiness. Appropriately, therefore, it is this matter that the Lord addresses explicitly in the story's concluding line.

Recall that this verse likens the Ninevites to dwellers of Eden: much like the *'ādām* who had not yet eaten from the forbidden tree, the *'ādām* who populate Nineveh, the Lord affirms, did not know the difference between good and evil. Hence, there would have been no justification for annihilating the city, unless the Ninevites had failed to repent in response to the prophet's admonition. Oddly, however, rather than merely saying that the Ninevites could not distinguish good from evil, God affirms that the city contains "twelve myriad people" who, before Jonah set them straight, "did not know their right from their left." Happily, however, still another inner-biblical allusion provides the key to both of these anomalous formulations.

The sinful Nineveh faces annihilation much like the prototypically wicked city of Sodom, and as widely noted, our text features multiple references to that story.[73] First, Jonah uses the root *hpk* when forecasting the destruction of Nineveh (Jonah 3:4), a verb used so often in connection with Sodom that the resonance becomes especially hard to deny.[74] Second, at the beginning of our story, the Lord states that Nineveh's evil "has risen up before me" (1:2), recalling a similar divine pronouncement that the cries of Sodom's victims "have come to me" (Gen 18:21). To be sure, the "rising" (*'ālĕtâ*; עלתה) of Nineveh's evil might better resonate with a different context, where God declares, by means of the same root *'lh* (עלה), that the cries of Egypt's Israelite slaves "have risen up (*watta'al*; ותעל) to me" (Exod 2:23).[75] Even if this is correct, however, our allusion-minded author, in all probability, would have intended to recall the oppressive conduct that characterizes *both* soon-to-be-disciplined, Edenic locations – not just Egypt but also Sodom.[76]

With this in mind, then, consider the story of Lot, the nephew of Abram who settles in Sodom (Gen 13). Before Lot moves to Sodom – and, crucially, immediately before the text compares that city to Egypt and "the Garden of the Lord" – Abram frames his kinsman's choice by saying, "If you go left I will go right, and if you go right I will go left" (13:9). It follows, in turn, that the terms "right" and "left" mark the distinction between the wicked but paradisiacal location embraced by Lot and the alternative region to be inhabited by Abram and his descendants. Fittingly, therefore, when our text refers to the lowly moral state of the Edenic city of Nineveh, it pointedly affirms that the people did not know the difference between "their right and their left." That is to say, before Jonah provided the warning, the Ninevites could not properly distinguish between a Sodom-like way of life and its alternative. Rather, only after the prophet enlightened them could they have been held accountable for their conduct, and by that time they had undergone a successful transformation.

As for Nineveh's 120,000 people, this number equals one-fifth of Abram's progeny, who stand in contrast to the inhabitants of Lot's paradigmatically evil location.[77] Note, however, that the region chosen by Lot encompassed not just Sodom but the entire Plain of the Jordan, which contained *five* sinful cities (Deut 29:22; Gen 19:20–22).[78] Accordingly, toward the goal of invoking just *one* of those cities, our author places the Ninevites at one-fifth of 600,000 – the larger number presumed to mark the total not just of Abram's descendants but also of the population of the corresponding area selected by his less virtuous nephew.

And yet, despite their similarity to the wicked residents of Sodom, the newly enlightened inhabitants of the paradisiacal Nineveh transform their character after hearing the reluctant words of Jonah. Hence, they succeed in eliciting the full measure of God's compassion – much to the consternation of a moralistic prophet who, profoundly troubled by the efficacy of repentance, could only embark on a defiant and relentless quest, however futile, for a radically different kind of world.

Peaceful Dove

A PACIFIST JONAH?

What, then, of the possibility that Jonah yearns for the *salvation* of Nineveh? Does the text really give rise to another reading, in which the prophet seeks out a paradisiacal world free of punishment and suffering? Whereas some of our book's allusions allow exclusively for a moralistic Jonah, the story itself does yield an alternative, pacifist conception of his motives. Indeed, crucially, still other allusions point strongly toward this additional layer of meaning.

To begin, consider that the term *yônâ*, when applied to a human being, tends to evoke not a raging oppressor but the more tranquil image of a dove, as when it signifies wholesome, gentle beauty in the Song of Songs.[1] In fact, the parallel between Jonah and the *yônâ* sent flying off the boat in the flood story in Genesis, despite the contrasts already noted, intensifies the prophet's association with that peaceful bird. Furthermore, in his only appearance in the Bible outside our book, Jonah relays a prophecy of restoration that comes to fruition despite the *unworthiness* of its beneficiaries (2 Kgs 14:23–27). If, accordingly, the passage in Kings bears significance for our story, it might well suggest that the prophet fancies redemption for the sinning Ninevites even in the *absence* of contrition.[2]

Another set of evidence, however, carries far greater importance. Specifically, our story offers numerous indications that Jonah, by withholding his pronouncement and pursuing an idyllic existence, actually wishes to salvage – and to inhabit – *the very Edenic reality embodied by Nineveh.*

By way of introduction, recall that the standard translation of the Lord's opening command, which renders *kî* in the sense of "because," might easily suggest that he is dispatching Jonah to proclaim destruction on the city ("Arise and go to the great city of Nineveh and *call out on it*, because their evil has risen up before me"). If the prophet understands his mission this way, it follows that, by running away, he is seeking to withhold the dire pronouncement. Jonah's actions – his journey toward "beauty" (*yāpô*) and his boarding a Tarshish-bound vessel – only add to the perception that he is driven by an aspiration toward Eden-like placidity. Recall, furthermore, that the text generates an analogy between Nineveh and Tyre, the Edenic coastal city supplied/signified by fortune-laden ships of Tarshish. This analogy contributes to the sense that Jonah, by loading treasures onto the Tyre-like vessel, wishes to maintain, rather than to obliterate, the resplendence of Nineveh. For even though the prophet heads in a direction away from the actual Assyrian city, the futility of his action proves no different from that of other manifestations of his escapist endeavor: much like Jonah's descent into unperturbed sleep during the storm, his ill-fated voyage offers no genuine promise of preventing the imminent disaster. Rather, his flight amounts to nothing more than a hopeless, deluded effort to avoid confronting a reality that distresses him.

The text, moreover, goes beyond this Tyre connection to provide some strong indications that the prophet's Edenic sanctuaries stand not as alternatives to the paradisiacal Nineveh, but as embodiments of it. First, the sea creature that swallows Jonah bears an equivalence to Nineveh, a city whose name and ideogram invoke the imagery of fish. According to our first reading of the story, this association merely helps identify the fish's belly as an alternative Edenic domain. This explanation, however, suffers from a serious drawback. To recognize such a connection, the reader must link the creature to Nineveh, and *then* link Nineveh to Eden based on an Edenic depiction of Assyria in Ezekiel 31 that makes no reference to Nineveh or to fish. The fish motif in Jonah, consequently, works far more effectively if the creature signifies the Assyrian city in and of itself.

Second, recall that the Eden-like *qîqāyôn* corresponds to the arrogant cedar that represents Assyria. Consider, then, that when the plant grows above Jonah, who is probably sitting not very far from Nineveh, the possibility arises that it might symbolize that very Assyrian city. At the end of the book, moreover, the Lord draws a direct comparison between the *qîqāyôn* and Nineveh, even as the analogy ultimately underscores a pointed difference between them. There would appear to be good reason, accordingly, to link the *qîqāyôn* to the city itself.[3]

Most important, however, is one essential inner-biblical connection that links Nineveh to both the ship and the plant – hardly, it would seem, just for the purpose of indirectly invoking the Garden of Eden. This connection warrants our especially close attention.

THE CITY OF NINEVEH, THE SANCTUARIES OF JONAH, AND THE ORACLES OF NAHUM

The book of Jonah bears a widely acknowledged correlation to the prophecies of Nahum, who likewise forecasts the destruction of Nineveh. On a basic level, this correlation underscores a contrast between the wrath of God in Nahum and the mercy that he displays in Jonah. For example, the divine-attribute formula in Nahum highlights the Lord's vengeance (Nah 1:3), whereas the one in Jonah emphasizes his mercy (Jonah 4:2). And a rhetorical question at the end of Nahum serves to condemn Nineveh, whereas the one at the end of Jonah affirms that the city merits divine compassion.[4] At the same time, however, some additional, notably meaningful parallels to Nahum – most of which have gone unremarked – help generate a formidable case that our prophet wishes to rescue the imperiled Assyrian city.

First, observe that the vengeance of God in Nahum's opening prophecy takes the form of cataclysmic events in nature (Nah 1:3–6), beginning with a raging storm.[5] Right after depicting these disasters, Nahum rhetorically asks, "Who can stand (*ya'ămôd*) before [God's] anger (*za'mô*)?" (1:6). Subsequently, he challenges Nineveh with the query, "Why do you plot (*tĕḥaššĕbûn*) against the Lord?" (1:9). This uncommon usage of *ḥšb* ("plot") occurs also in Jonah when, after the tempest arrives, the text tells us that the Tarshish-bound ship "plotted (*ḥiššĕbâ*) to break apart" (Jonah 1:4).[6] And after the sailors throw Jonah overboard, the text employs personification once more when, again recalling the language of Nahum, it states that "the sea stood back (*wayyaʿămōd*) from its rage (*zaʿpô*)" (1:15).[7]

These correspondences suggest that the vessel in Jonah stands in parallel to Nineveh in the text of Nahum, where, significantly, one finds no mention of the city's Edenic character. Most straightforwardly, the correlation thus suggests that Jonah, by setting out on the treasure-laden ship, sought to inhabit an *enduringly resplendent Nineveh* – not, as our first reading would have it, a *more authentic Eden* that would rise up on the Assyrian city's proverbial ashes. The Lord, consequently, casts a storm on this glamorous Nineveh-on-the-sea that "plots" to help Jonah avoid confronting the actual city – the "plot" thus nearly causing the vessel to break apart – and he only prompts the waters to "stand back" from their "wrath" when the crew expels both the ship's fortune and the recalcitrant, bliss-seeking prophet.

Crucially, moreover, in a later passage in Nahum, we find that "lots (*gôrāl*) were cast on the honored ones (*nikbaddêhā*)" among the ill-fated nations that sought to rescue Nineveh (Nah 3:10). Working off this motif, accordingly, our story – through the key, thrice-repeated expression "cast lots (*gôrāl/gôrālôt*)" (Jonah 1:7) – recounts how a lottery helped determine the fate of the dove-like prophet who, much like those nations, wished to *prevent* the city's destruction. Indeed, recall that this uncommon *niphal* plural denoting "the honored ones" of a nation likewise appears in the phrase "to dishonor (*lĕhāqēl*) all the honored ones of (*nikbaddê*) the land" (Isa 23:9) – a formulation that inspired our text's use of *lĕhāqēl* ("to get the weight/honor off") to describe the purging of the vessel's Edenic treasures (Jonah 1:5). It emerges, then, that the sea-storm passage in Jonah, if indirectly, associates the term *nikbaddêhā/nikbaddê* with the ship's precious cargo *and* Jonah's attempted escape, both of which mark the prophet's presumptuous effort to preserve the resplendent Nineveh.

Next, we turn to the paradisiacal plant that rises above Jonah – perhaps originating from the site of Nineveh – which shows unmistakable parallels to the cedar that represents Assyria. According to our first reading, this analogy to Assyria serves merely to confirm the *qîqāyôn*'s Eden-like character. Recall, however, that the worm that attacks the plant bears an association with ravaging locusts. With this in mind, observe that the locust motif dominates the concluding passage of the book of Nahum (3:15–17), beginning where the prophet envisions a fire consuming Nineveh like a swarm of locusts. For one thing, the presence of this image helps confirm that our text, too, means to evoke that motif. More important, however, it suggests that the locust-recalling worm, when it assails the *qîqāyôn*, attacks not merely a representation of Eden but also *an embodiment of Nineveh*, a city that, as Nahum affirms, faces destruction by a locust-like onslaught.

Observe, furthermore, that the locust image in Nahum quickly turns to signify something entirely different: the hapless soldiers of Nineveh who are designated to guard the city's borders (Nah 3:17). These "locusts," says the prophet, remain perched on the fences of Nineveh in the cool weather, but when the sun rises up (*šemeš zārĕḥâ*) they disappear, nowhere to be found. Evidently, then, our text draws on this motif when, after the withering of the *qîqāyôn*, it recounts that "on the rising of the sun" (*kizrōaḥ haššemeš*) Jonah was attacked by the scorching elements (Jonah 4:8). After all, the analogous phrase "on the rising of the dawn" (*baʿălôt haššaḥar*; 4:7), according to its deeper layer of meaning, refers not to any new occurrence but rather to the rise of the Star-of-Dawn-like plant recounted in the preceding verse. The expression "on the rising of the sun" thus likewise refers to the event reported immediately before it; that is, the shriveling of the *qîqāyôn* in the wake of the worm-attack. For much like the Assyrian city itself, the Nineveh-like plant – assailed by a locust-like entity – ceases to provide protection at sunrise, thereby leaving its lone denizen at the mercy of the ruthlessly onrushing heat.[8]

A PACIFIST PROPHET AND AN IMPERILED CITY

If, accordingly, our book offers indications that Jonah wishes to save Nineveh – his coveted sanctuaries symbolizing that very Edenic location – it remains to see if the story as a whole can sustain such a reading. Significantly, for as long as the text declines to explain Jonah's conduct, it indeed allows for – and probably even encourages – different interpretations of the prophet's motives.[9] After all, until Jonah finally explains why he escaped, nothing in the text itself requires our seeing him as a zealot. Furthermore, a majority of the allusions we have seen prove equally compatible with the alternative, pacifist conception of the prophet's conduct: most of these correlations relate to Jonah's defiant quest for an Edenic existence, which remains in effect according to this new approach.

In fact, even Jonah's connection to Cain, who hardly strikes a pacifist image, suits this second interpretation. Consider that Cain's disdain for repentance arises not from any apparent *objection* to its efficacy, but from a failure to appreciate the potential that it affords. The present reading, in turn, invites an especially befitting application of the Cain analogy. To wit, the initial, ambiguous divine command, instead of suggesting to Jonah that he must proclaim destruction on Nineveh ("and pronounce [doom] on it"), could alternatively have driven him to inspire the city's residents to reform their ways ("and call out to it that their evil has risen up before me"). Yet the prophet, much like Cain, *cannot muster any confidence* in the path of repentance. Consequently, he departs "from the face of the Lord" toward a fortune-laden embodiment of Nineveh, closing his eyes to the realities of sin and suffering while seeking to maintain – and to inhabit – the glorious existence epitomized by that very resplendent city. Indeed, this attitude toward repentance endures even when Jonah is forced to carry out his task. After the Lord, intent on exhorting Nineveh to transform itself, insists that the prophet convey "*to* it the calling that *I* am relating to you," Jonah's actual proclamation – "In another forty days Nineveh will be upended" – suggests that he remains stuck on the virtual inevitability of the city's collapse. Accordingly, the angst-ridden prophet continues, however fruitlessly, to pursue a trouble-free world, only to find that his paradisiacal aspirations, like those of Cain, cannot prevail over the will of God.

For obvious reasons, however, this reading appears to falter in the final chapter of the book. First, if Jonah wished to prevent the destruction of Nineveh, then his distress and indignation over its rescue would seem to defy explanation.[10] Moreover, if the prophet was seeking a peaceful outcome all along, then the conclusion of the story makes little apparent sense. The Lord, under such circumstances, should have had no need to teach Jonah, with the help of the *qîqāyôn*, that the mercy extended to Nineveh was genuinely warranted.

These objections, however, rest on decidedly questionable assumptions.[11] First, consider that, after the prophet constructs a *sukkâ*, we are informed that he sat under it waiting to see "what would happen in the city." Now according to the simple meaning of the story, Jonah knows quite well that God has rescinded the dire decree. Thus, some commentators suppose – as I do for our own first reading – that the text is now reporting, if rather obliquely, that the prophet hopes the Ninevites will regress and again provoke God's wrath. Other interpreters, however, draw a very different conclusion: that Jonah departed Nineveh immediately after his pronouncement and remains unaware of any ensuing developments. The distress that he exhibits, therefore, arises from what he *anticipates* will befall the city, rather than from anything that has actually transpired.[12]

If this latter alternative is correct, then what exactly is the fate that our angry protagonist thinks will befall Nineveh? According to the common understanding of Jonah's attitude, he expects, much to his frustration, that the city will survive. Our present reading, by contrast, suggests the opposite: Jonah, who seeks only peace and tranquility for both himself and Nineveh, harbors great skepticism that the Ninevites will manage to effect any change in their destiny. Consequently, he regards his pronouncement – which he had sought to avoid making – as little more than a step in the process of the city's annihilation, and his distress signals this deeply pessimistic outlook. The prophet, then, far from being distraught over the *salvation* of Nineveh, experiences anguish over an impending devastation that he feels helpless to prevent.

Immediately, however, we encounter an even more challenging difficulty. An indignant Jonah then lays out his complaint, in which he glumly articulates the merciful attributes of God. How could his statement possibly accord with our present reading, which affirms that the prophet *wants* the Lord to extend compassion to Nineveh? To address this problem, I propose that we take a close look at Jonah's remarks – leaving aside any added layers of meaning – and pay careful attention to the distinctly curious structure of his formulation.

"Was this not my word when I was still on my land?" Jonah asks. "That is why I took preemptive action in escaping toward Tarshish. For I know/knew (*kî yāda'tî*) that you are a gracious and compassionate God, slow to anger and abounding in kindness, who relents from causing harm."[13] Crucially, the prophet does not directly indicate the substance of his "word."

Rather, the *kî*-phrase here, much like the one uttered by God at the beginning of the book, yields an ambiguity that our skillful author, in all probability, consciously sought to generate.[14] On the one hand, according to the standard interpretation, Jonah fled because of his disdain for the mercy that he "knows" the Lord might yet extend – or has already extended – to the Ninevites. If this is correct, then Jonah's "word" consists of an objection to God's compassion, and the *kî*-phrase fittingly spells out the divine traits that the prophet is protesting.

On the other hand, Jonah might be saying something entirely different: when he initially withheld his pronouncement, far from trying to ensure Nineveh's destruction, he was *seeking* divine compassion for the sinful city. His "word," therefore, consisted of an *appeal* to the merciful attributes that he "knew" God possesses, but that he now believes will be of no use. The *kî*-phrase, then, in expounding the "word" of Jonah, suggests not that he is protesting God's merciful character, but rather that, before being forced to come to Nineveh, he had sought to *elicit* divine compassion by suppressing his prophecy of doom.[15]

Indeed, in support of this latter alternative, recall that Cain, when he moves to an area east of Eden, apparently yearns to enter the paradisiacal garden. Hence, when our prophet places himself east of Nineveh, we might easily conclude that he, too, longs to inhabit an Edenic domain *embodied* by the location that he is facing.[16] On this assumption, then, Jonah rejoices over the Nineveh-like *qîqāyôn* because, to his mind, it represents – as did the ship and the fish – the preservation of the Edenic environment afforded by the city itself, regardless of the morality of its inhabitants. The plant, however, much like those other Nineveh-like sanctuaries, proceeds to vomit Jonah out of its shelter, thereby signifying the inexorably fleeting nature of any such undeserved bliss.

To complete this second reading, we thus only need to account for the Lord's concluding remark, where he seems to be teaching Jonah, superfluously it would appear, that the mercy extended to Nineveh does not warrant protest. Let us, accordingly, consider the language of the book's final verse, in particular its opening clause, *"wa'ănî lō' 'āḥûs* on the great city of Nineveh." In line with the conventional reading, which attributes zealotry to Jonah, this phrase is typically rendered, "Should I not spare/ show compassion to the great city of Nineveh?"[17] That is to say, if the prophet wished to spare a plant in which he invested no effort and that he did not make great, why should God not spare a truly great city whose inhabitants cannot be held accountable for their moral failures?

At the same time, however, the phrase might just as well mean something else: "*Would* I not spare/show compassion to the great city of Nineveh?"[18] According to this translation – and in keeping with our present reading of the story – the Lord sharply rebukes the peace-seeking prophet for his resigned attitude and attendant escapism, born of his unwillingness to confront the uncertain consequences of human iniquity: You Jonah, declares God – who in your quest for bliss sought to spare an unmerited, manna-like plant that you did nothing to "make great" – did you really think that *I* wouldn't show compassion to the vast, blameless population of the genuinely great city of Nineveh?

In the final analysis, then, the book of Jonah yields multiple *sustained* interpretations. According to one reading, the prophet, driven by moralistic zeal, attempts to deny Nineveh an opportunity for salvation and instead seeks to occupy Edenic sanctuaries that meet his perfectionist ideals. Simultaneously, another reading ascribes to Jonah a desire for an untroubled, paradisiacal world, epitomized by an enduringly glamorous Nineveh and unencumbered by the ramifications of sin. Significantly, these two approaches complement one another, underscoring the dangers of either extreme and the necessity of a balanced and constructive attitude toward human imperfection and its implications.

Having arrived at this conclusion, we might well deem this pivotal part of our discussion complete. Nevertheless, recent scholarship has opened new avenues in the interpretation of the book's final chapter, which have significant implications for the present analysis. Specifically, there is excellent reason to embrace a different version of our second reading, one that attributes to the Lord – and ultimately to the story itself – a far harsher stance toward the sinful Assyrian city. Because of the prodigious multivalence that I attribute to the book, I am inclined to think that our author had that version in mind *in addition* to the one already presented. If, however, one of the two alternatives is to be preferred, it warrants emphasis that this new, more ambitious option has some striking advantages, which make it especially hard to exclude from the set of meanings generated by the story.

JONAH AND THE FALL OF NINEVEH

According to an increasingly popular view, the final verse in Jonah must be read declaratively rather than as a rhetorical question.[19] The Lord thus means to say that, in the end, he will in fact *not* spare Nineveh, a city populated by nothing more than "ignoramuses and beasts."[20] One the one hand, this reading accounts for the absence of an interrogative *hê* at the beginning of the sentence (*wa'ănî*). Indeed, I regard this consideration to be significant for two reasons. First, inasmuch as my analysis ascribes especially meticulous care to the book's composition, it suggests that any unconventional formulation – even if a philological justification can be marshaled for it – serves to generate added meaning.[21] Second, if I am correct that the story regularly employs multivalent expressions, this both enhances the probability that our author omitted the interrogative *hê* in order to generate a second, declarative meaning and allows an interrogative meaning, with the advantages that it affords, to remain in place simultaneously.

For a declarative rendering to be justified, however, it must accord with both the immediate context and the story more generally.[22] Now if, indeed, the Lord is intent on destroying Nineveh, it follows that Jonah, seeking a peaceful world, means to protest against that ominous prospect. Needless to say, this best fits our second reading of the story, which attributes to the prophet a pacifist motive. Recall, however, that in our first iteration of this second reading, Jonah, like Cain, pursues an Edenic existence because of his failure to embrace the possibilities afforded by repentance. If, however, the prophet is *correct* that the Lord means to condemn Nineveh, it becomes necessary to revisit some key parts of the story with that hypothesis in mind.

To begin with, this approach suggests that, when God initially dispatches Jonah, he actually does mean for the prophet to utter a pronouncement of doom ("and proclaim on it [destruction], because their evil has risen up before me"). At the beginning of chapter 3, then, when the Lord adamantly reaffirms that the prophet must perform his task, his concern must be the opposite of what I suggested earlier: God must be worried that Jonah, seeking to save Nineveh, might cleverly – and inaccurately – interpret his mandate to call for encouraging repentance. Consequently, God demands that the prophet "call out to it the calling that *I* am relating to you," meaning that he must be sure to proclaim that the city will be destroyed.[23] Jonah, however, by employing the ambiguous verb *nehpāket*, manages to include a subtle indication that there may be more than one way to actualize the "upending" of the city. The Ninevites, in turn, pick up on the helpful hint and repent of their evil ways toward the goal of transforming their destiny.

What effect, then, do their efforts generate? However obvious the answer might seem, let us pay careful attention to the final verse of the chapter, particularly its latter half: "and God relented from/had remorse regarding (*wayyinnāhem 'al*) the bad that he had said he would do to them, and did not do [it] (*wĕlō' 'āśâ*)." This formulation creates two problems. First, its language clearly draws on the text of Exodus 32:14, which affirms that the Lord, in the aftermath of the sin of the golden calf, "relented from the bad that he had said he would do to his people."[24] It thus begs explanation why our text, which weighs its terminology so carefully, finds it necessary to add the extra clause "and did not do [it]" at the end of the line. Second, in that same clause, what might account for the uncommon elision of the direct object "it"?[25]

To resolve these difficulties, I propose that, shunning all preconceptions, we render this line in keeping with its apparent literal meaning: "and God had remorse regarding the bad that he had said he would do to them *but had not done*."[26] According to this translation, the Lord – perhaps anticipating the moral regression and attendant destruction of Assyria – experiences regret that he did not simply annihilate Nineveh without involving our stubbornly idealistic prophet. After all, now that the people have repented, what is God to do when forty days are up? Can he justify destroying the city anyway, even though the moral picture, as things stand now, has become decidedly more ambiguous? Or does he have no choice but to allow Nineveh to survive, at least for the time being?

What is more, consider that the first half of this verse likewise features extraneous language and an atypical structure: "And God saw/took note of (*wayyar'*) their deeds, that (*kî*) they turned back from their evil ways." Why does the text say that God saw "their deeds" *and* "that they turned back from their evil ways"? Is this not redundant? Might there be, then, an alternative way of reading the line – perhaps without assigning to it this relatively uncommon appositional syntax? Moreover, what are the ostensibly favorable "deeds" that helped trigger a reversal of fortune for this long-sinning population? Could it be just their fasting and donning of sackcloth?[27] Could the expression "their deeds" merely refer to the *cessation* of their wicked behavior? Or is the text only making an oblique reference to unspecified deeds that it acknowledged earlier at best by implication?

In response to all these questions, I submit that the *kî*-phrase ("*kî* they turned back from their evil ways"), like others we have seen, is designed to bear two meanings. According to the simple rendering, the word *kî* yields the translation "that," and it introduces an elaboration of the irredeemably superfluous reference to "their deeds." In line with our present reading of the book, however, we may translate the verse as follows: "And God took note of their deeds *because* (*kî*) they had turned back from their evil ways."[28] In principle, the text might thus be emphasizing that, because the people repented, the Lord – despite his preference to destroy Nineveh – *had* to take note of their (unspecified) better deeds, and he in turn regretted not having annihilated them earlier. I am inclined, however, to favor an even more ambitious explanation: the verse recounts that, because the Ninevites desisted from their evil, God was prompted to inspect the *full array of their deeds* – past, present, and future – and came to regret that he had not obliterated them before allowing this ephemeral, last-minute show of deference to complicate the moral equation.

Either way, according to this approach, the verse stops short of indicating the Lord's actual decision. This omission, in turn, allows us to interpret the remainder of the book in strict chronological order. First, Jonah, who recognizes that the fate of Nineveh remains uncertain, becomes distressed that his proclamation might contribute to the fall of the city. He affirms, accordingly, that when he ran from pronouncing doom he was appealing to God's contrary disposition toward mercy. Then, after the Lord challenges his pacifist indignation, the prophet places himself east of Nineveh and builds a *sukkâ*, a would-be divine abode that signifies his wish to preserve the paradisiacal city.

With Jonah thus anxiously awaiting God's verdict, an Edenic, Nineveh-like *qîqāyôn* grows above him. Crucially, according to this reading, it is *not* the purpose of the plant to give the prophet the fleeting, mistaken impression that Nineveh will endure regardless of the morality of its inhabitants. Rather, the flourishing *qîqāyôn* signals to Jonah *the actual rejuvenation of Nineveh* in the wake of its abandonment of evil. Jonah then rejoices greatly over the growth of the plant, rightly perceiving that the Lord has, at least for now, decided not to destroy the repentant city.

Sadly, however, the peace-seeking prophet returns to his state of despair when the Nineveh-signifying *qîqāyôn* withers. After all – as was known to our book's audience – the great city represented by the *qîqāyôn* would, like the plant itself, eventually be attacked and devastated.[29] Jonah, accordingly, must learn that, notwithstanding the value of peace and the merits of compassion, the wickedness of a population may at times necessitate truly dire consequences. This, in turn, becomes the purpose of the story's concluding dialogue, where the Lord explains to the prophet why, in the end, he indeed will not spare the majestic Assyrian city.

Previously, I embraced a connection between the *qîqāyôn* and the manna, arguing that the plant signifies unmerited divine largesse, which cannot endure. On this basis, I explained that God, when he comments on the fate of the *qîqāyôn*, is saying that Jonah did nothing to earn it or to instill in it any "greatness." The city of Nineveh, by contrast, *is* a "great" entity, one whose amoral conduct did not quite justify its annihilation.

Observe, however, that whereas the Lord states explicitly that Jonah did not make the plant "great," he does not complete the thought by spelling out who made Nineveh "great." To fill this gap, I initially appealed to the manna analogy, suggesting that the great city deserved a chance for survival because the *Ninevites* built it up – in contrast to the *qîqāyôn* and the manna that came into being without any human effort. The present reading, however, which affirms that God is *condemning* Nineveh, requires that we abandon this entire explanation. For Nineveh's greatness – whatever amount of human toil brought it about – has now become an apparent strike against it, contributing in some way to the Lord's decision *not* to spare the city.

Why, then, does the text not say who made Nineveh great? The matter is left ambiguous, I submit, precisely to allow for a different, if hardly novel, explanation: it is *God* who made Nineveh into a great and powerful city.[30] This final verse thereby emphasizes the incongruity between Nineveh's greatness, on the one hand, and the wickedness of its inhabitants, on the other. After all, a people in whom the Lord invested much can only survive if its conduct proves befitting.[31] Hence, God declares that he will ultimately not spare the great city of Nineveh, because its moral standing falls well short of justifying the preservation of its majesty.

I thus propose the following interpretation of the Lord's concluding admonishment: You Jonah sought to spare a paradisiacal *qîqāyôn* whose idyllic character – like that of the city it signifies – was due to no personal investment of yours, the plant having risen up suddenly and having endured for just a short time. I, by contrast, will *not* spare Nineveh itself, a city that *I endowed* with greatness only to have it wasted on a vast population that cannot tell the difference between good and evil, not to mention a sizable bunch of out-and-out animals.

It emerges, then, that insofar as a pacifist Jonah flees his mission out of concern for the future of Nineveh, the story allows – intentionally, I suspect – for two variations of the Lord's position. According to one interpretation, the merciful God, no less than the prophet himself, yearns for the city to achieve salvation. A skeptical Jonah, therefore, must learn that, despite the genuine possibility of devastating punishment, repentance holds serious promise for a sinful people like the Ninevites. Alternatively, the Lord – taking the past, present, and future into account – seeks to bring about the destruction of Nineveh, whose conduct will, at some later point, inexorably necessitate that unfortunate outcome. The dejected prophet, accordingly, must be taught that, divine compassion notwithstanding, the presence of abiding evil may indeed justify the obliteration of a great and resplendent city.

Either way, this perspective on the book suggests that a *peace-seeking* Jonah, unwilling to confront the prospect of Nineveh coming to a violent end, dreamily seeks to ensure the preservation of its Edenic glory. By contrast, according to our initial, more conventional reading, it is a *zealous* Jonah who tries to escape his *restorative* mission, vainly pursuing a paradisiacal world whose moral perfection matches its aesthetic splendor. In the final analysis, the book thereby yields two fundamentally distinct understandings of the conduct of its protagonist that attribute to him opposite, extreme reactions to human imperfection and its ramifications. Neither extreme, however, accords with God's purposes. Instead, by shunning the prophet's utopian absolutism, the Lord endorses the human struggle for moral improvement – a painstaking process that necessarily entails sin and punishment, on the one hand, and repentance and forgiveness, on the other.

A Song of Thanks in Waters of Eden

AN AUTHENTIC AND MEANINGFUL PRAYER

Jonah's prayer inside the fish, no less than other parts of the story, generates a layer of meaning that bespeaks his passion for Eden. This poetic passage, in fact, features an especially pronounced form of multivalence: the prayer not only carries deeper significance but, almost from start to finish, also demands to be *rendered* in fundamentally different ways. In addition, its subtle meaning yields solutions to several long-standing problems in the text.

The prayer's references to Eden, furthermore, together with the literary devices that give rise to them, suggest an especially close affinity to the wider story. The passage is thus almost certainly authentic to the book, and any serious contention to the contrary must accordingly be abandoned. For it strains credibility that a different author, employing the same techniques, produced a hidden layer of meaning that so closely matches the deeper implications of the narrative. It is precisely the poem's multivalent formulations that have led many interpreters, unaware of that multivalence, to assign it to a different author and a different context.[1]

To begin, recall that Jonah, according to our approach, perceives not that the fish *portends* an ultimate liberation but that it embodies an enduring paradisiacal haven.[2] Fittingly, he offers an expression of gratitude appropriate for a complete deliverance. At the beginning of the prayer, he thus describes his salvation using verb forms that typically indicate the past tense:[3]

> I called to the Lord (*qārā'tî*) from my distress and he answered me
>   (*wayya'ănēnî*);
> From the belly of Sheol I cried out (*šiwwa'tî*). You heard my voice
>   (*šāma'tā qôlî*)!   (Jonah 2:3)

When Jonah speaks of his call from "distress" and God's response, he might in principle be referring to his initial reprieve from drowning. The *belly* of Sheol, however, quite clearly signals his predicament after the fish consumed him, before the creature's three-day transition into an Edenic sanctuary. It follows that when the prophet then affirms, in the past tense, that God heeded his cry (*šāma'tā qôlî*), he is referring to that very transition. Moreover, it is precisely here that Jonah begins speaking to God in second-person form ("You heard my voice!"), suggesting that this three-day process indeed brought him into the presence of the divine.

It remains to show how the prayer directly alludes to the Garden of Eden. Let us thus proceed to the remainder of the poem, which produces a layer of meaning that, in utterly remarkable fashion, consistently evokes a paradisiacal domain.

JONAH'S PRAYER AND THE GARDEN OF EDEN

Where Did God Cast Jonah? A Subtext of Restoration

Note that the first word of the next verse appears in the *wayyiqṭōl* form, which generally denotes an action that occurs in sequence with a prior one:

> You cast me (*wattašlîkēnî*) into the deep waters in the heart of the seas,
> Flowing waters surrounding me,
> All your breakers and waves passing over me.   (Jonah 2:4)

Recall, however, that the preceding line describes a favorable divine response to Jonah's cry, whereas the present one depicts God's casting of the prophet into the sea. Must we assume, then, that the *wayyiqṭōl* form here does not indicate any sort of progression?[4] Happily, the rest of the verse's terminology forestalls this problematic conclusion. For according to another layer of meaning, this entire line recounts the *salvation* that the Lord provided after hearing the prophet's cry from the belly of Sheol.[5]

First, let us review the pivotal allusion generated by the phrase "flowing waters surrounding me" (*wĕnāhār yĕsōbĕbēnî*). The combination of *nāhār* ("flowing water/river") and *sbb* ("surround"), we recall, occurs just two other times in Scripture. In Genesis (2:10–13), a *nāhār* that flows from Eden yields streams that surround (*sbb*) multiple locations, including a land filled with precious stones and metals. And in Ezekiel (31:4), *nĕhārôt* ("rivers") surround (*sbb*) and provide nourishment to the Eden-surpassing cedar that symbolizes Assyria. When Jonah, then, affirms that a *nāhār* surrounds (*sbb*) him, he likewise refers to paradisiacal waters that encase an Edenic abode.

As for the rest of the verse, consider first the phrase "the heart of the seas." On the one hand, this phrase recalls the expression "the heart of the sea" in the analogous song in Exodus (31:8). After all, according to the simple meaning of the line, the submerged prophet presents a suitable analogy to the drowning Egyptians. At the same time, however, the plural noun "seas" triggers a resonance with the key phrase "the heart of the seas" in Ezekiel, which depicts the watery surroundings of the Eden-like city of Tyre (Ezek 27:4, 25–27; cf. 28:2, 9).[6] It follows that, like *nāhār yĕsōbĕbēnî*, the expression "the heart of the seas" generates a crucial second layer of meaning, one that situates Jonah in an idyllic domain surrounded by waters of Eden.

In fact, even the expression "into the deep waters" (*mĕṣûlâ*) – whose straightforward meaning need not contradict this reading – hints at the prophet's salvation. Recall that our book plays on the consonant sequence *ṣl*, linking together the words *ṣēl* ("shade," of the root *ṣll*) and *lĕhaṣṣîl* ("to save," of the root *nṣl*) in connection with the Eden-like plant (Jonah 4:5–6). Likewise, by invoking the word *mĕṣûlâ*, our author generates a play both on *ṣll*, suggesting "shade" that protects, and on *nṣl* ("save"), a root that almost always displays only the consonants *ṣl*.[7]

Finally, the verse's concluding phrase, "all your breakers and waves passing over me," maintains the dual meaning of the line. On a simple level, this clause describes the threat that the sea posed to Jonah when he flailed in its raging waters.[8] Simultaneously, however, the expression "passing over" suggests that the waves now traverse above Jonah harmlessly – or even, in line with the analogy to Ezekiel 31, nourishingly – while he revels in a paradisiacal domain. Indeed, our text borrows this entire phrase from Psalm 42:8, where some premodern exegetes, for contextual reasons, do interpret it in a favorable way.[9] Quite possibly, then, our author sensed the ambiguity of the clause in that context – where the Psalmist, in a dire situation, poignantly expresses confidence in being saved by God and returning to the divine presence – and seized the opportunity to deploy the expression in Jonah's multivalent prayer.

So No Banishment, After All

In the next verse, the poem's references to Eden and attendant subtext persist unabated:

> I said (*wa'ănî 'āmartî*) that I was banished (*nigraštî*) from before your eyes.
> Yet I will continue (*'ak 'ôsîp*) to gaze upon your holy sanctuary.
>
> (Jonah 2:5)

The expression "I was banished" (*nigraštî*) has long presented a problem, because the source of this half-line, Psalm 31:23, employs the verb *nigzartî* ("I have been cut off") rather than *nigraštî*.[10] The prophet, furthermore, who was trying to *flee* "from the face of the Lord," hardly seems to have been denied the presence of the divine by being thrown overboard.[11] Our reading, however, offers a straightforward solution: even while running from God's judgmental presence, Jonah had sought to enter the kind of sacred, protective environment that characterizes an Edenic domain. Accordingly, precisely on being hurled out of the Zaphon-like ship, the prophet saw himself as having been excluded – like Cain before him – from the Lord's *protective* gaze. The text, moreover, invokes the term *nigraštî* to denote this exclusion, because both Genesis and Ezekiel 31 use the root *grš* to describe the barring of sinful individuals from the Garden of Eden (Gen 3:24; Ezek 31:11).[12]

Further, in Psalm 31, the expression *wa'ănî 'āmartî* – found at the beginning of the phrase in question – signals a contrast ("I, however, had thought") in keeping with the sense often generated by *wa'ănî*, including at the end of this very prayer in Jonah ("I, however [*wa'ănî*], will offer sacrifices to you with a voice of gratitude"; Jonah 2:10).[13] It bears emphasis, in turn, that in only our reading does *wa'ănî* suggest a similar contrast here. For if the preceding line describes Jonah's thrashing in the raging sea, then now the prophet merely expresses his consequent realization that he had been banished from God's presence. If, however, that prior verse speaks of Jonah's perceived *salvation* in the Edenic belly of the fish, then *wa'ănî* appropriately signals the *contrasting*, threatening situation that he recalls having faced when the crew cast him out of the vessel ("I, however, had thought that I was banished from before your eyes").

As for the second half of the verse, our multivalent reading of the prayer offers a uniquely helpful perspective. Whereas Jonah seems, most straightforwardly, to be expressing confidence that he shall "yet gaze upon [the Lord's] holy sanctuary," the context has impelled many scholars to interpret the phrase in negative terms. Thus, they either render it as a rhetorical question (e.g., "Would I ever gaze again upon your holy sanctuary?") or emend *'ak* (אך) to *'êk* (איך), which yields a translation such as, "How would I ever gaze again upon your holy sanctuary?"[14] Whatever the merits of these efforts, however, the apparently positive sense of the clause contributes smoothly to the poem's deeper layer of meaning. After all, according to our reading Jonah has already found his desired utopia, and he has been expressing gratitude for it in all but the preceding half-line. In turn, with *'ak* functioning as a term of contrast, the present phrase yields the triumphant meaning, "Nevertheless, I continue to gaze upon your holy sanctuary!" And of course, that sanctuary epitomizes an Edenic, divine abode.[15]

The Sacred Mountain and the Watery Abyss

On a simple level, the next two verses refer to Jonah's apparently hopeless situation in the violent sea, alluding to his salvation only in the final clause:

> Water engulfed me up to my neck (*'ad-nāpeš*),
> The Deep surrounding me (*těhôm yěsōběbēnî*),
> Reeds clinging to my head.
> I descended to the base of the mountains,
> The earth – its bars obstructing me forever.
> But you raised up my life from the Pit, O Lord my God!
> (Jonah 2:6–7)

At first glance, this passage leaves no room for a more sustained positive rendering. Such a conclusion, to be sure, would yield no real difficulty, because psalms of thanksgiving typically provide an account of the circumstances that threatened the speaker.[16] On close inspection, however, these verses do advance the poem's additional layer of meaning, referring again to the prophet's rescue in an Eden-like location.

This selection contains a number of perplexing images and expressions, some of which have contributed to serious doubts about the compatibility of the poem with the wider story.[17] Consider the following:

1. If Jonah is drowning in the Mediterranean, then how could "reeds," which do not grow in deep water, be "clinging to [his] head"?[18]

2. If, in fact, Jonah has descended to the vegetation at the bottom of the sea, then why does he speak of water engulfing him *'ad-nāpeš* (literally: "up to [my] life/breath") – a formulation that, in its original context (Ps 69:2), depicts a drowning individual whose breathing orifices are not yet submerged?[19]

3. The phrases *sûp ḥābûš lĕrō'šî* ("Reeds clinging to my head") and *qiṣbê hārîm* ("the base of the mountains"), unlike most of the poem's distinctive terminology, notably do not derive from any apparent formulations elsewhere in the Bible.[20]

4. The base of the mountains hardly seems like a suitable metaphor for Jonah's location in the middle of the sea.

5. Why does the prophet say that the earth's "bars" block him from entry, when his problem is ostensibly that he cannot reach dry land at all?

6. Why does he choose to say, "The earth – its bars *ba'ădî* (literally: 'are before/against me') forever," a weak formulation that, unlike every other clause in the prayer until the very end, contains no explicit verb?

7. Instead of "the earth – its bars" (*hā'āreṣ bĕrîḥêhā*), why does Jonah not just say "the bars of the earth" (*bĕrîḥê hā'āreṣ*), a smoother expression that would have presented a better parallel to "the base of the mountains" (*qiṣbê hārîm*)?

8. For that matter, does anything in particular account for this striking imagery of the earth's "bars"?

9. Why does the prophet extend this already unwieldy clause by adding the word "forever," if at worst he merely *perceived* that his dire situation was irreversible?

To resolve these difficulties, we return to the imagery in Ezekiel 31. Recall, first, that the phrase *nāhār yĕsōbĕbēnî* and the root *grš* parallel

Eden-related language in that chapter. Consider, then, that in the Ezekiel text (31:4), the *těhôm* ("Deep") stands in parallel to the "surrounding" *něhārôt* ("rivers"): the *něhārôt* nourish the Edenic cedar, and the *těhôm* sustains it from below. It follows that *těhôm yěsōběbēnî* in our verse, much like *nāhār yěsōběbēnî* earlier, signals the presence of a paradisiacal domain. Furthermore, Jonah's references to the "mountains" (*hārîm*) and the "earth" (*āreṣ*) draw on Ezekiel 31:12, which immediately follows the banishment (*grš*) of the cedar from its Eden-surpassing place of distinction. In that verse, Ezekiel depicts the great tree being cut down by foreign nations, its branches thereby falling "to the mountains (*hārîm*) and into all the valleys" and its boughs splintering "into all the watercourses of the earth (*hā'āreṣ*)." In similar fashion, Jonah thus states that, having been banished (*grš*) from an Edenic existence of his own, he too was figuratively cast down to the base of the mountains toward the water below the earth.

Ultimately, however, this analogy underscores an essential difference. In the Ezekiel text, the cedar eventually descends to the "Netherworld" and "Sheol," becomes covered by the "Deep," and is forced to join other denizens of the "Pit" (Ezek 31:14–15). Crucially, scholars compare this to Zaphon imagery whereby the sacred mountain stands above – and in opposition to – the Pit.[21] They also note a poetic parallel between Zaphon – whose sacred environs encompass "both the heights and the base" of the mountain – and the earth at its bottom, "both of which are suspended above Sheol/Abaddon/Tohu" (cf. Job 26:6–7).[22] Hence, whereas the branches of the Edenic cedar fall to the earth at the base of the mountains, it is only the chaotic region *below* this, to which the tree itself descends, that stands outside the boundary of the divine abode.

Evidently, then, our prophet, who sought out the *yarkětê ṣāpôn* when he was on the ship, again invokes the image of the divine mountain.[23] In these verses, he thus figuratively describes himself falling into the surrounding Deep, submerged in the water up to his neck. His head, however, remained atop the surface, entwined in reeds that, appropriately, grow *above* the water near the coast. Accordingly, he fell only to the *qiṣbê hārîm*; that is, the "bottom edge of the mountains," the root *qṣb* aptly denoting this sharply defined boundary.

And yet, despite being suspended in this precarious position, *Jonah descended no farther past that point.* For "the earth" at the base of the mountains, with the help of the bracing reeds (*ḥbš*), was there to *protect* him: it would not then, or ever, allow him to descend into the Pit. The clause that relates this protection thus marks the defining moment of this brief segment, its phraseology giving emphasis to this favorable turn. Consequently, the text declines to present a simple parallel between "the bars of the earth" and "the base of the mountains." Instead, it emphasizes the shift in the prophet's fortunes by isolating the word *hā'āreṣ*, calling attention to the pivotal role played by the earth: "While I descended to the base of the mountains/ The earth! Its bars are there for me (*ba'ădî*) forever!" The term *ba'ădî*, in addition to denoting obstruction, thus simultaneously yields its more common, favorable meaning, "for my sake."[24] Jonah, moreover, makes clear that, as he perceives the situation, these bars will protect him "forever" while he revels in the blissful grandeur of the divine mountain. After all, by saving him at the last minute, the Lord "raised up [Jonah's] life from the Pit" into whose clutches the prophet's head was about to descend.[25]

Finally, the imagery of the earth's "bars" contributes further to the poem's deeper significance. Recall that our book, in connection with both the Tarshish-bound ship and the paradisiacal plant, invokes the prophet Nahum's depictions of Nineveh. What, then, of the correspondingly Edenic belly of the fish? Consider that Nahum, when describing the locust-like blaze that devastates the "land" of Nineveh (*'arṣēk*), utters the phrase, "fire consumed your bars (*bĕrîḥāyik*)" (Nah 3:13). Those "bars," accordingly, fail to prevent the annihilation of the majestic Assyrian city. By contrast, Jonah affirms that the "bars" (*bĕrîḥêhā*) of "the earth" (*hā'āreṣ*) do protect *him* from being consumed, thereby enabling him to savor the blissful, Nineveh-like reality signified by the creature's belly.

In the final analysis, then, these verses do not merely describe the dire predicament faced by our protagonist. They also evoke paradisiacal imagery that, on a more profound level, depicts his salvation from the brink of the abyss. What is more, this layer of meaning accounts, rather elegantly, for a range of puzzling formulations in this highly challenging section of the prayer.

The Edenic Cedar and the Divine Sanctuary

The next verse of the poem, by contrast, speaks of Jonah's rescue far more straightforwardly:

When my spirit closed in on me I remembered the Lord,
And my prayer came to you, to your holy sanctuary!
(Jonah 2:8)

This line, furthermore, invokes Ezekiel 31 when it adopts the Psalmist's terminology, "When my spirit closed in on me" (*běhit'aṭṭēp 'ālay napšî/ rûḥî*; Ps 142:3). As scholars observe, the *hithpael* verb *běhit'aṭṭēp* (בהתעטף; of the root *'ṭp* [עטף]) resonates with *wayyit'allāp* (ויתעלף [and he felt faint"]; of the root *'lp* [עלף]) in Jonah 4:8, where our prophet loses the protection of the Eden-like plant.[26] *Wayyit'allāp*, for its part, parallels the verb *'lp* in Ezekiel 31:15, which denotes the wilting of Sheol-bound trees once shielded by the now-crumbling Edenic cedar. Appropriately, then, when depicting his brush with death, Jonah selects a poetic expression containing the analogous root *'ṭp* (עטף): just as the blissfully protective plant shrivels, thereby leaving the parched, despairing prophet to long for his demise, Jonah's dilemma in our chapter follows directly from his expulsion from an Edenic existence into surroundings that threaten his life.

As in the poem's opening verse, moreover, the prophet's descriptions of God's deliverance – both here and in the preceding line – use verb forms that commonly indicate the past tense: "you raised up (*watta'al*) my life from the Pit," and "my prayer came (*wattābō'*) to you, to your holy sanctuary." Now if Jonah does *not* perceive the fish as an enduring source of bliss and we take the apparent past tense of the verbs at face value, then these phrases can only serve as expressions of thanks for the short-term rescue granted by the creature and, perhaps, for the presumed deliverance still to come. According to our reading, by contrast, the prophet's intentions justify the apparent definitiveness of his gratitude. After all, the belly of the fish now grants Jonah the salvation that he had been seeking all along.

In addition, the second phrase ("my prayer came to you, to your holy sanctuary"), which seems to say that an earlier supplication uttered by the prophet had reached the divine abode, simultaneously allows for another interpretation: Jonah's "prayer" (*těpillâ*) – or perhaps better, his "praying" – presently transformed into an expression of thanks, now *takes place* in the divine location that the grateful prophet inhabits.[27] Indeed, the awkward sequence "to you, to your holy sanctuary" might well serve to generate this very dual meaning. That is, Jonah's prayer "came to [God]" in the standard sense of having elicited a favorable response. Yet at the same time, it quite literally "has come to [God's] holy sanctuary," for the prophet now expresses his gratitude inside the idyllic, sacred domain that he wished to occupy from the very beginning.

Jonah, the Sailors, and Authenticity of Devotion

We now reach the poem's final couplet, where the first line poses fundamental problems of interpretation:

> Those who keep to empty folly (*mĕšammĕrîm hablê-šāw'*)
> Abandon their goodness (*ḥasdām yaʿăzōbû*).
> I, however, will offer sacrifices to you with a voice of gratitude.
> I will fulfill my vows.
> Deliverance belongs to the Lord!   (Jonah 2:9–10)

The odd expression *mĕšammĕrîm hablê-šāw'*, adapted from a phrase in Psalm 31:7 (*haššômĕrîm hablê-šāw'*), is rightly understood to describe the pagan sailors, who according to Jonah remain "keepers of empty folly" despite their momentary recognition of the Israelite God.[28] The next phrase, however, *ḥasdām yaʿăzōbû*, has proved unyieldingly difficult, seeming to suggest – rather puzzlingly – that in one sense or another the "keepers" in question "abandon/will abandon" their "goodness." A majority of commentators, moreover, take this phrase to refer to unspecified goodness that these individuals *receive*; yet, in other instances where the root ʿ*zb* takes this object it refers to the provider of the *ḥesed*, not its beneficiary (Gen 24:27; Ruth 2:20).[29] Far simpler is the last line of the prayer. In that verse, Jonah gratefully affirms that he will offer sacrifices (*'ezbĕḥâ*) to the Lord and fulfill his vows (*'ăšer nādartî 'ăšallēmâ*), and commentators perceptively add that these actions parallel the sacrifice offered (*wayyizbĕḥû-zebaḥ*) and vows taken (*wayyiddĕrû nĕdārîm*) by the sailors at the end of chapter 1.[30]

All told, then, how shall we understand the force of this couplet? Consider, first, that if Jonah's sacrifices and vows recall those of the sailors and, moreover, this part of the poem *contrasts* these polytheists with the prophet, then when Jonah affirms that he will fulfill his vows, he is suggesting that his shipmates will *not* honor their own. Indeed, the text of chapter 1 leaves this question open when, after informing us that the sailors took vows, it ends abruptly with no indication that they fulfilled them. However, in seeking to contrast the *sacrifices* pledged by Jonah with those offered by the crew, our author confronted a more difficult challenge. After all, there is nothing to suggest any deficiency in the sailors' offering – nor would the context of chapter 1 have allowed for any failing – and the mere assertion by Jonah that he will accompany his sacrifices with a "voice of gratitude" would seem to fall short of generating any decisive contrast.

To appreciate, then, how Jonah conveys the alleged inadequacy of the crew's offering, we first direct our attention to the sixth chapter of Hosea, rightly identified as one source for the content of Jonah's prayer.[31] In that prophecy, Hosea imagines the Israelites exhorting one another to repent, anticipating a process of salvation that, reminiscent of the one experienced by Jonah, would reach its completion on the third day (Hos 6:2).[32] The Lord, however, invoking an uncommon usage of the noun *hesed*, responds that Israel's *commitment to God* (*hasdĕkem*) is as fleeting as the morning clouds, thus making harsh divine judgment unavoidable (6:4).[33] After all, he continues, "it is commitment (*hesed*) that I desire, not sacrifices (*zābaḥ*), and knowledge of God rather than burnt-offerings" (6:6). The Psalmist, moreover, likewise brings together the roots *ḥsd* and *zbḥ*, depicting a divine call toward "my devoted ones" (*ḥăsîdāy*) who make a covenant with God over "sacrifices" (*zābaḥ*; Ps 50:5).[34] Most important, consider the latter part of Psalm 116, which almost certainly provided the primary source material for the last verse of Jonah's prayer.[35] That passage contains mulitple affirmations that the Psalmist "will fulfill [his] vows to the Lord" (116:14, 18), a promise that he "will offer a sacrifice (*'ezbaḥ zebaḥ*) of gratitude" (116:17), and a grateful acknowledgment that the Lord dreads the death of "his devoted ones" (*ḥăsîdâw*; 116:15). It follows that the motifs of *zebaḥ* ("sacrifice") and *hesed* ("devotion") bear a close connection, suggesting that the value of sacrifices lies in the genuine commitment to the Lord maintained by those who offer them.

Accordingly, in our passage too, we should properly analyze *hasdām* in conjunction with the root *zbḥ* found both in the ensuing verse (*'ezbĕḥâ*) and earlier in chapter 1 (*wayyizbĕḥû-zebaḥ*). Jonah predicts that the adherents of "empty folly" on the ship, who keep (*šmr*) to their pagan convictions despite the terror-induced sacrifice (*zebaḥ*) that they brought to the one true God, will eventually "abandon their devotion" to the Lord (*ḥasdām yaʿăzōbû*). Indeed, this unique *piel* form of *šmr* – which may denote a more persistent sense of "keeping" – helps underscore the sailors' *sustained* adherence to their false gods.[36] Jonah means to affirm, then, that in the end, the lone offering brought by his shipmates will prove inconsequential. The prophet himself, by contrast, even when his three-day process of salvation is long over, will continue to offer sacrifices to God together with genuine expressions of gratitude – and unlike the crew he will be sure to fulfill his vows. After all, Jonah concludes, "deliverance belongs to the Lord," and to none other.[37]

The Concluding Couplet and the Story of Cain and Abel

What, then, of the added layer of significance that the prayer generates? Does anything in this concluding section further the poem's reference to a paradisiacal location? Remarkably, careful attention to its terminology yields an affirmative answer: the obscure phrase *měšamměrîm hablê-šāw'*, by way of perhaps the most astonishing parallel yet, makes an especially striking contribution to this deeper level of meaning.

The verb *šmr*, with *hbl* as the recipient of the action, brings to mind one particularly memorable biblical passage. After Cain, disdaining the option of repentance, proceeds to murder his brother, the Lord confronts him with the fateful question, "Where is your brother Abel (*hebel*)?" (Gen 4:9). Cain replies that he does not know. After all, he asks, "Am I my brother's keeper (*šmr*)?" (4:9). Moreover, at the beginning of that episode, Abel elicits a favorable divine response to the one sacrifice that he offers (4:4). Cain, by contrast, finds himself in need of self-improvement (4:5–7), a challenge that he defiantly refuses to embrace when he kills Abel (4:8) and proceeds, shortly thereafter, to roam wistfully outside the harshly unattainable utopian garden.

Our prophet, accordingly, in his effort to write off the sailors' sacrifice as a mere ephemeral burst of inspiration, makes a clever play on Cain's dismissive response to God's question. Jonah implies that, despite the Lord's acceptance of Abel's offering, a single sacrifice – without evidence of more sustained devotion – does not imply true commitment to God. Hence, no genuine sincerity may be attributed to the shipmen, whose lone offering proves nothing more than that of the slain brother of Cain. Rather, Jonah presumptuously affirms, people like these sailors who "abide by Abel-like initiatives of vanity" (*měšamměrîm hablê-šāw'*) – or, more simply, "perpetuate Abel-like folly" – eventually abandon their devotion to the Lord (*ḥasdām yaʿăzōbû*). By contrast, the prophet himself, embracing a wholly different path, adheres to the precedent set by Cain, spurning a theology that favors repentance and seeking an idyllic existence that is entirely unmerited. Yet whereas Cain fell short of entry into Eden, Jonah persuades himself that, unlike his unwitting mentor, he has now succeeded in reaching that elusive paradisiacal destination.

A PRAYER FROM THE DEPTHS
AND THE DEPTHS OF A PRAYER

I conclude, then, with a rendering of Jonah's prayer that gives voice to its implied layer of meaning:

I called to the Lord from my distress and he answered me;
From the belly of Sheol I cried out. You heard my voice!
You thus cast me into a safe haven in the midst of the seas,
Rivers [of Eden] surrounding me,
All your breakers and waves passing [harmlessly/nourishingly] above me.
I, however, had thought that I was banished from before your eyes.
And yet – I continue to gaze upon your holy sanctuary!
Water had engulfed me up to my neck,
The Deep surrounding me,
[Coastal] reeds holding fast to my head.
While I had descended to the base of the mountains,
The earth! Its bars protect me forever!
You thus raised up my life from the Pit, O Lord my God!
When my spirit closed in on me, I remembered the Lord;
And lo! My praying has come near to you – right into your holy sanctuary!
Those who perpetuate Abel-like folly
Will abandon their devotion [to you].
I, however, will offer sacrifices to you with a voice of [true] gratitude;
My vows I will fulfill –
For it is to the Lord that deliverance belongs!

Nautical and Hermeneutical Dilemmas

ON ACCOUNT OF WHOSE GOD?

We now turn our attention to several remaining salient formulations, chiefly in the book's opening chapter. When the sailors first confront Jonah, they begin by saying, "Tell us, please, *ba'ăšer lĕmî-hārā'â hazzō't lānû*" (Jonah 1:8). Previously, we adopted the common but philologically knotty translation of this phrase: "you, on an account of whom this disaster has befallen us!" Yet more straightforwardly, the line indicates a question: "on account of whom has this disaster befallen us?"

This interrogative rendering, however, yields an obvious difficulty of its own: if the lottery already revealed that Jonah is the source of the trouble, why would the crew ask him to identify a culprit? Some commentators propose, therefore, that the sailors – consistent with the emphasis of the preceding verses – are actually seeking to determine which *god* caused the storm. Accordingly, after Jonah is selected, they ask him, "On account of [what deity] has this disaster befallen us?" The prophet, by naming the Israelite God in his reply, then addresses that very question.[1]

Still, this proposal remains seriously problematic. The sailors, after all, cast lots to determine "on account of whom" the storm hit them (Jonah 1:7). The selection of Jonah, therefore, appears to indicate that he is the one. Consequently, when the men, on confronting him, refer again to the one "on account of whom" the threat arose, here too the expression would seem to mean the prophet.[2]

Our story's pervasive multivalence, however, suggests another alternative: the sailors seek to identify both a person *and* a corresponding deity who bear responsibility for the tempest. Thus, the relevant phrase in their interrogation of Jonah bears two meanings: you, on account of whom this disaster has befallen us, and, simultaneously, on account of what god of yours did the storm come about?

This alternative, in fact, draws support from the text's notably long-winded description of the lottery: "One man said to the next, 'Let us cast lots, and we shall know [or: and let us find out] (*wĕnēdĕʿâ*) on account of whom this disaster has befallen us.' And they cast lots, and the lottery fell on Jonah." Certainly, a more succinct formulation would have sufficed: "And the men cast lots in order to know (*lādaʿat*) on account of whom the disaster had befallen them, and the lottery fell on Jonah." The use of direct speech, however, enables the separation of the "casting" and the "knowing" into two independent clauses: "Let us cast lots, and let us know/find out." This divided formulation, in turn, suggests that, even after the lottery reveals the human culprit, more investigation is needed to identify the god that this individual provoked ("and let us find out . . .").

The sailors' quest to determine the relevant deity, moreover, accounts for their striking litany of questions. To wit, when they ask not only about Jonah's mission but also his place of departure, homeland, and people of origin, they seek, at least in part, to identify the location or group associated with the *god* whose wrath he incurred. The prophet, accordingly, begins his reply by saying, "I am an *ʿibrî*," thereby declaring that he is an Israelite and that his mission is to "cross over" to an Edenic domain. Then, in response to the remaining queries, he affirms his fear of "the Lord God of the heavens who made the sea and the land"; that is, *the universal deity who controls every part of the world*. Consequently, any effort to associate the god who caused the storm with a distinct location, as his shipmates wish to do, is inevitably doomed to fail.[3]

Our multivalent approach helps resolve still another difficulty. After Jonah's initial response, the sailors proceed to ask him, "What shall we do to you (*lāk*) so that the sea will quiet down from on us?" (Jonah 1:11). Yet this standard rendering of the question raises an evident problem: short of killing him, what *could* the sailors do to Jonah to resolve the issue, seeing that his use of the voyage to escape from God is what caused the storm?

However, we may easily incorporate another meaning that explains the sailors' uncertainty: "What," they are simultaneously asking, "might we do *for* you (*lāk*)" to enable you to fulfill the Lord's command, "so that the sea will quiet down from on [all of] us," including yourself?[4] After all, the narrator continues, "the men knew that he was escaping from the Lord, for he had told them" in the preceding line that he was "crossing over" to escape God's wrath.

What is more, this explanation adds significance to the notably suggestive way in which this passage deploys pronouns. The standard interpretation of the line, "What shall we do to you (*lāk*) so that the sea will quiet down from on us?" (Jonah 1:11), generates a contrast between "you," the prophet who would be harmed, and "us," the sailors whom the storm would no longer affect. Our additional reading of the word "us," however, keeps Jonah and the crew all in the same boat. What, then, will the actual solution be – the elimination of the prophet, which would save the crew, or the facilitation of Jonah's mission, which would save him too? To the sailors' multivalent question, then, Jonah answers, "Lift *me* and hurl *me* into the sea so that the sea will quiet down from on *you*, for I know that it is on account of *me* that this great storm is on *you*" (Jonah 1:12). Why, the question begs itself, must the prophet reiterate what, according to the standard reading, everyone knows already – that *he* is the cause of all this trouble? Indeed, what could Jonah be emphasizing when he says, "*I know* that it is on account of me"?[5] And why, for that matter, does he say that he is the cause of the "great storm," when both the sailors and the narrator referred, in a more general way, to the cause of the "disaster"?

Our approach offers a neat solution to these questions. In the entirety of his reply, Jonah means to resolve the very uncertainty implied by the two senses of the sailors' question: is he the culprit, so that they must dispose of him, or is the Lord prodding the sailors to ensure the fulfillment of the divine command? To this, the prophet responds that the crew should not seek to help satisfy the wishes of his God. Instead the focus belongs on Jonah alone. Although the sailors expressed doubts on the matter, I *know*, the prophet tells them, that the tempest is on account of *me* and my defiance, and not due to any failure of *yours* to facilitate my execution of God's orders. After all, it is not merely a "disaster" that is befalling us, as you the sailors called it, but a "great storm," whose one purpose, in pointed contrast to the "great storm" in Jeremiah, is to put the wrathful *yônâ* unmercifully in his place.

And yet, the horrified seafarers resist the inevitable zero-sum game and vigorously attempt to reverse course in order to save their passenger along with themselves. The text, accordingly, affirms that they attempted to "bring back to dry land" (Jonah 1:13) – the omission of a direct object allowing for two simultaneous explanations: the sailors tried to propel the *ship* back to shore, and equally important, they sought to calm the Lord's anger by leading *Jonah* back in the direction of Nineveh.[6] Their efforts, however, prove futile. For as the prophet hinted, as long as he remains with them in the vessel, the sea shall "continue to storm on [all of] them" (1:13).[7] It is only when the terrified, penitent sailors cast Jonah overboard that they succeed in separating their fate from his own (1:15), because it is only then that the Lord will resume the process of directing the prophet toward the fulfillment of his task.

WHO ARE THE RIGHTEOUS ONES?

Recall that Jonah, with the storm raging, goes off and descends into a deep slumber. The captain of the ship, in turn, after demanding of Jonah "How can you sleep?" verbosely continues, "Get up and cry out to your god – perhaps God will pay us heed so that we will not perish!" (Jonah 1:6). This latter part of the captain's exclamation, by the standards of our book, seems markedly extraneous. What would have been lost had he simply said, "How can you sleep? Get up and cry out to your god!" The text, moreover, employs the *hithpael* verb *yit'aššēt* (יתעשת) to mean "pay heed," a unique and striking application of the uncommon root *'št* (עשת; "think/consider").[8] What, then, might account for this choice of terminology?

To answer these questions, we turn again to Cain and Abel, focusing this time on the offerings that they bring at the beginning of the episode. The Lord, we are told, "paid heed" (*wayyiššaʿ* ; וישע) to Abel's offering, but he "did not pay heed" (*lōʾ šāʿâ*; לא שעה) to that of Cain (Gen 4:4–5). The possibility thus arises – because of our book's numerous connections to that passage – that *yit'aššēt* generates a parallel to those brothers' efforts to reach out to the Lord. That is, just as God "paid heed" (*šāʿâ*) to the devotions of

Abel but not of Cain, our captain anticipates that the Lord might "pay heed" (*yit'aššēt*) to the supplications of one traveler more readily than to those of the rest. If this is correct, then the captain means to contrast Jonah – who he hopes will assume the more effectual role of the righteous Abel – to the other men on the ship, whose unsuccessful prayers correspond to the rejected offering of Cain.

Nevertheless, this proposal raises two immediate problems. First, if our author sought to produce such an analogy, would not the root *š'h* (שעה) itself have presented a better option than the moderately similar-sounding *'št* (עשת)? Second, would a group of imperiled shipmen, facing the prospect of a sinking ship, really seek an association with the doomed figure of Abel, God's favorable response to his devotions notwithstanding?

Yet, there is one additional parallel that not only answers these questions but also helps confirm the validity of the correlation. It is indeed true that, if the captain sought a traveler whose prayers might compare to Abel's offering, he could not equate that individual with the murdered Abel himself. Instead, therefore, by means of the root *'št*, he cleverly invokes the surviving individual who arose in Abel's place. I refer, of course, to Cain's brother *šēt* (שת; "Seth"), whose name marks God's endowment (*št*) of Eve with "a son in place of Abel – for Cain had killed him" (Gen 4:25).[9] When the captain, then, utters the phrase "perhaps God will pay us heed (*yit'aššēt*)," he both invokes the impactful devotions of Abel (*wayyiššā'*) *and* expresses his wish that the Lord grant the sailors the standing of *šēt* – the one son of Adam and Eve who not only survives but also whose progeny endures even after the mounting, divinely commissioned floodwaters threaten to engulf all humanity. This interpretation also accounts for our verse's other apparently extraneous clause, "so that we will not perish": in the wake of the verb *yit'aššēt*, that phrase helps clarify the purpose of the desired connection to Seth – the lone child of Adam and Eve with whom a prayerful group of seafarers, facing annihilation, might reasonably seek to generate an association.

The sailors' concern that they might "perish" persists in the latter half of the chapter, where it serves yet another Cain-related role. After Cain murders Abel, God affirms the killer's guilt by way of the phrase, "the blood of your brother cries out to me from the ground" (Gen 4:10). It is hardly surprising, therefore, that the shipmen, whose ineffectual devotions instilled in them a Cain complex, are terrified by the prospect of ending Jonah's life, fearing that doing so would prompt the Lord to "place on [them] innocent blood" (Jonah 1:14). Accordingly, they cry out to God in an effort to distance themselves from Cain, pronouncing – in terms that recall their captain's quest for a connection to Seth – "*let us not perish* on account of the life of this man" (1:14).

Beyond this, let us examine more closely the sailors' plea, "do not place on us innocent blood." This formulation, we have seen, contributes to an allusion to Jeremiah, where the prophet warns of the consequences of killing a messenger of the Lord (Jer 26:15). Simultaneously, however, working off the bloodguilt motif in the Cain story, this part of our text also recalls passages that, in keeping with the objective of the sailors, speak of *absolution* from responsibility for engendering the loss of life.

First, the phrase in question resembles the formulation, "do not place innocent blood in the midst of your people Israel" (Deut 21:8), uttered during a ritual that atones for an unexplained death.[10] More remarkably, however, consider the term *wayyaḥtĕrû* used to denote the crew's efforts to row back to shore (Jonah 1:13). As in the case of *'št*, the use of *ḥtr* ("dig") to mean "row" amounts to a unique application of a biblical verb.[11] An explanation, however, is readily at hand. For among the handful of biblical passages featuring this root, undoubtedly the most memorable one concerns the law of the dangerous thief who, preemptively slain while digging a tunnel (*maḥteret*) to enter a home, consigns no "bloodguilt" to his killer (Exod 22:1). In a related passage, furthermore, Jeremiah warns his sinful audience that there may be no absolution for the deaths of the poor, whose "innocent blood" God discovered "not in the *maḥteret*" but on the hands of the people (Jer 2:34). Fittingly, therefore, the sailors in Jonah, who likewise seek to avoid responsibility for spilling "innocent blood," proceed to "dig" (*ḥtr*) feverishly in pursuit of dry land. For in the event that, unable to reach the shore, they would need to throw their passenger overboard, they seek to do so inside their own figurative *maḥteret*, where the blood of the slain individual – whose audacious deed, like that of the thief in Exodus, brought about the life-threatening predicament – would place no guilt on his terrified executioners.[12]

Finally, the sailors' concluding phrase yields two fundamentally different renderings (Jonah 1:14).[13] The common translation, "for you, O Lord, have done as you wished (*ka'ăšer ḥāpaṣtā 'āśîtā*)," appeals to the standard past-tense meaning of the *qāṭal* verb form. By contrast, the more compelling translation, "for you are the Lord, you do as you wish," places the verbs in the present tense. This alternative rendering draws, in part, on the *qāṭal* forms of these verbs used by the Psalmist in the verse *wē'lōhênû baššā-mayim kol ăšer-ḥāpēṣ 'āśâ* ("Our God is in the heavens; he does all that he wishes"; Ps 115:3), whose latter half almost certainly inspired this line in Jonah.[14] After all, when our prophet, in contrast to the decidedly more sincere sailors, claims to fear the Lord, he invokes the expression *'ĕlōhê haššāmayim* ("the God of the heavens"; Jonah 1:9), which generates a corresponding resonance with the first half of the Psalmist's formulation, *wē'lōhênû baššāmayim* ("Our God is in the heavens"). Our text, to underscore the difference between the defiant Jonah and the God-fearing shipmen, thus calls to mind that psalm, which contrasts the impotence of heathen deities with the supreme power of the biblical God: in our case, it is ironically the Gentile sailors who recognize that the God of Israel "does as he wishes," whereas the Israelite prophet's reference to "the God of the heavens" only highlights his own defiance of the Lord.

SACRED DOMAINS AND DIVINE NAMES

When Jonah affirms that he fears "the Lord God of (*'ĕlōhê*) the heavens," he utters the first of four varied references to "the Lord God" in our story. The phrase next appears right before Jonah's prayer, when he addresses "the Lord his God (*'ĕlōhâw*) from the belly of the fish." Then in the prayer itself, Jonah declares, "You raised my life up from the Pit, O Lord my God (*'ĕlōhay*)!" And in chapter 4, we find that "the Lord God (*'ĕlōhîm*) appointed a *qîqāyôn*" to provide shade for the prophet. This last example, we recall, brings to mind the recurring expression "the Lord God" in the Eden narrative in Genesis. More remarkably, however, on close inspection, *all four* instances of "the Lord God" in Jonah draw on that divine appellation in the Eden story. Significantly, moreover, this observation helps solve the vexing problem of our text's widely divergent ways of referring to the biblical God.[15]

We begin with the episode of the *qîqāyôn* itself. Most often, our book refers to the Israelite deity by the Tetragrammaton alone (rendered: "the Lord"), a name associated with divine presence/immanence and the magnanimous/redemptive qualities of God.[16] The *qîqāyôn* passage, however, repeatedly departs from this rule. Thus, after "the Lord God" prompts the growth of the plant, "the God" (*hā'ĕlōhîm*) appoints a worm to attack it. Then, "God" (*'ĕlōhîm*) sends an east wind to afflict Jonah, after which "God" (*'ĕlōhîm*) confronts the prophet about his anger. This movement from "the Lord God" to "the God" to "God" constitutes a progression, whose significance, according to our approach, lies in the Edenic symbolism of the passage.[17] Initially, that is, "the Lord God" causes the *qîqāyôn* to grow above Jonah, who experiences the redemptive divine presence under the plant's paradisiacal shelter. Next, in a moment of transition, "the God" takes away this Edenic haven. Finally, with the protective presence of the Lord firmly out of reach, the text recounts how "God," showing no sympathy toward Jonah's ideology, afflicts the prophet and challenges the validity of his indignation.

By contrast, it is only at the end, when the story redirects our attention to the salvation of Nineveh, that it fittingly returns to the standard expression "the Lord" (Jonah 4:10). For by appealing to divine mercy, the inhabitants of the city – in stark opposition to Jonah – succeed in retaining their idyllic domain. Indeed, consider that in chapter 3 the text likewise departs from the customary divine name "the Lord." First, it affirms that the Ninevites believed in "God" and were prompted to call out to "God" (3:5, 8). And then it recounts that, when the people repented and appealed to "the God's" merciful traits, "the God" took note and "the God" relented from his decree (3:9–10). It thus emerges that, whereas the sequence in the plant episode underscores Jonah's banishment from the magnanimous divine presence, the inverse movement in chapter 3 from "God" to "the God" signifies the divine salvation elicited by the chastened Ninevites, whose city, as the last verse of the book affirms, ultimately survives because of a show of mercy (*ḥws*) on the part of "the Lord."[18]

Another sequence bears similar significance. In chapter 1, when the storm hits, the sailors cry out "each man to his god." Next, they ask Jonah to call out to "your God," for perhaps "the God" in question will heed

Jonah's supplications. Then, the prophet affirms his fear of "the Lord God of the heavens." And finally, the crew – on two separate occasions – is said to fear "the Lord." Note that the first reference in this sequence, which alludes to the sailors' gods, specifies no particular divinity. By contrast, when the sailors refer to Jonah's God ("your God," "the God"), they begin the process of recognizing the merciful deity capable of saving them. When the prophet, in turn, reveals his connection to "the Lord God" who controls everything, he prompts the shipmen to attain genuine "fear of the Lord" – a phrase that, by the end, marks not just their identification of the Israelite God as the cause of the storm but also their intense veneration of him and gratitude for his deliverance. By pronouncing his own fear of "the Lord God," moreover, Jonah, according to one sense of his formulation, affirms his quest for the redemptive presence of the divine *in an Edenic domain*. That is, having hinted that he is "crossing over" in pursuit of a sacred realm on a paradisiacal vessel whose riches he personally bestowed, the prophet now declares that it is "the Lord God of the heavens" whom he reveres and whose blissful abode he accordingly seeks to inhabit.[19]

Finally, we turn to the two instances of "the Lord God" in chapter 2. The first example – "Jonah prayed to the Lord his God" – accompanies the beginning of Jonah's prayer from the *dāgâ*, a term that signals his conception of the fish as an Edenic haven. The second example – "You raised my life up from the Pit, O Lord my God" – marks the prophet's rescue from the brink of the netherworld and his belief that he will now reside permanently on the sacred mountain of the Lord.

It emerges, then, that our text, working off the Eden story in Genesis, deploys the expression "the Lord God" to mark *each* of Jonah's paradisiacal shelters: the Zaphon-like ship ("the Lord God of the heavens"), the blissful belly of the fish ("the Lord his God"), the metaphorical divine mountain ("the Lord my God"), and the Eden-like plant ("the Lord God"). Crucially, moreover, in conjunction with the progressions that we noted, this pattern accounts – in a comprehensive and satisfying way – for our book's strikingly divergent means of referring to the God of the Bible.

THE STORMING SEA AND THE GARDEN OF GOD

The text of Jonah, we have seen, generates numerous analogies to the exodus story, yielding an extended correlation that is fraught with contradiction: the prophet stands in parallel to the departing Israelites, yet at the same time he bears an ironic equivalence to the God-defying, Eden-inhabiting Egyptians. Accordingly, whereas Jonah is hurled into the raging waters like Pharaoh's army, the Lord carves out for him, as he did for the prophet's forebears, a path to salvation in the midst of the sea. After completing his song of gratitude, however, Jonah finds himself vomited out of the Egypt-like haven that he craved. In turn, like the manna-hoarding Israelites, the Eden-seeking prophet must learn a stark lesson concerning the rules that govern life's God-given rewards.

This complex allusion raises an important question about Jonah's request to be thrown overboard. Most straightforwardly, of course, the prophet means to end his life, both to save the ship and – as when he wishes for death in chapter 4 – to escape a reality that causes him anguish. Recall, however, that our text portrays a self-deceiving Jonah taking flight on a paradisiacal ship, and then, when the storm hits, descending into sleep in the most sacred part of the vessel. Might it be, then, that when the prophet asks the sailors to cast him out, he yearns for still another Edenic sanctuary by way of a divine salvation akin to the parting of the sea?

In a marvelously subtle way, the text suggests that Jonah hopes for precisely this outcome. To begin, note the language of Jonah 1:4: "And the Lord hurled a great wind toward the sea (*'el-hayyām*), and there was a great storm in the sea (*bayyām*), and the ship threatened to break apart." Why does this verse – with patent redundancy – make two references to the sea? Could it not have just said that a great wind, dispatched by God toward the sea, prompted a great storm? Or, alternatively, that God sent a great wind that in turn caused a great sea storm? Moreover, when the sailors cast the vessel's precious cargo overboard, the text does not simply say "they hurled the items off the ship," but that "they hurled the items that were on the ship *into the sea* (*'el-hayyām*)." Here too, then, what do we gain by the explicit mention of the sea? Beyond this, does the recurrence of the phrase *'el-hayyām* carry significance, particularly because it seems to yield two different meanings: "toward the sea" in the case of the great wind, and "into the sea" when referring to the cargo? Finally, might these instances of *'el-hayyām* bear a relationship to two later occurrences of the phrase, when Jonah asks to be "lifted" and hurled *'el-hayyām*, and the reluctant sailors indeed do "lift" him and hurl him *'el-hayyām*?

To answer these questions, recall that both the great wind and the great storm, in the service of the book's more conventional meaning, signify the divine wrath that Jonah seeks to bring on Nineveh – wrath that the Lord ironically turns against the prophet himself. The expression "great wind" derives from a story about the zealous Elijah, and the phrase "great storm" originates in a speech by Jeremiah, who depicts the impact of the rage of the *yônâ* ("oppressor") on sinful nations. Bearing in mind, then, that these violent weather conditions signify the Lord's fury, we may explain the force of our passage's extraneous references to "the sea": by the time the sailors confront Jonah, the sea has *gathered inside it* both the Tarshish-bound treasures and the wrath of God. The crew, after all, hurled the vessel's Edenic riches *'el-hayyām* ("into the sea"). And the Lord, for his part, hurled a great wind *'el-hayyām* – not merely "toward the sea" but "*into* the sea" – thereby engendering a great storm *bayyām* ("*in* the sea").[20] The raging, treasure-filled waters, in turn, *embody* the very Eden-like domain sought by Jonah, one that tolerates no evil and provides a glamorous, idyllic existence to its faultless inhabitants.

The prophet, consequently, asks the crew to "lift" him into the realm of the divine by hurling *him* into the sea (*'el-hayyām*), hoping that the paradisiacal waters will – to paraphrase his later words – encase him in an Eden-like sanctuary while the surging waves pass harmlessly above him. The sailors, accordingly, indeed lift Jonah and hurl him into the water (*'el-hayyām*), begging the Lord to absolve them of bloodguilt by granting the prophet his deliverance.[21] Hence, after asking God not to place on them innocent blood, the men fittingly declare, "for you are the Lord, you do as you wish" – an affirmation not merely that they recognize the Israelite deity. Instead, in closer conformity with the rest of the verse, these Gentiles are simultaneously affirming that the practical matter of Jonah's fate – on which their own culpability depends – lies entirely in the hands of the all-powerful, miracle-performing God of Israel.[22]

What is more, recall that the text employs the root *ṭl* ("hurl") four times in these verses. These instances of *ṭl*, we have seen, presage four later occurrences of *wayĕman* ("he appointed"), suggesting a correspondence to the *ṭal* ("dew") that provided a base for the *mān* ("manna"). It stands to reason, however, that the recurrence of the key root *ṭl* would also add meaning to the events that the verb helps recount. Ideally, moreover, such meaning would bear a suitable connection to the dew–manna allusion.

Consider, therefore, that our interpretation links together the various instances of "hurling," whereby the raging tempest, the ship's fortune, and the Eden-seeking prophet all end up in the sea. The recurring root *ṭl*, by signaling this linkage, thereby helps convey that the sea promises Jonah an environment characterized by divine zeal and Edenic splendor. More important, however, the root suggests that, even as these hurlings lay the foundation for the prophet's subaquatic paradisiacal encounter, they will ultimately accomplish no more than the *ṭal*, which provided a base for a divine gift that could not endure. Already in the book's opening chapter, these occurrences of *ṭl* – much like the later, corresponding references to the *mān* – thus signal the futility of Jonah's pursuit of Eden by underscoring the stark ephemerality of unearned divine favor.[23]

In the end, then, none of Jonah's Edenic sanctuaries afford him what he genuinely desires. For indeed, like the manna in the wilderness, unmerited divine bliss does not last for more than a short time. Rather, in keeping with God's purposes, life presents its travelers with relentless trials and vicissitudes, quite unlike the reality sought by our protagonist when setting out on his voyage to Eden. And in that challenging world favored by the Lord, neither the unforgiving perfectionist nor the dreamy idealist attains satisfaction. Both the moralistic Jonah and the pacifist Jonah, having failed in their pursuit of an idyllic existence, must therefore learn – each in his own way – to confront the truth about human imperfection and its implications. In line with the message of this timeless, splendidly crafted biblical story, it is by embracing the slow, painstaking work of moral improvement that human beings, for all their sinfulness, stand the best chance of savoring God's abundant gifts.

NOTES

1. Proposed explanations of the book's purpose appear in summary form in a number of treatments. See, e.g., Catherine L. Muldoon, *In Defense of Divine Justice: An Intertextual Approach to the Book of Jonah* (CBQMS 47; Washington, DC: Catholic Biblical Association of America, 2010), 6–30; T. A. Perry, *The Honeymoon Is Over: Jonah's Argument with God* (Peabody, MA: Hendrickson, 2006), xxv–xxxii; Uriel Simon, *Jonah: The Traditional Hebrew Text with the New JPS Translation* (JPS Bible Commentary; Philadelphia: Jewish Publication Society, 1999), vi–xiii; and esp. Thomas M. Bolin, *Freedom beyond Forgiveness: The Book of Jonah Re-Examined* (JSOTSup 236; Sheffield: Sheffield Academic Press, 1997), 57–63.

Broadly speaking, scholars have identified themes pertaining to divine mercy or sovereignty, repentance, universalism, and the role and limitations of prophets and prophecy. I argue that the book of Jonah underscores the efficacy of repentance – itself a product of divine mercy – while critiquing certain improperly balanced reactions to sin and the divine response that it provokes. A central theme pertaining to universalism or prophecy, by contrast, would not easily accord with the book's pervasive Eden-related motifs. Nonetheless, I do not exclude universalism as a possible secondary message.

My approach does not ascribe to the story any fundamental Israel-related theme, nor do I associate the book with any political or ideological concern presumed to typify the centuries-long postexilic Jewish experience. Regarding this methodological step, see the important remarks by Benjamin D. Sommer, "Dating Pentateuchal Texts and the Perils of Pseudo-Historicism," in *The Pentateuch: International Perspectives on Current Research* (ed. T. B. Dozeman, K. Schmid, and B. J. Schwartz; FAT 78; Tübingen: Mohr Siebeck, 2011), 85–108 (esp. 106–108). Rather, my non-Israel–centered reading suggests that the story of Jonah, much like wisdom texts, addresses questions that transcend sociohistorical boundaries. On the question of a relationship between Jonah and wisdom literature, see, inter alia, Bolin, *Freedom beyond Forgiveness*, 184–185, and the earlier material cited there.

Consistent with this conception of the book, scholars note that Edenic aspirations appear in postexilic texts in a variety of forms, "nationalistic/covenantal" and otherwise, and that Edenic depictions of a divine sanctuary – the likes of which we repeatedly encounter in Jonah – may evoke a heavenly abode without reference to any earthly temple. (See recently Peter T. Lanfer, *Remembering Eden: The Reception History of Genesis 3:22–24* [Oxford: Oxford University Press, 2012], 30, 131–132; and more generally the expansive study by T. Stordalen, *Echoes of Eden: Genesis 2–3 and Symbolism of the Eden Garden in Biblical Hebrew Literature* [BBET 25; Leuven, Belgium: Peeters, 2000]). Observe, therefore, that beyond offering no overt indication of any nationalistic or political objective, the book of Jonah – unlike numerous other texts that allude to Eden – avoids mention of Jerusalem, Mount Zion, and, for that matter, any specific holy mountain, even as it refers to God's "holy sanctuary" and invokes motifs that signify a divine abode. Rather, the Edenic sanctuaries in Jonah represent an idyllic, sacred domain that transcends any narrowly delimited space.

Finally, in line with sentiments expressed by Jack M. Sasson (*Jonah: A New Translation with Introduction, Commentary, and Interpretation* [AB 24B; New York: Doubleday, 1990], 326), I make no effort to attach any nuanced label to the genre of the work, although I maintain little objection to the rather general category "didactic story." See esp. James Limburg, *Jonah: A Commentary* (OTL; Louisville: Westminster/John Knox, 1993), 22–28; Steven L. McKenzie, "The Genre of Jonah," in *Seeing Signals, Reading Signs: The Art of Exegesis* (ed. M. A. O'Brien and H. N. Wallace; JSOTSup 415; London: T & T Clark, 2004), 159–171 (160–162). Note, however, the concerns raised by Kenneth M. Craig Jr. regarding "didactic story" as a technical classification (*A Poetics of Jonah: Art in the Service of Ideology* [Macon, GA: Mercer University Press, 1993], 159–165).

2. I am inclined to date the book of Jonah near the end of the fifth century BCE or later, because I offer strong evidence that it alludes to the Eden motif in the book of Joel and I am sympathetic to the assignment of Joel to the latter half of the fifth century. See esp. John Strazicich, *Joel's Use of Scripture and the Scripture's Use of Joel: Appropriation and Resignification in Second Temple Judaism and Early Christianity* (BINS 82; Leiden: Brill, 2007), 53–55.

3. I concur here with the position of Ehud Ben Zvi – endorsed by many others at least by implication – that the book of Jonah was intended for a sophisticated audience and that an appreciation of its depth requires careful study and repeated engagement of the text (*Signs of Jonah: Reading and Rereading in Ancient Yehud* [JSOTSup 367; Sheffield: Sheffield Academic Press, 2003], 9–11, 14–33).

To cite just one illustration, Jonah's indignation at the beginning of chapter 4 seems, at least initially, to result from God's reversal of his decree against Nineveh. Shortly thereafter, however, we find the prophet sitting anxiously near the city, apparently unaware of any decision about its fate. This widely noted incongruity invites a sober reassessment of Jonah's anger, and not one that gives way to a quick resumption of the story under a new set of clear-cut assumptions. Instead, this apparent discrepancy throws the chronology of events and their causal relationships into serious confusion, thereby demanding reengagement with the passage and sustained, careful reflection on the merits of different possible explanations.

For a broader articulation of this methodological premise and its relevance to inner-biblical allusion, see Cynthia Edenburg, "Intertextuality, Literary Competence, and the Question of Readership: Some Preliminary Observations," *JSOT* 35 (2010): 131–148. According to Edenburg, when a text features complex allusions that yield subtle meaning, this suggests that it was intended for a reading audience that "had the means to peruse and reread texts" in order to make the necessary associations (145–147).

4. Many of our book's resonances with prior biblical material were first noted in André Feuillet, "Les sources du livre de Jonas," RB 54 (1947): 161–186. Considerable advances, both in identifying allusions and in evaluating their significance, appear in the final two chapters of Jonathan Magonet, *Form and Meaning: Studies in Literary Techniques in the Book of Jonah* (BBET 2; Frankfurt: Peter Lang, 1976). More recent contributions include, inter alia, Simon, *Jonah*, xxxvi–xxxix; Hyun C. P. Kim, "Jonah Read Intertextually," JBL 126 (2007): 497–528; and Muldoon, *Divine Justice*. Most of these treatments support the view that inner-biblical allusions, even when distributed erratically through a text, function to generate meaning. Studies that operate on this assumption, moreover, have produced suggestive analyses of numerous biblical compositions, especially works of the postexilic period. I provide some substantial bibliography pertaining to allusions in Ruth and Esther in my essays, "Ruth and the David–Bathsheba Story: Allusions and Contrasts," JSOT 33 (2009): 433–452; "Ruth and Inner-Biblical Allusion: The Case of 1 Samuel 25," JBL 128 (2009): 253–272; and "Esther and Benjaminite Royalty: A Study in Inner-Biblical Allusion," JBL 129 (2010): 625–644.

To an extent, this methodological conclusion emerges from the craftsmanship exhibited by such compositions more generally: when a text seems carefully designed to maximize meaning – through its lexical and structural features, plot and character development, deployment of motifs, and more – it stands to reason that similarities to earlier texts likewise carry significance. Crucially, moreover, where multiple apparent allusions combine to yield a single striking interpretation, it becomes especially difficult to deny their presence and meaningfulness. Thus certain lexical analogies in Jonah, which other scholars have dismissed as mere products of stock terminology, play a significant role in my analysis. For example, Bolin affirms that similarities between the sea-storm narrative in Jonah and analogous accounts elsewhere in Scripture result from nothing more than "a time-honored literary convention that demands certain features and vocabulary" (*Freedom beyond Forgiveness*, 95). Based on a more comprehensive set of evidence, however, I argue that the relevant parallels make an important contribution to the development of our book's Eden theme.

Finally, let me stress that, where apparently meaningful inner-biblical correlations are convincingly present, they amount to hard data that may not be ignored either by those who seek to identify an author's intended theological message or by anyone embracing a hermeneutical model that calls for serious engagement of all varieties of signification. Put differently, only a hermeneutic that places limits on the types of evidence it will entertain could reasonably allow for ignoring intertextual signifiers, and importantly, even non-intentionalist treatments do not generally operate with such stark constraints. It emerges, accordingly, that in the interpretation of Jonah, the incorporation of intertextual evidence may scarcely be regarded as a mere hermeneutical option.

5. In short order, we will encounter examples of phonetic parallels between texts. The first one of these examples, involving the phrase *yarkĕtê hassĕpînâ* ("the nethermost part of the vessel"; Jonah 1:5), finds support in multiple earlier studies. Phonetic wordplay, moreover, is widely seen to characterize the text of Jonah itself, inner-biblical parallels aside. See esp. Baruch Halpern and Richard E. Friedman, "Composition and Paronomasia in the Book of Jonah," HAR 4 (1980): 79–92.

6. The most important discussion of the book's multivalence appears in the first two chapters of Ben Zvi, *Signs of Jonah*. More recently, see esp. chapter 8 of Perry, *The Honeymoon Is Over*, and the more general discussion in Diana V. Edelman, "Jonah among the Twelve in the MT: The Triumph of Torah over Prophecy," in *The Production of Prophecy: Constructing Prophets and Prophecy in Yehud* (ed. D. V. Edelman and E. Ben Zvi; BibleWorld; London: Equinox, 2009), 150–167. Perry makes considerable strides toward a *comprehensive* multivalent conception of the story, and in the present study I argue that the text indeed yields sustained multiple readings that flow smoothly from start to finish.

Significantly, my interpretation invokes multivalence of various kinds: semantic, syntactic, and thematic. Furthermore, whereas the text's deeper meanings typically add to its superficial sense without generating any sort of clash, these deeper meanings do stand in creative tension *with one another* – ultimately, to be sure, in the service of a single theological message. It thus bears emphasis that all these types of multivalence find considerable precedent in biblical interpretation. A notably detailed treatment, including the citation and evaluation of secondary works of both biblical and more general scholarship, appears in Jonathan Grossman, "Ambiguity in the Biblical Narrative and Its Contribution to the Literary Formation" (Hebrew; Ph.D. diss., Bar Ilan University, 2006). See especially chapter 8 of Grossman's study concerning the dialectical relationship that may obtain between different intended meanings of a biblical story, and note also his discussions of the multiplicity of meaning triggered by philological obscurity (chapter 5) and by inner-biblical allusion (chapter 6). All this material provides a foundation for the methods that I use. (Note also the English-language study by Allen M. Darnov, "Equivocal Narrative in the Hebrew Bible" [Ph.D. diss., Jewish Theological Seminary of America, 2007], and the literature cited therein.) As for the dialectical variety of multivalence, see also the instructive essay by Benjamin D. Sommer, "Is It Good for the Jews? Ambiguity and the Rhetoric of Turning in Isaiah," in *Birkat Shalom: Studies in the Bible, Ancient Near Eastern Literature, and Postbiblical Judaism Presented to Shalom M. Paul on the Occasion of His Seventieth Birthday* (ed. C. Cohen et al.; Winona Lake, IN: Eisenbrauns, 2008), 321–345; and cf. idem, "Reflecting on Moses: The Redaction of Numbers 11," *JBL* 118 (1999): 601–624 (622–624).

Finally, let me emphasize, echoing both Grossman and Sommer, that I speak of multivalence as a product not of reader subjectivity but of literary craftsmanship, whereby the text's multiple meanings generate a unified if multifaceted theological message. By no means do I regard the book of Jonah to be theologically indeterminate. In this connection, see also – albeit with important variation – the classic if controversial argument in chapter 6 of Meir Sternberg, *The Poetics of Biblical Narrative: Ideological Literature and the Drama of Reading* (ISBL; Bloomington: Indiana University Press, 1987).

7. Many of my claims draw on an accumulation of suggestive evidence. Such claims pertain to the presence of widespread multivalence; the prevalence of allusions, the complexity of their deployment, their meaningfulness, and the validity of numerous specific correlations; the presence and significance of keywords, different types of wordplay, and other literary features; and my actual interpretation of the story. I ask, therefore, that the reader allow the argument to build on all these fronts. In this connection, note esp. the remarks by Richard B. Hays concerning the force of cumulative, exegetically satisfying arguments in favor of allusion (*Echoes of Scripture in the Letters of Paul* [New Haven: Yale University Press, 1989], 31–32). Let me emphasize, moreover, that

if the author of Jonah intended for the book to be studied carefully and repeatedly, and doing so reveals a strikingly meaningful convergence of allusions, we hardly need to justify that conclusion by speculating about the mental process by which a reader makes instinctive textual associations.

In addition, let me caution against skepticism born of excessively restrictive methodological criteria. For example, the evidence suggests that a character may have more than one biblical counterpart and that textual correlations may draw on references that are distributed erratically (if judiciously) through a narrative. Cf., e.g., Mark E. Biddle, "Ancestral Motifs in 1 Samuel 25: Intertextuality and Characterization," *JBL* 121 (2002): 617–638; and contrast the restrictions proposed by Paul R. Noble, "Esau, Tamar, and Joseph: Criteria for Identifying Inner-Biblical Allusions," *VT* 52 (2002): 219–252.

Furthermore, when a passage – especially one already shown to be highly allusive – features a concentration of terms/motifs that appear likewise in an earlier composition, the presence of those elements may serve as a marker of allusion even if the later text does not deploy the terms/motifs "ungrammatically"; that is, in a way that generates some kind of incongruity. Indeed, in her pivotal study of literary allusion, Ziva Ben-Porat provides a central example where the reader, even after arriving at a "satisfactory local interpretation," would properly detect an allusion to another work purely on the strength of an analogous lexical sequence ("The Poetics of Literary Allusion," *PTL: A Journal for Descriptive Poetics and Theory of Literature* 1 [1976]: 105–128 [119]). The term *ungrammaticality*, by contrast, was coined by Michael Riffaterre to refer, in a more general way, to incongruities in a text that prompt the reader to seek implied significance (*Semiotics of Poetry* [Advances in Semiotics; Bloomington: Indiana University Press, 1978], 2). Even though Riffaterre later applies the term when discussing "intertextuality" (see, e.g., his essay "Syllepsis," *Critical Inquiry* 6 [1980]: 625–638 [625–628]), nowhere does he deny the common-sense observation that, even in the absence of an ungrammaticality, a set of terms in one text may call to mind a similar set in an earlier text. He affirms, rather, that without an ungrammaticality the reader will not *seek out other texts to help determine meaning*. If, accordingly, we apply Riffaterre's analysis to *allusion*, we must do so in a different way: once an earlier text is evoked with or without the help of an ungrammaticality – and innocuous explanations such as "stock terminology" and "common influence" are not applicable – the resulting textual correlation, much like an extraneous word or phrase in a single text, *amounts* to an ungrammaticality that calls for interpretation. In other words, although establishing an allusion does not require an appeal to ungrammaticality, the allusion itself constitutes a sign that, bearing no intrinsic meaning, generates implied significance. Regarding the proposed role of ungrammaticality in the identification of inner-biblical allusions, see recently Joseph R. Kelly, "Intertextuality and Allusion in the Study of the Hebrew Bible" (Ph.D. diss., Southern Baptist Theological Seminary, 2014), 135–141; Edenburg, "Intertextuality," 144–145; idem, "How (Not) to Murder a King: Variations on a Theme in 1 Sam 24; 26," *SJOT* 12 (1998): 64–85 (68–69, 72–73). Most often, lists of criteria for identifying inner-biblical allusions justly omit this requirement; see, e.g., chapter 5 of Kelly, "Intertextuality"; Hays, *Echoes of Scripture*, 29–32; and Jeffery M. Leonard, "Identifying Inner-Biblical Allusions: Psalm 78 as a Test Case," *JBL* 127 (2008): 241–265 (246). All of my important claims, in any event, meet any reasonable threshold in this regard, much as they do for more widely accepted criteria involving the distinctiveness, quantity, and thematic suggestiveness of proposed parallels.

Finally, on the matter of terminology, some scholars employ the expressions *intertextuality* and *allusion* almost interchangeably. For others, however, *intertextuality* refers not simply to an author's production of meaning through purposeful allusion to other texts but, to paraphrase one ambitious definition, to the impact of all encounters, textual and otherwise, on an individual's construal of signifiers. Such deployments of the term, which generally seek to conform to its initial usage by the literary theorist Julia Kristeva, are less pertinent to the methods of the present study. To avoid confusion, therefore, I typically speak of *inner-biblical allusion*, resorting to the adjective "intertextual" only where a suitable alternative is lacking. (The adjective "inner-biblical," which does not by itself indicate a textual relationship, is sometimes insufficient.) For a basic articulation of the relevant distinction, see Benjamin D. Sommer, "Exegesis, Allusion and Intertextuality in the Hebrew Bible: A Response to Lyle Eslinger," *VT* 56 (1996): 479–489 (486–489), and note the earlier studies cited there. More recent discussions include, inter alia, Kelly, "Intertextuality"; John Barton, "Déjà Lu: Intertextuality, Method or Theory?," in *Reading Job Intertextually* (ed. K. Dell and W. Kynes; LHBOTS 574; New York: T & T Clark, 2013), 1–16; David M. Carr, "The Many Uses of Intertextuality in Biblical Studies," in *Congress Volume Helsinki 2010* (ed. M. Nissinen; Leiden: Brill, 2012), 519–549; Geoffrey D. Miller, "Intertextuality in Old Testament Research," *CBR* 9 (2011): 283–309; and Stefan Alkier, "Intertextuality and the Semiotics of Biblical Texts," in *Reading the Bible Intertextually* (ed. R. B. Hayes, S. Alkier, and L. A. Huizenga; Waco, TX: Baylor University Press, 2009), 3–22. Note also that I use the expressions *allusion, correlation, relationship,* and *set of parallels* when referring to the totality of a connection between texts, and the terms *parallel* and *correspondence* when referring to a single common expression or motif. I may speak of a *link, connection, association, analogy, equivalence, resemblance, similarity, resonance,* or *reference* in either of these two senses.

8. James S. Ackerman, "Satire and Symbolism in the Song of Jonah," in *Traditions in Transformation: Turning Points in Biblical Faith* (ed. B. Halpern and J. D. Levenson; Winona Lake, IN: Eisenbrauns, 1981), 213–246; and less expansively idem, "Jonah," in *The Literary Guide to the Bible* (ed. R. Alter and F. Kermode; Cambridge, MA: Harvard University Press, 1987), 234–243. These studies provide an essential basis for my argument, even though I do not regard the story to be fundamentally satirical as does Ackerman. As for the significance of Jonah's sanctuaries, Ackerman provides just a brief conjecture: the prophet, he suggests, wishes to isolate himself in a protective, temple-like enclosure in an expression of the "Temple Presence theology" of the Zadokite priesthood – an objective that God shuns in favor of a more universalist stance ("Satire and Symbolism," 246; "Jonah," 242). Note, however, that Tarshish, Jonah's preferred destination, is hardly an enclosure like the ship, the fish, and the plant. Ackerman thus proposes, based on highly doubtful evidence, that Tarshish stands outside the boundaries of God's sovereignty and thereby offers a haven – albeit of a variety that, he concedes, stands in stark opposition to the kind of refuge provided by those other, divinely protected domains ("Satire and Symbolism," 233; "Jonah," 235).

Building in part on Ackerman's studies, Joel E. Anderson argues that the "re-creation" of Jonah in the womb of the fish spawns an analogy to the establishment of the postexilic temple ("Jonah's Peculiar Re-Creation," *BTB* 41 [2011]: 179–188). After all, prophets of this period occasionally describe that temple as a new creation and in other instances envision it as embracing all humanity, including non-Israelites. Accordingly, whereas Jonah resists his mission to save the Gentiles of Nineveh and longs for a temple that serves Israelites alone, the Lord insists that, in the newly fashioned reality represented by the reconstructed temple, sanctuary under the shelter of the divine shall be attainable to everyone.

Problematically, however, the proposed link between the postexilic temple, the re-creation motif, and the embrace of non-Israelites draws on just a small handful of select, diverse biblical passages, and the synthesis of these ideas in Jonah emerges from the text far from easily. This difficulty becomes particularly apparent when one asks what precisely the Eden-like temple signifies in Jonah's prayer. On the one hand, Anderson affirms, the "use of creation/temple imagery" serves "to anticipate the inclusion of Gentiles," because God's "true [cosmic] Temple, of which the Jerusalem temple is merely a symbol, encompasses all of the created order, and thus extends to all people, Jew and Gentile alike." On the other hand, the objective of our prophet, who utters the prayer, is allegedly to *exclude* non-Israelites from the sacred existence toward which he sees himself heading. It hardly seems likely that Jonah's words signal both his own limited view of the role of the temple and the book's more inclusive conception of it.

Finally, a rabbinic source (*Midr. Psalms* 26:7) affirms that Jonah underwent a process of purification in the sea and in the belly of the fish and that he subsequently entered the Garden of Eden alive (*The Midrash on Psalms*, vol. 1 [trans. William G. Braude; Yale Judaica Series; New Haven, CT: Yale University Press, 1959], 363). This affirmation appears in the context of a comparison between Jonah and Elijah, and it stands to reason that Elijah's ascent to the heavens (2 Kgs 2:11) influenced the analogous claim about our prophet. Regarding this rabbinic perspective, see Yehuda Liebes, "Jonah as the Messiah Ben Joseph" (Hebrew), *Jerusalem Studies in Jewish Thought* 3 (1983/4): 269–311 (269–270) and Pnina Galpaz-Feller, *Jonah – Journey to Freedom: A New Reading of the Book of Jonah* (Hebrew; Jerusalem: Carmel, 2009), 128–129. It is worth asking if the midrash perceived certain traits shared by Jonah and Elijah, particularly their zeal for unadulterated truth and justice, to have prompted their direct passage to a spiritual realm. This would resonate with my contention that, according to one meaning of the story, Jonah is drawn toward a pristinely sacred existence precisely because of his zealotry. In that connection, see Liebes, "Messiah Ben Joseph," 304–311; and cf. Arthur J. Seltzer, "Jonah in the Belly of the Great Fish: The Birth of Messiah Ben Joseph," *JNSL* 25 (1999): 187–203.

9. Cf. Gen 2:11–12, a passage that, to be sure, does not include Tarshish-stones among the riches that it associates with Eden. For a recent discussion, see Lanfer, *Remembering Eden*, 142–146.

10. Ackerman, "Satire and Symbolism," 232–233, 242; "Jonah," 235. Contrast Lowell K. Handy, who affirms that Tarshish must have been a specific location known to our book's audience (*Jonah's World: Social Science and the Reading of Prophetic Story* [BibleWorld; London: Equinox, 2008], 28). In connection with this idealized image of Tarshish, Ackerman adopts the phrase "distant paradise" from C. H. Gordon, "Tarshish," *IDB* 4:518–519. Cf. Terence E. Fretheim, *The Message of Jonah: A Theological Commentary* (Minneapolis: Augsburg, 1977), 40; and R. Reed Lessing, *Jonah* (Concordia Commentary; St. Louis: Concordia, 2007), 73. For a summary of speculations regarding the actual location of Tarshish see, inter alia, Sasson, *Jonah*, 78–79.

11. Ackerman, "Satire and Symbolism," 229–230; "Jonah," 235. The link to Zaphon is proposed likewise by Halpern and Friedman ("Composition and Paronomasia," 84 n. 11), endorsed by Willie S. van Heerden ("Humour and the Interpretation of the Book of

Jonah," OTE 5 [1992]: 389–401 [395]), and cited as a serious option by Duane L. Christensen ("The Song of Jonah: A Metrical Analysis," JBL 104 [1985]: 217–231 [226]), Philip J. Nel ("The Symbolism and Function of Epic Space in Jonah," JNSL 25 [1999]: 215–224 [218]), and Yvonne Sherwood (*A Biblical Text and Its Afterlives: The Survival of Jonah in Western Culture* [Cambridge: Cambridge University Press, 2000], 248 n. 152).

Fundamentally, the word *yarkâ* appears to mean "side" or "extreme part"; see the relevant entries in BDB and *HALOT*. Even if *yarkĕtê ṣāpôn* initially referred to the "sides/slopes" of Zaphon, its opposition to *yarkĕtê bôr* ("the nethermost reaches of the Pit"; Isa 14:13–15) suggests that it probably evolved to mean the "uppermost reaches" or "heights" of Zaphon. I thank Prof. Moshe J. Bernstein for prompting me to clarify this point.

12. See extensively Richard J. Clifford, *The Cosmic Mountain in Canaan and the Old Testament* (HSM 4; Cambridge, MA: Harvard University Press, 1972), esp. 131–160.

13. Here and elsewhere, my renderings of the biblical text bear the influence of the NJPS translation.

14. Ackerman, "Satire and Symbolism," 242.

15. These formulations, cited by Anderson ("Jonah's Peculiar Re-Creation," 183), appear, respectively, in Gordon J. Wenham, *Genesis 1–15* (WBC 1; Waco, TX: Word Books, 1987), 399; and Othmar Keel, *The Symbolism of the Biblical World: Ancient Near Eastern Iconography and the Book of Psalms* (trans. T. J. Hallett; New York: Seabury, 1978), 118. Cf. also Anderson's citations of Michael Fishbane, *Biblical Interpretation in Ancient Israel* (Oxford: Oxford University Press, 1985), 369–370, 386. Among many other expressions of this idea, see recently Stordalen, *Echoes of Eden*, chapters 13 and 15; Lanfer, *Remembering Eden*, chapter 5.

16. These parallels, noted long ago by Feuillet ("Sources," 176–181), have drawn only limited attention. An English summary of Feuillet's essay appears in Benoit Trépanier, "The Story of Jonas," CBQ 13 (1951): 8–16.

17. I am referring specifically to *ḥōbēl* in the sense of a "ship pilot."

18. Bolin, in his important if skeptical treatment of the Ezekiel correlation, does not cite this particular parallel (*Freedom beyond Forgiveness*, 91–95). Gerhard C. Aalders, who resists the analogies presented by Feuillet because of their perceived threat to the historicity of Jonah, dismisses the present parallel without meaningful argument (*The Problem of the Book of Jonah* [Tyndale Old Testament Lecture; London: Tyndale Press, 1948], 22–23). Magonet (*Form and Meaning*, 139–140 n. 66) discounts this parallel because the coastal rulers in Ezekiel act out of grief whereas the king of Nineveh seeks to display contrition. We will see, however, that contrasts of this sort contribute meaningfully to a number of our book's inner-biblical allusions, in line with Magonet's own approach elsewhere in his study (e.g., 102–103).

The proposed correlation to Ezekiel fares equally poorly in German-language treatments. Wilhelm Rudolph tersely dismisses the connection because of a perceived thematic incompatibility (*Joel–Amos–Obadja–Jona* [KAT 13.2; Gütersloh: Gerd Mohn, 1971], 328), and Hans W. Wolff sees the parallels as coincidental, arguing that, had our passage been dependent on the Ezekiel text, Jonah would have used the port city of Tyre rather than that of Joppa – especially because of Tyre's relative proximity to the prophet's hometown of Gath-Hepher (*Studien zum Jonabuch: Mit einem Anhang von Jörg Jeremias: Das Jonabuch in der Forschung seit Hans Walter Wolff* [Neukirchen-Vluyn: Neukirchener, 2003], 27). Like others, however, Rudolph and Wolff do not account for the striking convergence of the sea-storm parallels and the notably similar conduct displayed by the coastal rulers and the king of Nineveh. (Regarding the significance of Joppa and its relationship to the Ezekiel text, see the following discussion.) Gottfried Vanoni, for his part, cites the parallels to Ezekiel but confesses his inability to find meaning in them (*Das Buch Jona: Literar- und formkritische Untersuchung* [ATSAT 7; St. Ottilien: EOS, 1978], 147).

19. In Ezek 27 and Isa 23, treasure-filled ships of Tarshish supply or signify Tyre, a city that juts out into the sea.

20. Beyond the assumption that Joppa ought to bear literary significance, it is intrinsically unlikely that Jonah would head there for no important reason, because other port cities would probably have offered better options for the Gath-Hepherian prophet. Cf. Wolff, *Studien*, 27; Meik Gerhards, *Studien zum Jonabuch* (Biblisch-Theologische Studien 78; Neukirchen–Vluyn: Neukirchener, 2006), 67.

Sasson (*Jonah*, 80) embraces an older proposal that, by hurrying to a city that stood outside Israelite control, Jonah thought that he could escape the presence of God. See also Sasson (*Jonah*, 83–84) for citations and discussion regarding the *śākār* provided by Jonah, which, on the assumption that it refers to the cost of the whole voyage, is said to underscore the prophet's haste to run away. As a general matter, I regard the book's distinctive terminology and motifs to be of more concrete significance, often hinting at added layers of meaning through allusion to other biblical texts. Thus, Joppa marks something more specific than a port city outside Israel, and its use goes beyond highlighting Jonah's already stated motive to escape from the Lord.

It bears mention that the motifs in this verse are widely observed to contribute to a chiastic pattern, but I do not appeal to structural considerations as a sole justification for any striking feature of the text. Regarding the book's literary structures, see the helpful synopsis in Simon, *Jonah*, xxiv–xxx. The patterns observed by scholars typically accord with the arguments in this study without difficulty.

21. Indeed, even the many occurrences of *yph* in the Song of Songs are more scattered.

22. Regarding the implications of the phrase "its fare," see the discussion in Sasson (*Jonah*, 83–84).

23. The matter finds limited acknowledgment in some treatments, such as Ackerman, "Satire and Symbolism," 222–223. Ships of Tarshish appear in 1 Kgs 10:22 (cf. 2 Chr 9:21); 1 Kgs 22:49 (cf. 2 Chr 20:36–37); Isa 2:16; 23:1, 10, 14; 60:9; Ps 48:8; and, of course, Ezek 27. (The Psalms text alludes to the resplendence of these ships by means of their implied comparison to the surpassing "beauty" of Zion.) Cf. also Jer 10:9. In Ezekiel, Psalms, Jonah, and 2 Chr 20:37, these ships are said to "break apart." Cf. Sherwood (*Biblical Text and Afterlives*, 250 n. 155), who notes the surprisingly scarce mention of these biblical passages in scholarship on Jonah.

24. As argued recently by Aaron Koller, the biblical root in question denotes arrival or entry, not setting out or journeying ("לבוא and להיכנס: "Synchronic and Diachronic Perspectives on the Semantics of לבוא in Ancient Hebrew" [Hebrew], *Leshonenu* 75 [2013]: 149–164). See also the somewhat different formulation of the problem in Sasson (*Jonah*, 82–83) and his proposed solution. In 2 Chr 9:21 and 1 Kgs 22:49 (cf. 2 Chr 20:36), it is the verb *hlk* that fittingly indicates the departure of Tarshish-bound ships.

Note further that, according to our verse, Jonah descended into the ship "to go with *them*" to Tarshish, yet the text contains no explicit plural antecedent for the pronoun. The phrase "with them," moreover, seems extraneous, and the entire last line of the verse, which reiterates that Jonah fled in the direction of Tarshish, seems to accomplish no more than to help generate a widely perceived chiastic structure. Dare I suggest, accordingly, that, on another level of meaning, this latter part of the verse stresses that the prophet, seeking to escape his divinely ordained mission in favor of a Tarshish-like, paradisiacal existence, sought to arrive (*lābōʾ*) at his Edenic destination "with them" – that is to say, with *the ship and its treasures*?

25. Correspondence between *śîn* and *sāmek* is well attested in the biblical period; see, e.g., Paul Joüon and T. Muraoka, *A Grammar of Biblical Hebrew* (StudBib 14; 2 vols.; Rome: Pontifical Biblical Institute, 1996), 28–29. Note also the term *ʾeškārēk* ("your tribute"; Ezek 27:15) used to denote valuables provided to Tyre by foreign merchants, which bears at least some limited resemblance to the word *śĕkārāh* ("its fare") in the Jonah text.

Of possible significance is Ezekiel's acknowledgment, in the chapter following his proclamations against Tyre, that, in spite of his predictions, the invading Babylonian army did not destroy the city and thus left without pillaging any *śākār* ("wages") for its troops (Ezek 29:18). Perhaps, then, by filling a Tyre-like vessel with its *śākār*, Jonah seeks a resplendent domain epitomized by that *enduringly* affluent coastal kingdom.

26. The author's quest to generate the additional sense of shedding honor also accounts for the absence of a direct object after *lĕhāqēl*, which would have limited the phrase's range of meaning. A recent discussion of this omission of a direct object appears in Carl J. Bosma, "Jonah 1:9 – An Example of Elenctic Testimony," *CTJ* 48 (2013): 65–90 (76–77). See also Phyllis M. Trible, "Studies in the Book of Jonah" (Ph.D. diss., Columbia University, 1963), 210–211 n. 1; Bolin, *Freedom beyond Forgiveness*, 79–80.

27. The second one of these phrases raises serious problems of interpretation (see esp. Hans Wildberger, *Isaiah 13–27* [CC; Minneapolis: Augsburg Fortress, 1977], 408–409), but the remaining examples provide sufficient basis for my broader point.

28. A summary of alternatives appears in Wildberger, *Isaiah 13–27*, 406.

29. Feuillet ("Sources," 176–177) makes the connection, although Magonet (*Form and Meaning*, 80–82) is skeptical. The common terms do seem to suggest at least a shared template, and the acknowledgment of God that follows the salvation in the psalm accords with a key theme in our text. Cf. recently Tova Forti, "Of Ships and Seas, and Fish and Beasts: Viewing the Concept of Universal Providence in the Book of Jonah through the Prism of Psalms," *JSOT* 35 (2011): 359–374 (368). Significantly, it emerges from my analysis of Jonah that a root as distinctive as *štq* almost invariably generates a meaningful allusion to another text, unless it bears some alternative special significance. Thus I am inclined to think that our text alludes to the psalm, thereby calling attention to the sailors' emerging recognition of the Lord.

30. Cf., with variation, Sasson, *Jonah*, 115.

31. Isaiah speaks of the Tyrians attempting to preserve their resplendent existence, whereas Jonah sought to attain such an existence on the Zaphon-like vessel. If, however, our prophet actually seeks to *preserve* the Edenic environment embodied by the Tyre-like Nineveh, as I believe the story suggests according to one layer of meaning, then the parallel emerges even stronger.

32. This suggestion, of course, embraces an understanding of Jonah's fear of the Lord that, as in the case of the word *ʿibrî*, goes beyond the surface meaning of the expression. Later, we return to the multivalent force of the text's reference to Jonah's "fear," whose sense should properly take into account other parallels still to be considered.

33. See, e.g., the approaches presented in Sasson, *Jonah*, 121.

34. This explanation, furthermore, accounts for Jonah's reference to himself as a Hebrew rather than an Israelite. For another approach and some citations of earlier scholarship, see Meir Sternberg, *Hebrews between Cultures: Group Portraits and National Literature* (ISBL; Bloomington: Indiana University Press, 1998), 206–208, 216.

35. John C. Holbert, "'Deliverance Belongs to [Y-ahweh]!' Satire in the Book of Jonah," *JSOT* 21 (1981): 59–81 (68); cf. Lessing, *Jonah*, 110; Gerhards, *Studien*, 141. Except for this observation, Holbert does not address our story's connection to Eden. (Here and elsewhere, I modify transliterations of the Tetragrammaton because of personal religious constraints.)

36. The arrogance of Tyre, in fact, has justly been identified as the governing motif of all of Ezekiel's prophecies on that kingdom; see Ian D. Wilson, "Tyre, a Ship: The Metaphorical World of Ezekiel 27 in Ancient Judah," *ZAW* 125 (2013): 249–262 (254–255).

37. See Halpern and Friedman, "Composition and Paronomasia," 81–82, and the recent extensive study by Jan-Dirk Döhling, "Das Wüten der Welt: Zur literarischen und narrativen Funktion der Schöpfungsdynamik in Jona 1 und 2," *BN* 157 (2013): 3–32 (cf. idem, "Jona und des Meeres Wellen: Zum problemgeschichtlichen Horizont und zum traditionsgeschichtlichen Hintergrund," *BN* 158 [2013]: 17–37).

38. Concerning renderings akin to "city of God-like magnitude," see Sasson, *Jonah*, 228. Sasson's own inclination (228–230) is that the expression, in one way or another, links Nineveh to the divine in a nonmetaphorical sense. According to my suggestion, the phrase, in line with this chapter's emphasis on the humbling of Nineveh's "great" people, means to attribute godlike *pretensions* to the city. Indeed, Magonet (*Form and Meaning*, 32) observes that the text's descriptions of Nineveh's greatness constitute one of the story's "growing phrases" (cf. Jonah 1:2; 3:2; 4:11). In my opinion, this "greatness" bespeaks the wicked city's arrogance already at the beginning of the book, and the present, more expansive expression intensifies the story's disapproving characterization of Nineveh's self-perception.

In fact, scholars note the apparently unnecessary inclusion here of *hāyětâ* ("was"), a word that could easily have been elided (cf. Sasson, *Jonah*, 228, and the literature cited there). Perhaps, then, our phrase, in line with at least two other occurrences of *hyh* in Jonah (4:5, 10), bears the secondary meaning, "and Nineveh *had become* a city of divinely great pretensions" – a step beyond the merely "great" self-image implied in the book's opening scene. I propose another secondary meaning of the phrase in a later note.

39. See the extensive discussion and citations in Sasson, *Jonah*, 234–237.

40. The root *yph* also appears in Ps 48:3, where the text describes the beauty of Mount Zion and compares it to the *yarkětê ṣāpôn*. In the psalm, the magnificence of Zion proves overwhelming to foreign kings, and the city's superiority finds expression when God breaks apart ships of Tarshish by means of an east wind (48:5–8).

41. Muldoon, *Divine Justice*, 134–137. Regarding the identity of the plant, a peripheral matter for our purposes, the most elaborate discussion appears in Bernard P. Robinson, "Jonah's Qiqayon Plant," *ZAW* 97 (1985): 390–403.

42. Peter Weimar senses the relationship between these texts in a limited way (*Eine Geschichte voller Überraschungen: Annäherungen an die Jonaerzählung* [SBS 217; Stuttgart: Katholisches Bibelwerk, 2009], 140).

43. Eric W. Hesse and Isaac M. Kikawada likewise propose a connection between the plant and the Garden of Eden ("Jonah and Genesis 11–1," *AJBI* 10 [1984]: 3–19 [5]). Cf. also

the eighteenth-century commentary by Rabbi Elijah ben Solomon of Vilna (Moshe Schapiro, *The Book of Yonah: "Journey of the Soul": An Allegorical Commentary Adapted from the Vilna Gaon's Aderes Eliyahu* [Artscroll Judaica Classics; Brooklyn, NY: Mesorah, 1997], 93–94, and less clearly in the English adaptation on pp. 75–76).

44. Accounts of correspondences between Jonah and the Cain story appear in Vanoni, *Buch Jona*, 143, and in the later, more elaborate discussions by Gerhards (*Studien*, 138–140) and Weimar (*Geschichte*, 174–178). In English-language scholarship, the correlation was first noted by Hesse and Kikawada ("Jonah and Genesis 11–1," 5), who argue that our story progresses in inverse parallel to Genesis 1–11. The purpose of the book, they contend, is thus to affirm that the Lord's mercy extends to all people "as long as they conform to the spirit of the Mosaic covenant, even accidentally." For "in what better way could the author have reestablished the ground for the covenant than to have paralleled the book of Jonah with the first eleven chapters of Genesis in reverse order, taking us back to the God of creation?" This reading, however, has gained little traction in subsequent treatments, despite wide recognition of a more confined correlation between Jonah and the flood story.

Based in part on the study by Hesse and Kikawada, Lessing develops a similar thesis concentrating mostly on connections to the story of Noah (*Jonah*, 38–48). For other recent discussions of the link between our story and Noah's flood, see Noah Greenfield, "Jonah's Ark and Noah's Fish: Reading the Book of Jonah after the Flood," *AJBI* 33 (2007): 37–72; Timothy R. Koch, "The Book of Jonah and a Reframing of Israelite Theology: A Reader-Response Approach" (Ph.D. diss., Boston University, 2003), 285–291; Kim, "Jonah Read Intertextually," 499–504; Anderson, "Jonah's Peculiar Re-Creation," 184–185; and cf. the discussion by Albert H. Kamp, which addresses both creation and flood imagery (*Inner Worlds: A Cognitive Linguistic Approach to the Book of Jonah* [trans. D. Orton; BINS 68; Leiden: Brill, 2004], 205–217).

45. Cf. already Rudolph, *Joel–Amos–Obadja–Jona*, 328; Rabbi Elijah of Vilna (Schapiro, *Allegorical Commentary*, 73).

46. Regarding this last parallel, cf. Perry, *The Honeymoon Is Over*, 88.

47. Scholars often assume that Cain starts out near the eastern boundary of Eden where his parents allegedly made their home and that he then moves to a location farther east where he lives an unsettled life outside the range of God's protection (cf. Gen 4:14: "and I will be hidden from your face"). See, inter alia, Wenham, *Genesis 1–15*, 110; Kenneth A. Mathews, *Genesis 1–11:26* (NAC 1A; Nashville: Broadman & Holman, 1996), 278. The text, however, neither specifies where Adam and Eve settled nor any particular place from which Cain was banished. Rather – at least according to the author of Jonah – after Cain learns that God will not enable the land to produce for him, he moves *toward* Eden, longing to enter that blissful divine realm. Accordingly, both the Cain story and the analogous sin narrative about Adam and Eve fittingly culminate in the protagonists' exclusion from Eden itself. For lists of parallels between the two stories, see esp. Alan J. Hauser, "Linguistic and Thematic Links between Genesis 4:1–16 and Genesis 2–3," *JETS* 23 (1980): 294–305; Wenham, *Genesis 1–15*, 99–100.

48. Halpern and Friedman, "Composition and Paronomasia," 85–86. For additional sources and for a discussion of alternatives regarding who or what is doing the vomiting, see Brent A. Strawn, "On Vomiting: Leviticus, Jonah, Ea(a)rth," *CBQ* 74 (2012): 445–464 (455–459).

49. I am aware that the phrase in question may be compared to a similar one (albeit one that, significantly, lacks the preposition "from") in 1 Kgs 19 pertaining to Elijah – an

analogy that underscores Jonah's reluctance to carry out his task as a prophet. It becomes abundantly clear, however, that our story employs expressions that allude to multiple texts, and I am convinced that the present phrase is one of them. Cf. Vanoni, *Buch Jona*, 129 and n. 24; Gerhards, *Studien*, 141–142. For Gerhards, as well as for Weimar (*Geschichte*, 174–178), the phrase "away from the Lord" is central to the Jonah–Cain analogy, but the pivotal Garden of Eden connection plays only a peripheral role in their analyses.

50. See esp. Magonet, *Form and Meaning*, 73–74.

51. Our text invokes the face of God as a symbol of both judgment and protection, and I suspect that it attributes both meanings to the passage in Genesis also. (The expression "away from the Lord" may literally be rendered "from the face of the Lord.") The motif signals divine judgment when the evil of Nineveh rises up "to the face [of the Lord]," the defiant Jonah runs from "the face of the Lord," and Cain leaves "the face of the Lord" after God issues a sentence on him. (Cf. Gen 18:22, 25; Deut 19:17; 1 Kgs 3:16; Mathews, *Genesis 1–11:26*, 226–227, 278.) As for divine protection, Jonah later reflects on having been "banished" from the Lord's gaze (Jonah 2:5), whereas Cain worries about being hidden from the Lord's protective "face" (Gen 4:14).

Victor P. Hamilton contrasts Jonah, who left God's presence "voluntarily and in his own self-interests," with Cain, whose departure marks his "life of alienation from God" (*The Book of Genesis: Chapters 1–17* [NICOT; Grand Rapids, MI: Eerdmans, 1990], 235). This explanation, however, mandates a focus on the judging/commanding divine presence in the case of Jonah and on the protective divine presence in the case of Cain. My analysis, by contrast, suggests that both Jonah and Cain head away from God's judgment while yearning for a blissful existence under his protection.

A substantive analogy between Jonah's departure "from the face of the Lord" and that of Cain is likewise drawn by the twelfth-century theologian Judah Halevi, who identifies the relevant sacred location as the land of Israel, which he regards to be "[just] a step below the Garden of Eden" (Yehudah Halevi, *The Kuzari: In Defense of the Despised Faith* [trans. N. D. Korobkin; Jerusalem: Feldheim, 2013], 157–158).

52. Cf. Ackerman, "Jonah," 41; Anderson, "Jonah's Peculiar Re-Creation," 186–187. The connection was already drawn by the eleventh- to twelfth-century Spanish polymath Abraham bar Ḥiyya Savasorda, who adds the crucial observation that the trees of Eden, much like the *qîqāyôn*, rose up quickly and without any human effort (Abraham bar Chiyyah, "*Hegyon Hanefesh Ha'atzuvah* [Meditation of the Sad Soul]," in *The Journey of the Soul: Traditional Sources on* Teshuvah [ed. and trans. L. S. Kravitz and K. M. Olitzky; Northvale, NJ: Jason Aronson, 1995], 131–174 [170]).

53. Ackerman, "Satire and Symbolism," 242; "Jonah," 241. Images that show a serpent specifically are reproduced in Keel, *Symbolism*, 51–52.

54. Galpaz-Feller, *Journey to Freedom*, 103; Gershon Hepner, *Legal Friction: Law, Narrative, and Identity Politics in Biblical Israel* (Studies in Biblical Literature 78; New York: Peter Lang, 2010), 694–695. In many rabbinic Bibles, there appears a parenthetical insertion in Rashi at Jonah 2:1 which, in the name of a lost, centuries-old commentary called *Sod Mesharim*, draws this lexical connection between *wayĕman* and the manna. Some discussion of these insertions in Rashi and their obscure origins appears in Chaim Lieberman, *The Tent of Rachel* (Hebrew; New York: Empire Press, 1980), 310–329.

55. Additionally – if rather less definitively – the arguably extraneous word *lammāḥŏrāt* ("the next day") in Jonah 4:7, which marks the worm incident, resonates with a similar

term in Joshua 5:12 where the text recounts the *permanent* withholding of the manna on the day that followed the paschal offering (*mimmāḥŏrāt*).

56. I am indebted to Rabbi David Silber who, in a personal communication, identified the basic significance of the manna connection.

57. See esp. Alastair Hunter, "Jonah from the Whale: Exodus Motifs in Jonah 2," in *The Elusive Prophet: The Prophet as a Historical Person, Literary Character and Anonymous Artist* (ed. J. C. de Moor; OTS 45; Leiden: Brill, 2001), 142–158 (147–150). The verb "swallow" (*blʿ*) in v. 1 may resonate with the affirmation that the land "swallowed" (*blʿ*) the Egyptians (Exod 15:12), but Hunter proposes an alternative connection to Ps 69:16: "Let the deep (*měṣûlâ*) not swallow (*blʿ*) me."

58. Regarding all these connections, cf. Magonet, *Form and Meaning*, 70.

59. Ibid., 74–75.

60. The keyword is noted by, inter alia, Magonet, *Form and Meaning*, 16; Halpern and Friedman, "Composition and Paronomasia," 81.

61. At the very end of this study, I explain why these references to the *ṭal* appear where they do and how precisely they relate to the idea introduced here. Bolin (*Freedom beyond Forgiveness*, 174) proposes a different connection between Jonah and Num 11 that involves Moses's frustration and wish for death, but it does not appear relevant to my present claim.

62. See, inter alia, Ackerman, "Satire and Symbolism," 235–236; Anderson, "Jonah's Peculiar Re-Creation," 182–183; Yael Shemesh, "'And Many Beasts' (Jonah 4:11): The Function and Status of Animals in the Book of Jonah," *JHS* 10.6 (2010): 9 (online: http://www.jhsonline.org/Articles/article_134.pdf).

63. See, e.g., Marvin A. Sweeney, *The Twelve Prophets* (Berit Olam; 2 vols.; Collegeville, MN: Liturgical Press, 2000), 317. This is also the apparent intention of Ackerman ("Satire and Symbolism," 235), contra the paraphrase by Sasson (*Jonah*, 155).

64. See recently Shemesh, "Status and Function of Animals," 12, and the earlier treatments cited there.

65. Indeed, Sasson (*Jonah*, 176) observes that elsewhere in Scripture the imperfect *polel* form of *sbb* denotes protection (e.g., Deut 3:10). Ps 55:11, however, contains an apparent counterexample. The sixteenth-century commentator Rabbi Moses Alshekh provides his own favorable reading of v. 4b–c, noting the resonance with the rivers of Eden in Genesis (*The Book of Jonah: The Voyage of the Visionary: The Commentary of Rabbi Moshe Alshich on the Book of Jonah* [trans. R. Shahar; Alshich Tanach Series 3; Jerusalem: Feldheim, 1992], 59). Cf. Seltzer, "Messiah Ben Joseph," 197.

66. Regarding the term's consistently unfavorable connotation and its striking appearance in the present context, see recently Strawn, "On Vomiting," 445–447, 453–454. Phyllis L. Trible suggests that the verb "underscores the repugnance that Jonah's words have elicited" (*Rhetorical Criticism: Context, Method, and the Book of Jonah* [GBS, OTG; Minneapolis: Augsburg Fortress, 1994], 172).

67. Halpern and Friedman, "Composition and Paronomasia," 85.

2. WRATHFUL MORALIST

1. Scholars, to be sure, have generally shied away from interpreting this occurrence of *kî* in the sense of "that." See, e.g., Simon, *Jonah*, 4. Exceptions include André Lacocque and Pierre-Emmanuel Lacocque (*Jonah: A Psycho-Religious Approach to the Prophet*

[SPOT; Columbia: University of South Carolina Press, 1990], 1), and the medieval commentators Abraham Ibn Ezra and Eliezer of Beaugency (*Mikrao't Gedolot 'Haketer': A Revised and Augmented Scientific Edition of 'Mikra'ot Gedolot' Based on the Aleppo Codex and Early Medieval MSS* [Hebrew; ed. M. Cohen; 17 vols.; Ramat Gan, Israel: Bar Ilan University Press, 1992–2013], The Twelve Minor Prophets: 156–157). For discussion of the issue and another alternative, see Sasson, *Jonah*, 75. Based on a more general philological treatment by A. Schoors ("The Particle כִּי," in *Remembering All the Way: Collection of Old Testament Studies* [ed. B. Albrektson; OTS 21; Leiden: Brill, 1981], 240–276 [256–259]), Sasson affirms that *kî* cannot mean "that" and thereby introduce the substance of what Jonah is expected to convey. Schoors's intent, however, is merely that *kî* cannot serve to introduce the actual words of the speaker. For an example of a verb denoting speech that is followed by *kî* in the sense of "that," see Gen 3:11: "Who told you that (*kî*) you are naked?"

As for *'ālêhā*, which most straightforwardly means "on it," Sasson (*Jonah*, 72–75) cites the widespread view that *'al* may also mean "to," especially in Late Biblical Hebrew, before offering his own argument that the present expression indicates a (repentance-inducing) proclamation of doom. My own analysis acknowledges both the suggestiveness of Sasson's rendering and the fundamental ambiguity of the language.

2. Regarding the absence of an explicit direct object see, inter alia, Simon (*Jonah*, 4), who affirms that the expression, understood to mean "cry out against it," requires no "complement."

Several scholars maintain that, at this stage, the reader may perceive Jonah's mission to entail a proclamation of doom. See Sternberg, *Poetics*, 318–320; Hauser, "In Pursuit of the Dove," 21–22; and Lessing, *Jonah*, 362–363. See also Ben Zvi's discussion (*Signs of Jonah*, 34–39), which provides an especially important foundation for my own analysis.

3. See, e.g., Feuillet, "Sources," 179–186, esp. 181–182; Simon, *Jonah*, xxxvii–xxxviii. Note also the sources collected by Bolin (*Freedom beyond Forgiveness*, 141–142 n. 75).

4. We should properly acknowledge the related motifs in Jer 18:7–10, whose "verbal and thematic links [to Jonah] have been noticed for centuries" (Bolin, *Freedom beyond Forgiveness*, 141).

5. Cf. Craig, *Poetics*, 71.

6. Sasson (*Jonah*, 323 n. 3), Ben Zvi (*Signs of Jonah*, 42), and Benjamin Gesundheit ("Studies in the Book of Jonah" [Hebrew], in *U-ve-Yom Tzom Kippur yehatemun: Studies on Yom ha-Kippurim* [ed. Amnon Bazak; Alon Shevut, Israel: Tevunot, 2004/5], 151–197 [160]) acknowledge the phrase in Jeremiah, albeit without explicitly referencing Jonah's wrath in 4:1. Even if, as most scholars maintain, the phrase *ḥărôn hayyônâ* should properly read *ḥereb hayyônâ* ("the *sword* of the oppressor"), an independent reference to the oppressor's *ḥărôn* ("rage") appears immediately thereafter in the verse in Jeremiah. For references and discussion see Jack R. Lundbom, *Jeremiah: A New Translation with Introduction and Commentary* (AB 21B; New York: Doubleday, 2004), 280.

7. Elijah's zeal is signified, inter alia, by the storm (*sě'ārâ*) that carries him up to the heavens in a fiery chariot (2 Kgs 2:1, 11). It is quite possible, accordingly, that when selecting the phrase *sa'ar-gādôl*, our author had that text in mind in addition to the one in Jeremiah.

8. Most of these correspondences are listed by, inter alia, Feuillet ("Sources," 168–169), Magonet (*Form and Meaning*, 68–69), Vanoni (*Buch Jona*, 145–146), Hagia Witzenrath (*Das Buch Jona: Eine literature-wissenchaftliche Untersuchung* [ATSAT 6;

St. Ottilien: EOS, 1978], 78–82), Lessing (*Jonah*, 48–52), Weimar (*Geschichte*, 170–74), and
Muldoon (*Divine Justice*, 97–98). A convenient table displaying these and still other
suggested parallels appears in Vanoni, "Elija, Jona und das Dodekapropheton: Grade der
Intertextualität," in *Wort [J-HWHs], das geschah . . . " (Hos 1,1): Studien zum Zwölfprophetenbuch* (Herders Biblische Studien 35; Freiburg: Herder, 2002), 113–121 (118–119). A
further analogy is proposed between Elijah's forty-day walk to Mount Horeb (1 Kgs 19:8)
and Jonah's warning that Nineveh will be destroyed in forty days (see, e.g., Muldoon,
Divine Justice, 98 n. 150), but these hardly seem to correspond thematically. Rather, the far
more important parallel to this motif in Jonah is apparently the forty days of rain in the
story of Noah.

There does, however, remain one instructive parallel that merits some supplementary
discussion (cf. Sweeney, *Twelve Prophets*, 326; Weimar, *Geschichte*, 171). When our text
recounts the king's display of submission, it states that "he removed his mantle from upon
him" (*wayya'ăbēr 'addartô mē'ālâw*; Jonah 3:6). This terminology recalls the aftermath of
Elijah's escape, when the prophet, on the Lord's instructions, designates Elisha his
successor by approaching him and throwing his mantle toward him (*wayya'ăbōr 'ēliyyāhû
'ēlâw wayyašlēk 'addartô 'ēlâw*; 1 Kgs 19:19). In a different context, moreover, Elijah uses
this mantle to part the waters of the Jordan (2 Kgs 2:8). It seems, therefore, that Elijah's
mantle symbolizes the exceptional power that he must ultimately transfer to Elisha, and
that the mantle of the Ninevite king, correspondingly, signifies the supreme power that he
is prepared to renounce as a show of deference to God. Elijah, furthermore, before shying
away from his mission still another time, uses his mantle to hide his face from the Lord (1
Kgs 19:13). Thus, whereas Elijah covers himself with his mantle in the process of resisting
his divine mandate, the king of Nineveh sheds his own mantle in order to show *acceptance*
of God's authority.

Consider, then, that the Ninevites' submission to the Lord, much like that of the
Gentile sailors, underscores the contrasting behavior of Jonah, who persists in contesting
God's merciful ways (cf. Magonet, *Form and Meaning*, 19; Craig, *Poetics*, 61–62.). Let me
suggest, therefore, that when the king sheds his Elijah-recalling mantle, he stands in
pointed opposition to Jonah, the zealous Elijah-figure in our own story. For when our
Elijah-like prophet refuses to carry out his task, he resembles the Ninevite leader in his
prior, mantle-clad state, when the sinfulness and arrogance of his kingdom aroused God's
wrath. In the end, then, the entire connection between these two stories underscores the
moralistic zeal of Jonah, which prompts him to rebuff the divine command.

Indeed, that our prophet needs to be *humbled* like the Ninevites, not merely taught a
lesson in theology, likewise emerges from the book's deployment of the key root *gdl*,
denoting "greatness." Every occurrence of *gdl* in the story highlights, directly or otherwise,
the Lord's suppression of either the self-importance of the Ninevites or the brazenness of
Jonah. Twice the text refers to "great" people in Nineveh who, facing destruction,
capitulate to God (Jonah 3:5, 7). Four times it calls Nineveh "great," emphasizing either the
city's need to be humbled or the salvaging of its grandeur in the wake of its submission (1:2;
3:2–3; 4:11). A "great wind" and a "great storm," with pointed irony, underscore God's
pushback against Jonah's zealotry (1:4, 12). The sailors, both before and after throwing their
passenger overboard, show "great" fear of the Lord (1:10, 16) – in sharp contrast to the
fleeing Jonah whose recalcitrance belies his claim to be God-fearing. The ejection of Jonah
from a "great fish" (2:1, 11) thwarts his presumption of having attained Eden. After the Lord

rescinds his decree against Nineveh, the "greatly bad" feeling that overtakes the still oppositional prophet (4:1) provokes a divine challenge. And when the tenacious Jonah then rejoices "greatly" over an unmerited paradisiacal plant that he did nothing to make "great" (4:6, 10), God promptly causes it to dry up.

9. There is hardly sufficient basis to conclude that Jonah and the equally zealous Elijah stand in opposition to one another. For discussion and citations, see recently Muldoon, *Divine Justice*, 98–101.

10. Recent discussions appear in Koch, "Book of Jonah," 285–291; Kim, "Jonah Read Intertextually," 499–504; Lessing, *Jonah*, 38–48; and Anderson, "Jonah's Peculiar Re-Creation," 184–185.

11. To be sure, the root *qll* in Jonah, which appears in the *hiphil* infinitive form *lĕhāqēl,* bears a more important correspondence to *lĕhāqēl* in Isa 23.

12. Cf., with variation, Fretheim, *Message of Jonah*, 107–108.

13. Cf., e.g., Anderson, "Jonah's Peculiar Re-Creation," 185; contra Simon, *Jonah*, 29.

14. Hauser ("In Pursuit of the Dove," 32) embraces both this interpretation and, simultaneously, the inference that the Ninevites became inspired after just one day of admonishment. The cumulative evidence leads me to conclude that the text, at least primarily, seeks to underscore Jonah's reluctance.

15. The verb also appears a second time in this sense, albeit with all three root letters present (*wayyiyyāḥel*; Gen 8:12).

16. As noted by Sasson (*Jonah*, 231), numerous modern commentators, beginning with Julius A. Bewer (*A Critical and Exegetical Commentary on Jonah* [ICC; Edinburgh: T. & T. Clark, 1912], 52), sense that Jonah delayed making his pronouncement, but they do not derive this from the word *wayyāḥel*. By contrast, Meir Zlotowitz cites multiple rabbinic commentators who do translate *wayyāḥel* this way, and he acknowledges the similar usage of *yḥl* in the Noah story, albeit without suggesting any literary relationship (*The Twelve Prophets: Yonah/Jonah: A New Translation with a Commentary Anthologized from Midrashic and Rabbinic Sources* [Artscroll Tanach Series; Brooklyn, NY: Mesorah, 1978], 121).

17. Cf. Itzhak Amar, "Similar [Motifs] in the Story of Jonah and the Story of Noah" (Hebrew), *Megadim* 45 (2006/7): 73–86 (79); Koch, "Book of Jonah," 289; Ben Zvi, *Signs of Jonah*, 122; Lessing, *Jonah*, 46; and Thomas M. Bolin, "Jonah 4,11 and the Problem of Exegetical Anachronism," *SJOT* 24 (2010): 99–109 (105–106). All these scholars note the analogy albeit without drawing this particular contrast.

18. To my discussion, cf. esp. R. J. Lubeck, "A Look at Jonah 3:2–4," *Trinity Journal* 9 (1988): 37–46.

19. The root *dbr* occurs again in connection with the king of Nineveh (Jonah 3:6), thereby underscoring, in conjunction with the analogous recurrence of *qr'* and *qwm* (3:5–6), a contrast between the Ninevites' submission and Jonah's recalcitrance. Cf. Magonet, *Form and Meaning*, 21; Craig, *Poetics*, 62; and Limburg, *Jonah*, 81.

20. Cf. Simon, *Jonah*, 26. The phrase in Exodus employs *'ănî* for the first-person singular. Regarding our text's use of the alternative *'ānōkî*, see the following discussion. The only other similar phrase appears in Daniel 10:11, a text that is generally believed to postdate Jonah.

21. The term likewise appears in the abrupt clause *'ibrî 'ānōkî* ("I am a Hebrew"; 1:9). Sasson, accordingly (*Jonah*, 117), cites a suggestion that the alternative *'ănî* tends to be employed "as a lighter choice [specifically] when appended to verbs."

22. Cf. the important discussion of this issue in Ben Zvi, *Signs of Jonah*, 34–39.

23. Accordingly, "forty" appears to be the correct reading, not "three" as in the LXX. For an elaborate discussion, see R. W. L. Moberly, "Preaching for a Response? Jonah's Message to the Ninevites Reconsidered," *VT* 53 (2003): 156–168.

24. Cf. Magonet, *Form and Meaning*, 65; Greenfield, "Jonah's Ark," 41.

25. Cf. Koch, "Book of Jonah," 287; Greenfield, "Jonah's Ark," 44.

26. The beginning of this translation follows the basic approach of Sasson (*Jonah*, 5, 252–253), who argues that the edict should properly start right after *wayyō'mer* (which I have rendered "saying"). In several ways, however, the formulation in the text thereby remains less than ideal. First, as Sasson notes, this sense of *wayyaz'ēq* typically involves the *summoning* of troops or people. Second, when *wayyaz'ēq* indicates a pronouncement, it is always followed by a direct object. Third, this would constitute an uncommon instance where the (untranslated) infinitive *lē'mōr*, which appears before the clause "let them not taste anything," does not operate in conjunction with a finite verb that signals the approaching onset of speech. Finally, according to this rendering, instead of opening with "in Nineveh" the edict might better have said, in the appropriate place, "the people and the animals *of Nineveh* ('ăšer běnînĕwê)." Other translations, furthermore, which begin the edict right *after* "in Nineveh," yield most of the same difficulties.

I propose, therefore, that an additional meaning is implied: "And *he prompted crying out* [among the citizens] in Nineveh, saying on the authority of the king and his nobles, 'The people and the animals. . . .'" This rendering of *wayyaz'ēq* accounts for both the absence of a direct object and the presence of the phrase "in Nineveh" near the beginning, and it also links *lē'mōr* to the earlier word *wayyō'mer*. To be sure, according to this translation, *wayyō'mer* would best have appeared after "in Nineveh" rather than before it.

27. Cf. Trible, *Rhetorical Criticism*, 217–218; Bolin, "Exegetical Anachronism," 100–101.

28. The word *ribbô* occurs several times in Late Biblical Hebrew, but our author typically prefers a more classical Hebrew style. Among many discussions of language in Jonah, see Simon, *Jonah*, xxxix–xli, and Muldoon, *Divine Justice*, 48–63. I return to this matter near the end of the study.

29. See, e.g., Sasson (*Jonah*, 255–256), who makes a preliminary effort at investing this wordplay with meaning.

30. As noted by Sasson (*Jonah*, 256) and others, *'al-yir'û* might also play on the root *r''*, so that the clause would bear the added meaning "let them not act wickedly." However, this strikes me as a peripheral reason for the word choice.

31. See, e.g., Moshe Greenberg, *Ezekiel 21–37: A New Translation with Introduction and Commentary* (AB 22A; New York: Doubleday, 1997), 723.

32. The verse reads, "For the Lord has comforted Zion; he has comforted all her ruins; he has made her wilderness like Eden and her desert like the Garden of the Lord; exultation and joy (*śimḥâ*) shall be found in her, gratitude and the voice of melody." Cf. the appearance of *śmḥ* in Joel (2:21, 23) concerning the restoration of the Eden-like city of Jerusalem (2:3). A helpful list of appearances of the root in the Twelve Minor Prophets appears in Craig, *Poetics*, 141.

33. Sasson, *Jonah*, 255.

34. See, e.g., the discussion in Simon, *Jonah*, xxxvii.

35. The lexical analogy to *'al-yir'û* in the Exodus passage was brought to my attention by Menachem Leff and is acknowledged in Gesundheit, "Studies," 181.

36. For extensive summary and discussion, see recently Seth D. Postell, *Adam as Israel: Genesis 1–3 as the Introduction to the Torah and Tanakh* (Cambridge: James Clarke, 2012), 32–41, 124–129.

37. Sweeney, too, proposes that the three days in our passage conform to the three days that precede entry into the divine presence in Exodus (*Twelve Prophets*, 317). Note also that a similar three-day period precedes the arrival at Mount Moriah in the account of the binding of Isaac (Gen 22:4). Regarding that story's connections to the revelation at Sinai, see Jonathan Grossman, "'He Saw the Place from Afar' – The Binding of Isaac as Background for the Covenant of the Basins and Other Stories" (Hebrew), *Megadim* 25 (1995/6): 79–90 (79–86); and the elaborate table provided by Neria Klein, "The *shofar* of Isaac at Mount Sinai" (Hebrew); online: http://www.etzion.org.il/dk/5770/1224maamar3.html.

38. I have fallen short in my substantial efforts to recover the source of this proposal, which came to my attention some time ago. It is possible that the extraneous word *hāyĕtâ* in Jonah 3:3 also works together with the three-day motif, so that on a deeper level that verse means to say, "Nineveh was/had come to be a great distance [from returning] to God, a walk of three days."

39. Regarding the three days *and nights* mentioned in our text, I am inclined to accept a widely cited proposal by George M. Landes that, based on comparative evidence, this motif signifies the travel distance between the "upper" and "nether realms" ("The 'Three Days and Three Nights' Motif in Jonah 2:1," *JBL* 86 [1967]: 446–450 [448–450]). According to the present analysis, this span of time would thus mark the transformation of the fish from "the belly of Sheol" into an Edenic enclosure.

40. Extensive discussion and citations of earlier scholarship appear in Siegfried Bergler, *Joel als Schriftinterpret* (BEATAJ 16; Frankfurt: Peter Lang, 1988), 213–245; Kim, "Jonah Read Intertextually," 512–516; Strazicich, *Joel's Use of Scripture*, 146–156; and most recently the expansive treatment by Joseph R. Kelly, "Joel, Jonah, and the [Y-HWH] Creed: Determining the Trajectory of the Literary Influence," *JBL* 132 (2013): 805–826.

41. Cf., inter alia, Gesundheit, "Studies," 161, 187.

42. Note that this verse, within the space of four words, refers twice to the prospect of God "turning" (*swb*). This redundancy evidently results from the author's wish to allude both to the parallel expression in Joel and to the phrase "turn back (*swb*) from your fury" in the story of the golden calf.

43. For citations of scholarship see Strazicich, *Joel's Use of Scripture*, 146; Kelly, "Literary Influence," 806–810 nn. 4–12. The most important argument in favor of the priority of the Jonah text is that, whereas our author was clearly working off the relevant passage in Exodus, the same cannot be said of the author of Joel. Thus, it is proposed, our text contains an adaptation of the divine-attribute formula found in Exodus, and the new phrasing of the formula – along with other motifs – influenced the passage in Joel. See Magonet, *Form and Meaning*, 79; Strazicich, *Joel's Use of Scripture*, 151; and the admirably cautious endorsement of this position in Kelly, "Literary Influence," 819–820, 825.

To be sure, as noted by Thomas B. Dozeman, the phrase "Why should they say among the peoples" in Joel 2:17 resonates with the formulation "Why should they say in Egypt" in Exod 32:12 ("Inner-Biblical Interpretation of [Y-ahweh]'s Graciousness and Compassionate Character," *JBL* 108 [1989]: 207–223 [222]). Nevertheless, that line in Joel bears a far closer parallel to a nearly identical phrase in Ps 79:10 (cf. 115:2), and so it cannot be said definitively that it also draws on the formulation in Exodus. See also Kelly ("Literary

Influence," 818) regarding a possible connection between Joel 4:21 and Exod 34:7, and the earlier discussions cited there.

The evidence that I introduce here strongly supports the more common view, which affirms the priority of Joel.

44. These overt references to Eden appear in Gen 2–4, 13; Isa 51; Ezek 28, 31, 36; and the present passage in Joel.

45. Cf. BDB: 724 (I 2b), 725 (II 1b).

46. See, e.g., the discussion by Sasson (*Jonah*, 278–279), who also observes, as have many others, that *qdm* appears three times in this chapter (vv. 2, 5, 8). All occurrences of this key root generate allusions to Eden.

47. This bears an analogy, of course, to the land's withholding of its vigor in the story of Cain (Gen 4:12).

48. A recent discussion of the phrase appears in Yoo-ki Kim, "The Function of היטב in Jonah 4 and Its Translations," *Bib* 90 (2009): 389–393. See esp. p. 390 regarding the present alternative and its philological difficulty, which makes it implausible as a primary meaning. A version of the proposal first appears in Ibn Ezra in the name of the tenth-century Karaite exegete Yefet ben Eli (Steven Bob, *Go to Nineveh: Medieval Jewish Commentaries on Jonah Translated and Explained* [Eugene, OR: Pickwick, 2013], 38). It is likewise mentioned by the eleventh- to twelfth-century commentator David Kimḥi and later embraced by the fifteenth- to sixteenth-century figure Don Isaac Abarbanel (Bob, *Commentaries*, 61, 104). For *hêṭēb* as a noun, cf. Isa 1:17. I thank Prof. Richard C. Steiner for this reference.

49. By contrast, the prophet Nahum depicts Nineveh itself as a once indomitable den of preying lions that will nonetheless fall (Nah 2:12–14). I discuss connections between Jonah and Nahum in the next chapter.

50. See, e.g., Sasson, *Jonah*, 292.

51. Regarding the *yrd* motif, cf., inter alia, Halpern and Friedman ("Composition and Paronomasia," 84–85), who also appear to hint at this last suggestion.

52. Halpern and Friedman ("Composition and Paronomasia," 85) note the wordplay but affirm that it bears no apparent thematic significance.

53. This wordplay may also extend to Jonah's construction of a סֻכָּה (*sukkâ*), a defiant act that stands in contrast to the repentant conduct of the Ninevites. See Alan Cooper, "In Praise of Divine Caprice: The Significance of the Book of Jonah," in *Among the Prophets: Language, Image, and Structure in the Prophetic Writings* (ed. P. R. Davies and D. J. A. Clines; JSOTSup 144; Sheffield: JSOT Press, 1993), 144–163 (154–155).

On a related note, observe that, initially, the people of Nineveh merely call a fast and "don" (לבש) sackcloth, which may bespeak mourning rather than a plea for deliverance (cf. the perception articulated by the courtiers of David in 2 Sam 12:21). The Ninevite king, by contrast, in the context of a series of reversals, "*covers* himself with sackcloth" (ויכס שק). Then, he provides a set of instructions that call for repentance and prayer, on the chance that a transformation of the conduct of the population might prompt a corresponding nullification of the divine decree. Indeed, as I have suggested, the verb *wayyaz'ēq* might well indicate that it is the king who prompts the Ninevites to cry out to God, their own initial reaction having reflected sorrow rather prayer. Fittingly, therefore, the king insists that, much like him, the people not merely "don" sackcloth but exhibit a reversal by "covering" themselves in sackcloth (ויתכסו שקים). In a notably fundamental way, the Ninevite leader thus expands on the deferential reaction of the citizenry – in pointed contrast to the Judean king in Jer 36 who, we recall, undercuts his subjects' submission to God. The subtly different reactions of the Ninevites and their king, moreover, give expression to the ambiguity of Jonah's pronouncement, which suggests inevitable doom, on the one hand, and the opportunity for a transformation, on the other.

54. The presence of wordplay in these verses is noted in a general way by, inter alia, Simon, *Jonah*, xxxii.

55. Because of the significance of the phrase *rûaḥ qādîm*, our author had little choice but to separate the words *rûaḥ* and *ḥărîšît*. Note also that the *wāw* that breaks up the *rêš–ḥêt* combination in the word *rûaḥ* is nonconsonantal.

56. The wordplay in noted by, inter alia, Halpern and Friedman ("Composition and Paronomasia," 86). Arguably, the unexpected preposition *l-* (-ל) that follows *lĕhaṣṣîl* contributes to the play on *ṣll*. Indeed, the two words that denote "to save him," if read as one (*lĕhaṣṣillô*), would yield the meaning "to shade him."

57. The hot wind that afflicts Jonah, to be sure, reinforces the impact of the worm attack, which might suggest that straight letter-repetitions would have been preferable in that case too. Crucially, however, the worm and the scorching weather, joined together by the repetition of the word *wattak* ("and it attacked"), are both commissioned by God. They embody, accordingly – as in the case of the manna – a single, premeditated one-two punch that thwarts any prospect of lasting unmerited divine favor. By contrast, God initially commissions the plant to endorse, however fleetingly, a human initiative whose fate was as yet undetermined.

As for the word *wattak*, note that the Lord protects Cain – who wished to preserve his life – from those who would "attack" (*hakkôt*) him during his wanderings east of Eden (Gen 4:15). Fittingly, therefore, after Jonah, facing the prospect of a world that falls short of his ideals, expresses a wish for *death*, God prompts a life-threatening "attack" on the prophet as he sits to the east of an Edenic domain.

58. Regarding *ḥărîšît* see the discussion in Sasson (*Jonah*, 302–304), who ultimately speculates that the word means "big, powerful" based on an analogy to *rûaḥ qādîm ʿazzâ* in Exod 14:21 – a passage that, as we have seen, indeed served as a source for our author. We should also consider the common suggestion that *ḥărîšît* gives the sense of "silent" (in line with one meaning of the root *ḥrš*), especially in view of the link between the plant episode in Jonah and the Elijah story in 1 Kgs 19: in that story God teaches Elijah a lesson by means of a "great wind" followed soon after by a sound of silence. Cf. the Targum and, inter alia, the discussion in Simon, *Jonah*, 44; and see Perry regarding the implications of the Elijah connection (*The Honeymoon Is Over*, 60–64). For that matter, might the ominous "sound" of God walking in the Garden of Eden during the *rûaḥ* of the day have constituted a similarly quiet rustle?

59. Cf. BDB: 361: "wood, wooded height."

60. It thus bears adding *ḥōreš* to the impressive list of biblical terms provided by Stordalen that relate to a garden (*Echoes of Eden*, 36–40).

61. Regarding the various renderings of the root *ḥws* in this context, see at length Sasson, *Jonah*, 309–310.

62. Needless to say, there have been many attempts to explain the analogy between the plant and Nineveh (see, e.g., Muldoon, *Divine Justice*, 139–149, and Perry, *The Honeymoon Is Over*, 144–159), and it would be impossible to specify the strengths and weaknesses of every suggestion. For present purposes, it suffices to observe that any explanation would

ideally account for God's seeming mischaracterization of Jonah's desire for the plant; the specific content of the contrast drawn between the plant and Nineveh; the selection of the plant motif for the purposes of this climactic scene, in a way that does not merely justify its de facto presence in the story; and the relevance of the book's final scene to the theme of the story more generally.

63. Kim ("Function," 390) is correct in affirming that, in addition to the philological difficulty of this rendering in both instances – which is why I relegate it to a secondary meaning – "it does not produce as good a sense" in the present verse.

64. Concerning the play on the root *gdl* see, inter alia, Sasson, *Jonah*, 308–310.

65. In the next chapter, I revisit this assumption that it is the Ninevites who "made [the city] great." On the more general matter of human labor in biblical theology, see recently Amos Frisch, "The Biblical Attitude toward Human Toil," in *Jewish Bible Theology: Perspectives and Case Studies* (ed. I. Kalimi; Winona Lake, IN: Eisenbrauns, 2012), 101–108. According to the present analysis of Jonah, the book advances a favorable view of labor at least in a post-Edenic world, even placing constructive work in parallel to the quest for moral improvement.

66. See extensively R. Mark Shipp, *Of Dead Kings and Dirges: Myth and Meaning in Isaiah 14:4b–21* (Academia Biblica 11; Atlanta: SBL Press, 2002), 67–79, 130–131 n. 6.

67. See, e.g., Wildberger, *Isaiah 13–27*, 645–646; cf. Muldoon, *Divine Justice*, 136.

68. See esp. Ackerman, "Satire and Symbolism," 230, 242.

69. This particular analogy is drawn by Muldoon, *Divine Justice*, 136.

70. The notable repetition of *'lh* is acknowledged by Wildberger, *Isaiah 13–27*, 67.

71. On the difficulty of the formulation see, e.g., Simon, *Jonah*, 45.

72. Recall that the phrase *ben-'ămittay* (Jonah 1:1) – which features the only other occurrence of *ben/bin* in Jonah – is widely seen to bear a secondary, descriptive meaning ("the truthful one"). Moreover, other than in the ubiquitous phrase "Joshua *bin-nûn* ('son of Nun')," the word *bin* – with its distinctive vowel – appears just two times elsewhere in the Bible, and one of those occurrences likewise serves this uncommon descriptive function rather than indicating age or filial relationship (Deut 25:2).

73. See, inter alia, Yair Zakovitch, "Through the Looking Glass: Reflections/Inversions of Genesis Stories in the Bible," *BibInt* 1 (1993): 139–152 (147–149).

74. Cf. Gen 19:21, 29; Deut 29:22; Isa 13:19; Jer 49:18; Amos 4:11; Lam 4:6.

75. The distinct expression "before me" in our text, taken together with Jonah's subsequent escape "from before the Lord," might well serve to underscore a similarity between the noncompliant prophet and the God-defying Ninevites.

76. In addition to these parallels, Jonah's reluctance to save Nineveh is typically contrasted to Abraham's efforts to save Sodom; see Zakovitch ("Reflections/Inversions," 148–149) for discussion and some other proposed connections.

77. Simon (*Jonah*, 47), endorsing a position that the number 120,000 includes only the Ninevite children, speculates that these children composed one-fifth of the population. There is no apparent basis, however, for presuming such a ratio of children to adults. My own analysis, in any event, yields a preference for the alternative view that the number includes all the Ninevites. To be sure, on the simplest level of interpretation, I accept that the text might well mean to invoke the innocence of the children and animals of Nineveh, because this explanation accounts in a plausible way for the reference to these animals.

Koch ("Book of Jonah," 286) draws a speculative connection between 120,000 here and the number 120 in the flood story (Gen 6:3), "the length of time allotted to mortal life by the Lord"; cf. Lessing, *Jonah*, 44. See also the discussion in Sasson, *Jonah*, 311–313.

78. The five sinful cities identified in these contexts appear as a group in Gen 14:2.

3. PEACEFUL DOVE

1. The term appears in Song 1:15; 2:14; 4:1, 5:2; 5:12; 6:9. On the varying resonances of Jonah's name see, inter alia, Hauser, "In Pursuit of the Dove," 22; Bolin, *Freedom beyond Forgiveness*, 71–72; Ben Zvi, *Signs of Jonah*, 41–42; Gesundheit, "Studies," 160; and Kim, "Jonah Read Intertextually," 502–503, 507–512. See also the novel connection to the word *yônîm* in Isa 60:8 proposed by Lacocque and Lacocque (*Jonah*, 18–20).

2. Cf., with variation, Simon, *Jonah*, xxxvi. Among many efforts to connect our story in a meaningful way to Jonah's appearance in the passage in Kings, see Kim, "Jonah Read Intertextually," 504–507. It bears mention that the phrase "the word of the Lord" occurs in connection with Jonah's prophecy in that context, much as it does at the beginning of chapters 1 and 3 of our book (cf. Sasson, *Jonah*, 227; Ben Zvi, *Signs of Jonah*, 46; and Muldoon, *Divine Justice*, 116–117).

3. Significantly, even before Muldoon's identification of the plant with the cedar that signifies Assyria, some scholars – on the basis of the contrast drawn at the end of the book – drew a direct connection between the process undergone by the plant and the fate of Nineveh. See Philippe Guillaume, "The End of Jonah Is the Beginning of Wisdom," *Bib* 87 (2006): 243–502 (47); Perry, *The Honeymoon Is Over*, 167–169; and cf. my discussion in the final section of this chapter.

4. For sources, discussion, and some additional proposed connections, see the extensive treatment by Kim ("Jonah Read Intertextually," 507–512). More recently, William W. Hallo has argued that our book presents a parody of other prophetic oracles on Nineveh, chiefly those of Nahum ("Jonah and the Uses of Parody," in *Thus Says the Lord: Essays on the Former and Latter Prophets in Honor of Robert R. Wilson* [ed. J. J. Ahn and S. L. Cook; LHBOTS 502; New York: T & T Clark, 2009], 285–291).

5. Cf. Cooper, "In Praise of Divine Caprice," 163 n. 1; Muldoon, *Divine Justice*, 138.

6. Outside of Jonah and Nahum, this usage of *ḥšb* occurs only in Hos 7:15, Dan 11:24, and Prov 24:8. A related usage, without a negative connotation, occurs in Ps 73:16 and Prov 16:9.

7. The change from *za'mô* in Nahum, which denotes God's anger, to *za'pô* in Jonah, which denotes the storming sea, is understandable; cf. BDB s.v. *z'm* ("indignation") and *z'p* ("storming, raging, rage").

8. Fittingly, moreover, if the scorching *rûaḥ qādîm* in Jonah indeed corresponds to the locust-like fire in Nahum, then in all likelihood it alludes simultaneously to the *rûaḥ qādîm* in Exod 10:13 that, at the onset of morning, deposits a swarm of ravaging locusts onto the Edenic land of Egypt.

In addition, it warrants consideration that the *sōkēk* ("shelter") in Nah 2:6, which serves an apparent protective function near the wall of Nineveh, bears a connection to the *sukkâ* of Jonah who, according to the present reading, seeks to rescue the city. Note also that in Nah 2:8 the sound of *yônîm* ("doves") bemoans the destruction of Nineveh, suggesting that our *yônâ* might bear a similarly favorable attitude toward the city, and that an oft-noted orthographic similarity between the names יונה and נינוה might likewise suggest that the prophet identifies with Nineveh. Regarding these last two points, see, inter alia, Mark E. Biddle, "Obadiah–Jonah–Micah in Canonical Context: The Nature of Prophetic Literature and Hermeneutics," *Int* 61 (2007): 154–166. In Zephaniah 3:1, the city compared to a *yônâ* is probably not Nineveh but Jerusalem, despite the prophet's reference to Nineveh just beforehand.

9. On this particular point, cf. esp. Hauser, "In Pursuit of the Dove," 21.

10. Indeed, according to Hauser ("In Pursuit of the Dove," 22, 35), Sternberg (*Poetics*, 319–320), and Lessing (*Jonah*, 362–363), Jonah's reaction reorients the reader's perception of the prophet's motive for fleeing his mission.

11. For an alternative reading of Jonah's distress, and for multiple interpretations of God's remarks at the end of the book, see Perry, *The Honeymoon Is Over*, 139–141, 166–172.

12. A summary of approaches to the problem, including textual emendation, appears in Sasson, *Jonah* 287–289.

13. Our author prefers using the participle *yôdēaʿ* ("know") to indicate an unambiguous present tense, as in 1:12 and 3:9 (although the latter occurrence admittedly derives from a formulation in Joel). The *qāṭal* forms here and in 4:11, by contrast, allow either present- or past-tense renderings, and in each case we find use for both alternatives.

14. Regarding the lack of clarity in Jonah's words, cf. Ben Zvi, *Signs of Jonah*, 59.

15. Cf. the discussions by Perry, *The Honeymoon Is Over*, 139–141; "Changing God's Mind: Abraham versus Jonah," in *Universalism and Particularism at Sodom and Gomorrah: Essays in Memory of Ron Pirson* (ed. D. Lipton; Ancient Israel and Its Literature 11; Atlanta: SBL Press, 2012), 43–52 (47–48). In the first of these studies, Perry does not quite say that Jonah was *appealing* to divine mercy by running away. Rather, he suggests that Jonah withheld his warning because he did not believe that God would consider sparing Nineveh, even though, as the prophet now ruefully acknowledges, he knew deep down that God is merciful. In his later treatment, by contrast, Perry affirms that Jonah, knowing that the Lord is inclined to forgive, was indeed seeking to elicit such compassion and that the prophet became encouraged to return to Nineveh after he saw that God answered his prayer for personal salvation.

16. This helps explain, moreover, why the verse recounts Jonah's departure from "the city" to a location east of "the city," instead of employing a pronoun or other more succinct formulation. (The problem is duly noted by Sasson [*Jonah*, 287]). In this way, the text underscores the standing of the city in the eyes of the prophet, who wishes Nineveh to retain its Edenic character and, after worriedly leaving its confines in the wake of his pronouncement, remains in close proximity to it in hopes of inhabiting the paradisiacal domain that it embodies. Like the Eden-seeking Cain, then, who was compelled to leave the divine presence after disdaining the prospect of self-improvement, Jonah leaves the paradisiacal "city" of Nineveh harboring deep skepticism about the possibilities of repentance and places himself to the east of that very Edenic "city," yearning fruitlessly for an idyllic existence.

17. Any distinction between "Should I" and "May I" is peripheral for our present purposes. Regarding these alternatives, see Terence E. Fretheim, "Jonah and Theodicy," *ZAW* 90 (1978): 227–237; Craig, *Poetics*, 69–70.

18. Cf. the suggested translation in Perry, *The Honeymoon Is Over*, 166. To be sure, Perry does not elaborate on this rendering and adjusts it shortly thereafter.

19. Cooper, "In Praise of Divine Caprice," 158–163. Scholars who support Cooper's exclusive declarative rendering include Muldoon (*Divine Justice*, 140–149) and Guillaume

("End of Jonah"), the latter of whom also attributes such a reading to the LXX (cf. idem, "Caution: Rhetorical Questions!," *BN* 103 [2000]: 11–16; "Rhetorical Reading Redundant," *JHS* 9.6 [2009; online: http://www.jhsonline.org/Articles/article_108.pdf]). Ben Zvi ("Jonah 4:11 and the Metaprophetic Character of the Book of Jonah," *JHS* 9.5 [2009; online: http://www.jhsonline.org/Articles/article_107.pdf]) and Perry (*The Honeymoon Is Over*, 166–172) regard a declarative translation to be one of multiple alternatives intended by the author. Cf. also Carolyn Sharp, *Irony and Meaning in the Hebrew Bible* (ISBL; Bloomington: Indiana University Press, 2008), 184; George M. Landes, "Textual 'Information Gaps' and 'Dissonances' in the Interpretation of the Book of Jonah," in *Ki Baruch Hu: Ancient Near Eastern, Biblical, and Judaic Studies in Honor of Baruch A. Levine* (ed. R. Chazan, W. W. Hallo, and L. H. Schiffman; Winona Lake, IN: Eisenbrauns, 1999), 273–293 (291–292).

20. Cooper, "In Praise of Divine Caprice," 158. On the possibility that *běhēmâ* here means "human beings with beastlike sensibilities," see Sasson (*Jonah*, 319) for sources and discussion. It bears emphasis that, in view of the book's extensive multivalence, the phrase "people who do not know their right from their left" would seem to call for a condemnatory reading at least according to one layer of meaning. The phrase "and many animals" would thus follow suit.

21. See Ben Zvi ("Metaprophetic Character," 7–10) for examples of rhetorical questions that do not begin with *hê*, and for an affirmation that a striking formulation of this sort is probably designed to yield multiple meanings.

22. Prior declarative readings retain certain disadvantages. Cooper's interpretation requires reading Jonah in conjunction with Nahum, to the point where he must assume that our book not only draws on other biblical texts but "was never intended to be read apart from [its] canonical context" ("In Praise of Divine Caprice," 159–163). (In this connection, it warrants acknowledging the growing literature pertaining to the formation and unity of the Book of the Twelve. The present study relates to those issues only insofar as my analysis, which ascribes significance to almost every textual nuance in Jonah, resists any notion that the book was altered to serve the purposes of the collection to which it belongs.)

According to Muldoon's reading, Jonah does not initially understand the crucial symbolism of the *qîqāyôn*, which represents Nineveh (*Divine Justice*, 140). Thus, the prophet's intense emotional reactions to the plant's growth and demise reflect (apparently) nothing more than a misapprehension that it serves merely to provide shade. The presence of these emphatic reactions in the story, therefore, remains in need of basic explanation. The same problem obtains for Perry's declarative reading, which does not address these components of the account (see *The Honeymoon Is Over*, 167–169), and for that of Guillaume (who does, to be sure, make some effort to explain Jonah's reaction to the plant's demise; see "End of Jonah," 247–248).

Ben Zvi ("Metaprophetic Character," 10–13) grants that earlier parts of the story lead to an interrogative reading of the final verse; however, he affirms that the book's intended readership would have perceived an additional, declarative reading – one that balances the portrait of a merciful God who saves Nineveh with that of a punishing God who eventually destroys it. Yet even if some postmonarchic works, as Ben Zvi argues, require the reader to balance conflicting expressions of theology, it would seem far preferable that any proposed meaning of a verse in a narrative book like Jonah accord with at least one viable conception of the storyline.

23. To be sure, the switch from *'ālêhā* ("on it") in chapter 1 to *'ēlêhā* ("to it") in chapter 3 amounts to a drawback for this reading, because it is precisely in the latter instance that God wishes to stress the need for a proclamation of doom *on* the city. The switch to *'ēlêhā* thus serves the purposes only of our first reading and the first version of our second reading, according to which God insists that Jonah speak *to* the Ninevites to encourage them to repent.

24. See, inter alia, Sasson, *Jonah*, 263.

25. Sasson (*Jonah*, 264) proposes that the phrase as it stands (*wĕlō' 'āśâ*) has the advantage of paralleling *wĕlō' nō'bēd* ("and we will not perish") at the end of the preceding verse. Lessing (*Jonah*, 294) speculates that the clause, particularly with the omission of the pronoun "it," has the effect of ending the section with an emphasis on God's compassion. More suggestively, Zakovitch ("Reflections/Inversions," 148) notes that the expression resonates with God's assertion that he would not destroy Sodom should righteous people be found in it (*lō' 'e'ĕśê*; Gen 18:29–30).

26. This always struck me as the straightforward meaning of the formulation, even when I could make no sense of it in context.

27. On the syntactic difficulty of this explanation, see Simon, *Jonah*, 33–34.

28. Sasson (*Jonah*, 263) likewise presents this as a serious possibility. The statement, he suggests, thereby "reassures us that God's mercy is not showered prematurely on undeserving folk."

29. Cf. Guillaume ("End of Jonah," 247) and Muldoon (*Divine Justice*, 139) regarding the death of the plant as a symbol of Nineveh's future destruction. The fall of Nineveh, moreover, occupies a central place in Ben Zvi's argument in favor of the book's multivalence.

30. Perry refers to both alternatives, favoring this latter one (*The Honeymoon Is Over*, 156; "Changing God's Mind," 50–51). In this connection, it warrants mentioning Rüdiger Lux's argument that our book emphasizes God's relationship to the entire creation – in particular several "great" entities that he brought into being – and that the present verse, accordingly, means to underscore the value of the "great" city of Nineveh in the eyes of the Lord (*Jona: Prophet zwischen 'Verweigerung' und 'Gehorsam': Ein erzälanalytische Studie* [FRLANT 162; Göttingen: Vandenhoeck & Ruprecht, 1994], 203–204). Lux's observation, to be sure, follows the conventional reading whereby God is expressing why he *saved* the city.

31. Cf., e.g., the "vineyard" prophecy at the beginning of Isa 5, where the prophet underscores the Lord's investment in the people of Israel and his consequent inclination to abandon them when they disappoint him.

4. A SONG OF THANKS IN WATERS OF EDEN

1. George M. Landes, while accepting that the prayer derives from a different source, began the process of appreciating its relationship to the narrative ("The Kerygma of the Book of Jonah: The Contextual Interpretation of the Jonah Psalm," *Int* 21 [1967]: 3–31). Since then, many commentators have endorsed the prayer's authenticity. See esp. chapter 3 of Bolin (*Freedom beyond Forgiveness*) and the literature cited there. My analysis shows that the prayer is constructed – as is the rest of the book – to imply that Jonah is pursuing a sacred, Edenic domain and that the poem shares other subtle motifs with the surrounding prose.

My analysis also suggests that the book was composed entirely by a single author, who incorporated no source material apart from phraseology adopted from earlier biblical books. For extensive discussion, citations, and an argument to the contrary, see James D. Nogalski, *Redactional Processes in the Book of the Twelve* (BZAW 217; Berlin: de Gruyter, 1993), 255–262.

2. Cf. Ackerman, "Satire and Symbolism," 235; "Jonah," 237; Greenfield, "Jonah's Ark," 67. Landes, too, acknowledges that Jonah seems "quite happy inside the fish" ("Information Gaps," 283–284). By contrast, according to the more standard view, the fish's belly is merely the "instrument of salvation" (Sasson, *Jonah*, 202). Cf., inter alia, Sweeney, *Twelve Prophets*, 319. For discussion and some additional citations, see Craig, *Poetics*, 85–87.

3. On the general matter of tenses in the prayer, see the remarks by Sasson (*Jonah*, 162–164; cf. 206–207), who inclines toward present-tense renderings and, attributing a timeless quality to the poem, affirms that it need not give expression to Jonah's actual situation. I argue, by contrast, that the deeper meaning of the prayer accords with the prophet's experiences in a precise way. An alternative present-tense translation appears in Trible, *Rhetorical Criticism*, 163–164. An argument in favor of a past-tense rendering appears in Craig, *Poetics*, 85–86.

4. See esp. Sweeney (*Twelve Prophets*, 320), who attributes a pointed irony to this syntactic anomaly.

5. The recognition that it is God who, by means of the fish, has "cast" Jonah into a protective environment resolves certain apparent inconsistencies with the narrative; see the difficulties noted by Nogalski (*Redactional Processes*, 254–255).

6. Feuillet, "Sources," 178.

7. Perry (*The Honeymoon Is Over*, 31) likewise connects *mĕṣûlâ* to these later terms, the analogy signaling Jonah's perception of the fish as an eventual source of rebirth.

8. See, e.g., Holbert, "Satire in Jonah," 71.

9. This is the position of Ibn Ezra and the fourteenth-century commentator Menaḥem ha-Meiri (Cohen, *Haketer*, Psalms Part 1: 135). Ibn Ezra pointedly affirms that context does not permit an unfavorable reading.

10. See esp. the suggestion by Shalom M. Paul that *nigraštî* evokes the "turbulent undulation" of the waves, a sense of *grš* that occurs, inter alia, in Ezek 27:28 (*Divrei Shalom: Collected Studies of Shalom M. Paul on the Bible and the Ancient Near East, 1967–2005* [CHANE 23; Leiden: Brill, 2005], 487). Indeed, we have seen that this passage in Ezekiel was prominently on the mind of the author of Jonah. Whereas my proposal identifies a more important motive for the use of *nigraštî*, it does not preclude the simultaneous validity of Paul's observation.

My analysis, moreover, confirms the standard view that Ps 31 predates Jonah's prayer, contra J. Henk Potgieter, "'David' in Consultation with the Prophets: The Intertextual Relationship of Psalm 31 with the Books of Jonah and Jeremiah," OTE 25 (2012): 115–126 (122).

11. Sweeney (*Twelve Prophets*, 321) underscores this incongruity.

12. Perry (*The Honeymoon Is Over*, 88) makes the connection to Genesis, albeit with a different objective in mind.

13. The last verse in Jonah likewise uses *wa'ănî* as a term of contrast.

14. See the discussion in Sasson, *Jonah*, 179–181.

15. Cf. the rendering, "I nevertheless want to continue to gaze upon your holy sanctuary" in Sasson (*Jonah*, 180), which, to be sure, retains the standard unfavorable conception of Jonah's present circumstance.

16.   Regarding the widely noted compatibility of Jonah's prayer with the form of a song of thanksgiving, see recently the convenient table provided in James D. Nogalski, *The Book of the Twelve: Hosea–Jonah* (SHBC 18.1; Macon, GA: Smyth & Helwys, 2011), 428. A summary of perspectives on the poem, along with a new approach, appears in the recent study by Amanda W. Benckhuysen, "Revisiting the Psalm of Jonah," *CTJ* 47 (2012): 5–31.

17.   For one of many (moderately varied) summations of such difficulties in connection with the prayer more generally, see Ackerman, "Satire and Symbolism," 213–214.

18.   This problem has prompted the speculation that the term may also refer to seaweed, but no such usage is attested elsewhere. See esp. Hans W. Wolff (*Obadiah and Jonah: A Commentary* [trans. M. Kohl; CC; Minneapolis: Augsburg, 1986], 136) and Sasson (*Jonah*, 184–185), who emphasize the anomaly.

19.   The most elaborate account of biblical parallels to Jonah's prayer, including many speculative correspondences, appears in Sasson, *Jonah*, 168–201. The present parallel is acknowledged on p. 183.

20.   Cf. Sasson, *Jonah*, 184, 187.

21.   See, e.g., Wildberger, *Isaiah 13–27*, 645–646; cf. Muldoon, *Divine Justice*, 136. The most notable biblical Zaphon imagery for these purposes appears in Isa 14, whose relationship to Ezek 31 we have already seen.

22.   The quoted material appears in Ackerman, "Satire and Symbolism," 230. The poetic parallel was initially highlighted by J. J. M. Roberts, "ṢĀPÔN in Job 26:7," *Bib* 56 (1975): 554–557 (556–557).

23.   Significantly, even without recognizing the Eden imagery that pervades our book, Clifford (*Cosmic Mountain*, 81 n. 55) acknowledges the resonance between the imagery in Jonah's prayer and that of the cosmic mountain standing above the watery abyss.

24.   The term *bĕ'ad* most often means "for the sake of."

25.   On a more basic level of interpretation, I am inclined to accept a recent argument by Shalom M. Paul that the base of the mountains and the earth signify the netherworld itself (cf. "Sheol" in v. 3), whose bars prevent the prophet from escaping ("Jonah 2:7: The Descent to the Netherworld and Its Mesopotamian Congeners," in *Puzzling Out the Past: Studies in Northwest Semitic Languages and Literatures in Honor of Bruce Zuckerman* [ed. M. J. Lundberg, S. Fine, and W. T. Pitard; Leiden: Brill, 2012], 131–134; see also the discussion in Wolff, *Obadiah and Jonah*, 136). The more ambitious layer of meaning proposed here, however, resolves several additional problems, and it accords with the motifs of Eden and the divine mountain, which pervade the subtext of the book.

Perhaps, in fact, these two senses of the imagery operate simultaneously rather than contributing to independent layers of meaning. That is, Jonah's body figuratively descends to the base of the mountains and to the watery earth, both of which represent *the actual netherworld*, and the bars of the earth block the prophet from getting out. Yet at the same time, the expression *qiṣbê hārîm*, in keeping with standard Zaphon imagery, signals the boundary between the *sacred* mountain and the abyss, where the bars of the earth – with the help of coastal reeds – keep Jonah's head above the surface. Thus, in line with the twin images of Chaos and Eden borne by the fish's multivalent belly, the mountains and the earth contribute to a composite image of the prophet entering – and then being rescued from – a chaotic region and being prevented, at any point, from falling *entirely* into the Pit beyond the protective scrutiny of the Lord ("I had thought that I was banished from before your eyes / And yet – I continue to gaze on your holy sanctuary!").

26. See esp. Sasson (*Jonah*, 305), who adds that "both these verbal forms have the word *nepeš* in close proximity." Cf. Simon, *Jonah*, 23; Lessing, *Jonah*, 400.

27. For *tĕpillâ* as the act of prayer rather than the content of the utterance, see, e.g., Isa 1:15: "Though you pray at length (*tarbû tĕpillâ*) I will not listen."

28. See recently Lessing, *Jonah*, 200–201, 219–220.

29. For a summary of interpretations of *ḥasdām*, see Sasson, *Jonah*, 198–199.

30. See, e.g., Magonet, *Form and Meaning*, 43.

31. See Nogalski (*Redactional Processes*, 268–269) who, inter alia, makes the connection that I present here; and cf. the recent discussion by Emmanuel K. E. Antwi, who endorses Nogalski's proposals (*The Book of Jonah in the Context of Post-Exilic Theology of Israel: An Exegetical Study* [ATSAT 95; St. Ottilien: EOS, 2013], 63). The kernel of the observation appears earlier in Michael L. Barré, "Jonah 2,9 and the Structure of Jonah's Prayer," *Bib* 72 (1991): 237–248 (240).

32. Landes ("Kerygma," 447–448) draws a connection between this span of three days and the one in our text.

33. Cf., e.g., Nogalski, *Redactional Processes*, 269.

34. On the similarity between the relevant formulations in the psalm and the Hosea text, see Yehuda Keel, *The Book of Hosea* (Hebrew; *Da'at Mikra*; Jerusalem: Rabbi Kook Institute, 1990), 47 n. 93*.

35. Cf., e.g., Sasson, *Jonah*, 199. In the opinion of Leslie C. Allen, this psalm also resonates with the corresponding devotions of the sailors at the end of chapter 1 (*The Books of Joel, Obadiah, Jonah, and Micah* [NICOT; Grand Rapids, MI: Eerdmans, 1976], 212).

36. Sasson, *Jonah*, 197.

37. It would not have escaped our author's notice that, shortly thereafter in Hosea (7:11), the prophet compares the Northern Kingdom of Israel to a silly *yônâ* that seeks out the help of Egypt and Assyria. Notably, these are two of the Eden-like lands that our *yônâ* pursues because of his own lack of genuine fealty to God. For suggested connections between Jonah's name and that verse, see Wolff, *Obadiah and Jonah*, 99; Raymond F. Person Jr., *In Conversation with Jonah: Conversational Analysis, Literary Criticism, and the Book of Jonah* (JSOTSup 220; Sheffield: Sheffield Academic Press, 1996), 64.

5. NAUTICAL AND HERMENEUTICAL DILEMMAS

1. This explanation appears in the medieval commentaries of Rashi (Bob, *Commentaries*, 10) and Joseph Qara (Cohen, *Haketer*, The Twelve Minor Prophets: 159) and is one of two simultaneous meanings advocated by Abarbanel (Bob, *Commentaries*, 81). (On multivalence in Abarbanel's exegesis more generally, see Jonathan Grossman, "Abarbanel's Stance towards the Existence of Ambiguous Expressions in the Bible" [Hebrew], *Beit Mikra* 52 [2007]: 126–138.) I offer a different multivalent reading in what follows. A discussion of the problem that engages a range of medieval rabbinic commentaries appears in Leah Frankel, *Studies in Scripture 2* (Hebrew; Jerusalem: Eliner Library, 2001/2), 330–332.

A declarative reading appears in the medieval commentary of David Kimḥi (Cohen, *Haketer*, The Twelve Minor Prophets: 159) and has since become standard. Exceptions to the modern consensus include Landes, "Information Gaps," 279–280, and Döhling, "Das Wüten der Welt," 19–20. Indeed, Döhling, in a more limited variation of the argument that I offer here, attributes a double meaning to the sailors' question.

2. All told, these difficulties have led some critics – with support from the LXX – to deny the authenticity of the line, seeing it as an accidental duplication of an essentially identical phrase that appears in the previous verse. On the entire issue, see Sasson (*Jonah*, 112–113) and his citations of earlier treatments. Note also his argument that the more standard rendering accounts for the shift from *běšellěmî* to *ba'ăšer lěmî*.

3. Moreover, Jonah's goal of emphasizing his relationship specifically to the God of Israel accounts for his placement of the direct object before the verb in the second clause of his response: "*it is the Lord God of the heavens* whom I fear," not any other deity. Cf. the elaborate argument advanced by Bosma ("Jonah 1:9") that the prophet pointedly seeks to exclude other deities from responsibility for the storm.

4. Cf. Abarbanel and the nineteenth-century commentary of Rabbi Meir Leibusch (Weiser) Malbim (Bob, *Commentaries*, 85, 121); and recently Rob C. Barrett, "Meaning More than They Say: The Conflict between [Y-HWH] and Jonah," *JSOT* 37 (2012): 237–257 (242–243).

5. Regarding these two questions, see the speculations offered by Sasson (*Jonah*, 125). In view of the multivalence that I perceive in the text more generally, I am sympathetic to a proposal by William J. Horwitz that the phrase יודע אָני ("I know"), with its notable *qāmeṣ* under the *'ālep*, bears the added translation "the ship knows," especially because of the analogous personification in the phrase "the ship plotted to break apart" in 1:4 ("Another Interpretation of Jonah 1:12," *VT* 23 [1973]: 370–372).

6. In accordance with their interpretation of the sailors' question in verse 11, Abarbanel and Malbim favor the latter explanation of the present phrase (Bob, *Commentaries*, 86, 122). Cf. the variation of this in Wolff, *Obadiah and Jonah*, 119.

7. Verse 11 contains a similar line albeit without the expression "on them." The added prepositional phrase here thus underscores that the sailors, despite their uncertainty in that earlier context, now recognize that they will remain at the mercy of the storm until they dispose of Jonah.

8. See the discussion in Sasson, *Jonah*, 104.

9. I am indebted to Dr. Ditza Berger for this observation.

10. Magonet, *Form and Meaning*, 72–73.

11. The use of this verb, in fact, is seen as possibly the most enigmatic choice of terminology in the book; see esp. the recent discussion by Christian Meredith, "The Conundrum of חתר in Jonah 1:13," *VT* 61 (2014): 147–152.

12. Note the observation by Sherwood (*Biblical Text and Afterlives*, 247 n. 148) that "the same verb is used in Amos 9:2 to describe the burrowing activities of those who dig into Sheol, in the frantic attempt to escape God's wrath."

13. See the discussion in Sasson, *Jonah*, 136–137.

14. Sasson (*Jonah*, 135), among others, cites both this text and Ps 135:6, where a similar phrase appears. For the reason I provide here, Ps 115:3 would appear to be our author's actual source-text.

15. Sasson (*Jonah*, 18) expresses skepticism that a genuine solution is possible – an assessment that I challenge here. For a sampling of the many treatments of the issue, see the literature cited in his discussion. A full solution would properly account, in a consistent way, for the deployments of each divine designation: "the Lord," "God," "the God," and "the Lord God." I am not aware of any prior suggestion that does so successfully.

16. Regarding these implications of the divine name, cf., inter alia, Christopher J. H. Wright, "God, Names of," *ISBE* 2:504–509 (507); and see also the next note.

17. Cf. with variation the discussion by Sasson (*Jonah*, 147–149, 291), who identifies a progression from the most to the least "personal" of divine names in the four verses that employ *wayĕman*. A version of the progression that I describe here appears already in Magonet (*Form and Meaning*, 33–38), and my discussion accords with much of his analysis in this respect. Ultimately, however, Magonet resorts to multiple systems of meaning to account for the varying divine names.

18. Significantly, it is the Ninevite king who first uses the term "the God": as I have suggested, it might well be that the mournful, not-yet-repentant population fails to recognize the possibility of eliciting divine compassion. It is likewise understandable why the text switches to the term "the Lord" only in the book's final verse, rather than on the rescinding of the decree in chapter 3. In the story's concluding line, in an expression of divine immanence and magnanimity, the Lord directly communicates his merciful disposition toward a large population of unwitting sinners – in stark opposition to the compassionless ideology of the moralistic prophet. Chapter 3, by contrast, concentrates on the role of the Ninevites' repentance, rather than that of God's mercy, in the city's salvation. Accordingly, it maintains the transitional designation "the God," which limits the emphasis on divine benevolence.

19. It is quite possible, as many have proposed, that, in chapter 3 as well, the progression from "God" to "the God" marks – in addition to the eliciting of divine mercy – the Ninevites' emerging *recognition* of the Israelite deity.

20. Indeed, observe that when the sailors ask the prophet, "What shall we do to/for you so that the sea will quiet down from on us?" the verse concludes by saying, "for the sea was/is becoming increasing stormy (*sōʿēr*)." Most commentators assume that it is the narrator who adds this ominous remark. (For discussion, see Sasson, *Jonah*, 123–124.) Possibly, however, on another level of meaning, the text places this apparently redundant clause into the mouths of the sailors in order to attribute to them a more subtle intent: if you Jonah really seek a divine abode that brooks no imperfection, then perhaps we can arrange for you an existence inside the raging waters, where the unforgiving wrath of God awaits your eager embrace.

21. All of Jonah's efforts to reach Eden in chapter 1 are ironically marked by descent. His wish to be lifted into a divine realm by being cast down into the water is arguably the sharpest example of this irony.

Sasson (*Jonah*, 124–125) suggests several possible reasons for the inclusion of the phrases "lift me" and "they lifted." Among these reasons, he proposes that the verb might hint at "forgiveness" – a usage that likewise occurs twice in the Cain story (Gen 4:7, 13). Such a resonance would accord with Jonah's anticipation of a favorable outcome, whereby he would find himself forgiven.

22. Recall, furthermore, that the phrase "for you are the Lord, you do as you wish" – whose verbs may equally indicate the past tense – derives from a verse near the beginning of Ps 115. Significantly, that psalm occupies a place in a sequence, following a depiction of the divine power that figuratively prompted the sea to "flee" at the time of the exodus. I submit, accordingly, that when the sailors allude to Ps 115 in their plea for Jonah's survival, they fittingly invoke the exodus by affirming that the Lord "did as [he] wished" when he parted the sea.

23. In further support of this interpretation, let me offer one additional, more ambitious proposal. Whereas our book mostly uses a classical Hebrew style, it features a sprinkling of terms and other linguistic features characteristic of Aramaic and/or a late stage of Biblical Hebrew. Consistent with this varied style, my reading of Jonah suggests that, in select instances, the text invokes newer usages and expressions because of the literary value that they afford. For example, the verb *'št* ("think/consider"; *hithpael* "pay heed") and the word *ṭa'am* in the sense of "authority" – both of which, I have argued, contribute genuine meaning to the story – find analogs in Aramaic only. Similarly, the adjective *ḥărîšît*, notwithstanding the parallel to *ḥōreš* in Ezekiel 31, would best have evoked a tree-lined location in the minds of readers who regularly used the Aramaic noun *ḥûrĕšā'* to mean a wooded area. (*ḥûrĕšā'* does not appear in Biblical Aramaic, but it is the standard targumic rendering of Hebrew *ya'ar* ["woods"].) In all probability, then, our author not only made judicious use of late terminology but also appealed to the Aramaic proficiency of the book's audience to help communicate meaning.

With this in mind, I propose that the key root *ṭl* is meant to evoke *ṭll*, meaning "to provide shade or covering." Often employed in Aramaic noun forms denoting shade or shelter, *ṭll* occurs as a verb once in Biblical Aramaic (Dan 4:9) and once in Late Biblical Hebrew, evidently as a loan word from the Aramaic (Neh 3:15). Significantly, *hiphil* forms of Hebrew *ṭll*, although unattested, would closely resemble the four *hiphil* forms of *ṭl* that appear in Jonah. Crucially, moreover, *ṭll* bears an equivalence to the Hebrew root *ṣll* used to denote the shade of the *qîqāyôn*, where the text also links *ṣll* to *nṣl* ("save") by means of wordplay. Indeed, in connection with the fish as well, the word *mĕṣûlâ* ("the deep waters") generates a meaningful resonance with these two roots. If the occurrences of *ṭl* in our passage, accordingly, likewise bear this additional sense of "providing shade/salvation," then the text, on a more profound level of meaning, *directly* affirms that the great wind, Tarshish-bound treasures, and Eden-seeking prophet descended into a place of shade and protection.

BIBLIOGRAPHY

Aalders, Gerhard C. *The Problem of the Book of Jonah*. Tyndale Old Testament Lecture. London: Tyndale Press, 1948.

Abela, Anthony. "When the Agenda of an Artistic Composition Is Hidden: Jonah and Intertextual Dialogue with Isaiah 6, the 'Confessions of Jeremiah' and Other Texts." Pages 1–30 in *The Elusive Prophet: The Prophet as a Historical Person, Literary Character and Anonymous Artist*. Edited by Johannes C. de Moor. OTS 45. Leiden: Brill, 2001.

Abusch, Tzvi. "Jonah and God: Plants, Beasts, and Humans in the Book of Jonah (An Essay in Interpretation)." *JANER* 13 (2013): 146–152.

Ackerman, James S. "Jonah." Pages 234–243 in *The Literary Guide to the Bible*. Edited by Robert Alter and Frank Kermode. Cambridge, MA: Harvard University Press, 1987.

———. "Satire and Symbolism in the Song of Jonah." Pages 213–246 in *Traditions in Transformation: Turning Points in Biblical Faith*. Edited by Baruch Halpern and Jon D. Levenson. Winona Lake, IN: Eisenbrauns, 1981.

Alexander, T. Desmond. *Jonah: An Introduction and Commentary*. TOTC. Leicester: Inter-Varsity Press, 1988.

Alkier, Stefan. "Intertextuality and the Semiotics of Biblical Texts." Pages 3–22 in *Reading the Bible Intertextually*. Edited by Richard B. Hayes, Stefan Alkier, and Leroy A. Huizenga. Waco, TX: Baylor University Press, 2009.

Allen, Leslie C. *The Books of Joel, Obadiah, Jonah, and Micah*. NICOT. Grand Rapids, MI: Eerdmans, 1976.

Almbladh, Karin. *Studies in the Book of Jonah*. SSU 7. Stockholm: Almqvist and Wiksell, 1986.

Alshekh, Moses. *The Book of Jonah: The Voyage of the Visionary: The Commentary of Rabbi Moshe Alshich on the Book of Jonah*. Translated by Ravi Shahar. Alshich Tanach Series 3. Jerusalem: Feldheim, 1992.

Amar, Itzhak. "Similar [Motifs] in the Story of Jonah and the Story of Noah" (Hebrew). *Megadim* 45 (2006/7): 73–86.

Anderson, Joel E. "Jonah's Peculiar Re-Creation." *BTB* 41 (2011): 179–188.

———. "[Y-hwh]'s Surprising Covenant *Hesed* in Jonah." *BTB* (2012): 3–11.

Antwi, Emmanuel K. E. *The Book of Jonah in the Context of Post-Exilic Theology of Israel: An Exegetical Study.* ATSAT 95. St. Ottilien: EOS, 2013.

Band, Arnold J. "Swallowing Jonah: The Eclipse of Parody." *Prooftexts* 10 (1990): 177–195.

Bar Chiyyah, Abraham. "*Hegyon Hanefesh Ha'atzuvah* (Meditation of the Sad Soul)." Pages 131–174 in *The Journey of the Soul: Traditional Sources on Teshuvah.* Edited and translated by Leonard S. Kravitz and Kerry M. Olitzky. Northvale, NJ: Jason Aronson, 1995.

Barré, Michael L. "Jonah 2,9 and the Structure of Jonah's Prayer." *Bib* 72 (1991): 237–248.

Barrett, Rob C. "Meaning More than They Say: The Conflict between [Y-HWH] and Jonah." *JSOT* 37 (2012): 237–257.

Barton, John. "Déjà Lu: Intertextuality, Method or Theory?" Pages 1–16 in *Reading Job Intertextually.* Edited by Katharine Dell and Will Kynes. LHBOTS 574. New York: T & T Clark, 2013.

Bauks, Michaela. "Intertextuality in Ancient Literature in Light of Textlinguistics and Cultural Studies." Pages 27–46 in *Between Text and Text: Intertextuality in Ancient Near Eastern, Ancient Mediterranean and Early Medieval Literature.* Edited by Michaela Bauks, Wayne Horowitz, and Armin Lange. JAJSup 6. Göttingen: Vandenhoeck & Ruprecht, 2013.

Benckhuysen, Amanda W. "Revisiting the Psalm of Jonah." *CTJ* 47 (2012): 5–31.

Ben-Porat, Ziva. "The Poetics of Literary Allusion." *PTL: A Journal for Descriptive Poetics and Theory of Literature* 1 (1976): 105–128.

Ben Zvi, Ehud. "Jonah 4:11 and the Metaprophetic Character of the Book of Jonah." *JHS* 9.5 (2009). Online: http://www.jhsonline.org/Articles/article_107.pdf.

———. *Signs of Jonah: Reading and Rereading in Ancient Yehud.* JSOTSup 367. Sheffield: Sheffield Academic Press, 2003.

Berger, Yitzhak. "Esther and Benjaminite Royalty: A Study in Inner-Biblical Allusion." *JBL* 129 (2010): 625–644.

———. "Ruth and Inner-Biblical Allusion: The Case of 1 Samuel 25." *JBL* 128 (2009): 253–272.

———. "Ruth and the David–Bathsheba Story: Allusions and Contrasts." *JSOT* 33 (2009): 433–452.

Bergler, Siegfried. *Joel als Schriftinterpret.* BEATAJ 16. Frankfurt: Peter Lang, 1988.

Berlin, Adele. "Rejoinder to John A. Miles, Jr., with Some Observations on the Nature of Prophecy." *JQR* 66 (1976): 227–235.

Bewer, Julius A. *A Critical and Exegetical Commentary on Jonah.* ICC. Edinburgh: T. & T. Clark, 1912.

Biddle, Mark E. "Ancestral Motifs in 1 Samuel 25: Intertextuality and Characterization." *JBL* 121 (2002): 617–638.

———. "Obadiah–Jonah–Micah in Canonical Context: The Nature of Prophetic Literature and Hermeneutics." *Int* 61 (2007): 154–166.

Bob, Steven. *Go to Nineveh: Medieval Jewish Commentaries on the Book of Jonah Translated and Explained.* Eugene, OR: Pickwick, 2013.

Bolin, Thomas M. *Freedom beyond Forgiveness: The Book of Jonah Re-Examined.* JSOTSup 236. Sheffield: Sheffield Academic Press, 1997.

———. "Jonah 4,11 and the Problem of Exegetical Anachronism." *SJOT* 24 (2010): 99–109.

———. "'Should I Not Also Pity Nineveh?' Divine Freedom in the Book of Jonah." *JSOT* 67 (1995): 109–120.

Bosma, Carl J. "Jonah 1:9 – An Example of Elenctic Testimony." *CTJ* 48 (2013): 65–90.

Braude, William G., trans. *The Midrash on Psalms*. Vol. 1. Yale Judaica Series. New Haven, CT: Yale University Press, 1959.

Carr, David M. "The Many Uses of Intertextuality in Biblical Studies." Pages 519–549 in *Congress Volume Helsinki 2010*. Edited by Martti Nissinen. Leiden: Brill, 2012.

———. *Writing on the Tablet of the Heart: Origins of Scripture and Literature*. New York: Oxford University Press, 2005.

Cary, Philip. *Jonah*. BTCB. Grand Rapids, MI: Brazos Press, 2008.

Christensen, Duane L. "Anticipatory Paronomasia in Jonah 3:7–8 and Genesis 37:2." *RB* 90 (1983): 289–293.

———. "The Song of Jonah: A Metrical Analysis." *JBL* 104 (1985): 217–231.

Clifford, Richard J. *The Cosmic Mountain in Canaan and the Old Testament*. HSM 4. Cambridge, MA: Harvard University Press, 1972.

Coetzee, Johan H. "And Jonah Swam and Swam and Swam: Jonah's Body in Deep Waters." *OTE* 17 (2004): 521–530.

———. "Where Humans and Animals Meet, Folly Can Be Sweet: Jonah's Bodily Experience of Containment – The Major Drive behind his Conduct." *OTE* 20 (2007): 320–332.

Cohen, Menachem, ed. *Mikrao't Gedolot 'Haketer': A Revised and Augmented Scientific Edition of 'Mikra'ot Gedolot' Based on the Aleppo Codex and Early Medieval MSS* (Hebrew). 17 vols. Ramat Gan, Israel: Bar Ilan University Press, 1992–2013.

Cooper, Alan. "In Praise of Divine Caprice: The Significance of the Book of Jonah." Pages 144–163 in *Among the Prophets: Language, Image, and Structure in the Prophetic Writings*. Edited by Philip R. Davies and David J. A. Clines. JSOTSup 144. Sheffield: JSOT Press, 1993.

Craig, Kenneth M., Jr. "Jonah and the Reading Process." *JSOT* 47 (1990): 103–114.

———. *A Poetics of Jonah: Art in the Service of Ideology*. Macon, GA: Mercer University Press, 1993.

Crouch, Walter B. "To Question an End, to End a Question: Opening the Closure of the Book of Jonah." *JSOT* 62 (1994): 101–112.

Darnov, Allen M. "Equivocal Narrative in the Hebrew Bible." Ph.D. diss., Jewish Theological Seminary of America, 2007.

Del Castillo, Arcadio. "Tarshish in the Book of Jonah." *RB* 114 (2007): 481–498.

Dell, Katharine J. "Reinventing the Wheel: The Shaping of the Book of Jonah." Pages 85–101 in *After the Exile: Essays in Honor of Rex Mason*. Edited by John Barton and David J. Reimer. Macon, GA: Mercer University Press, 1996.

Dentan, Robert C. "Literary Affinities of Exodus 34:6f." *VT* 13 (1963): 34–51.

Döhling, Jan-Dirk. "Das Wüten der Welt: Zur literarischen und narrativen Funktion der Schöpfungsdynamik in Jona 1 und 2." *BN* 157 (2013): 3–32.

———. "Jona und des Meeres Wellen: Zum problemgeschichtlichen Horizont und zum traditionsgeschichtlichen Hintergrund." *BN* 158 (2013): 17–37.

Dozeman, Thomas B. "Inner-Biblical Interpretation of [Y-ahweh]'s Graciousness and Compassionate Character." *JBL* 108 (1989): 207–223.

Edelman, Diana V. "Jonah among the Twelve in the MT: The Triumph of Torah over Prophecy." Pages 150–167 in *The Production of Prophecy: Constructing Prophets and Prophecy in Yehud*. Edited by Diana V. Edelman and Ehud Ben Zvi. BibleWorld. London: Equinox, 2009.

Edenburg, Cynthia. "How (Not) to Murder a King: Variations on a Theme in 1 Sam 24; 26." *SJOT* 12 (1998): 64–85.

—. "Intertextuality, Literary Competence, and the Question of Readership: Some Preliminary Observations." *JSOT* 35 (2010): 131–148.

—. "The Story of the Outrage at Gibeah (Jdg. 19-21): Composition, Sources and Historical Context" (Hebrew). Ph.D. diss., Tel Aviv University, 2003.

Ego, Beate. "The Repentance of Nineveh in the Story of Jonah and Nahum's Prophecy of the City's Destruction: A Coherent Reading of the Book of the Twelve as Reflected in the Aggada." Pages 155–164 in *Thematic Threads in the Book of the Twelve*. Edited by Paul L. Redditt and Aaron Schart. BZAW 325. Berlin: de Gruyter, 2003.

Feintuch, Yonatan. "Judah and Jacob, Ahab and Ahasuerus: Notes on the Methodology of the Use of Allusion as an Exegetical Technique" (Hebrew). *Megadim* 44 (2006): 9–24.

Ferreira, Johan. "A Note on Jonah 2.8: Idolatry and Inhumanity in Israel." BT 63 (2012): 28–38.

Feuillet, André. "Le sens du livre de Jonas." RB 54 (1947): 340–361.

—. "Les sources du livre de Jonas." RB 54 (1947): 161–186.

Fewell, Danna N. *Reading between Texts: Intertextuality and the Hebrew Bible*. Literary Currents in Biblical Interpretation. Louisville: Westminster/John Knox, 1992.

Fishbane, Michael A. *Biblical Interpretation in Ancient Israel*. Oxford: Oxford University Press, 1985.

Forti, Tova. "Of Ships and Seas, and Fish and Beasts: Viewing the Concept of Universal Providence in the Book of Jonah through the Prism of Psalms." *JSOT* 35 (2011): 359–374.

Frankel, Leah. *Studies in Scripture 2* (Hebrew). Jerusalem: Eliner Library, 2001/2.

Fretheim, Terence E. "Jonah and Theodicy." ZAW 90 (1978): 227–237.

—. *The Message of Jonah: A Theological Commentary*. Minneapolis: Augsburg, 1977.

Frisch, Amos. "The Biblical Attitude toward Human Toil." Pages 101–108 in *Jewish Bible Theology: Perspectives and Case Studies*. Edited by Isaac Kalimi. Winona Lake, IN: Eisenbrauns, 2012.

Frolov, Serge. "Returning the Ticket: God and His Prophet in the Book of Jonah." *JSOT* 86 (1999): 85–105.

Galpaz-Feller, Pnina. *Jonah – Journey to Freedom: A New Reading of the Book of Jonah* (Hebrew). Jerusalem: Carmel, 2009.

Gerhards, Meik. *Studien zum Jonabuch*. Biblisch-Theologische Studien 78. Neukirchen–Vluyn: Neukirchener, 2006.

Gesundheit, Benjamin. "Studies in the Book of Jonah" (Hebrew). Pages 151–197 in *U-ve-Yom Tzom Kippur yehatemun: Studies on Yom ha-Kippurim*. Edited by Amnon Bazak. Alon Shevut, Israel: Tevunot, 2004/5.

Goldstein, Elizabeth. "On the Use of the Name of God in the Book of Jonah." Pages 77–83 in *Milk and Honey: Essays on Ancient Israel and the Bible*. Edited by Sarah Malena and David Miano. Winona Lake, IN: Eisenbrauns, 2007.

Gordon, C. H. "Tarshish." Pages 517–518 in vol. 4 of *The Interpreter's Dictionary of the Bible*. Edited by George A. Buttrick. 4 vols. Nashville: Abingdon, 1962.

Greenberg, Moshe. *Ezekiel 21–37: A New Translation with Introduction and Commentary*. AB 22A. New York: Doubleday, 1997.

Greenfield, Noah. "Jonah's Ark and Noah's Fish: Reading the Book of Jonah after the Flood." *AJBI* 33 (2007): 37–72.

Grossman, Jonathan. "Abarbanel's Stance towards the Existence of Ambiguous Expressions in the Bible" (Hebrew). *Beit Mikra* 52 (2007): 126–138.

——. "Ambiguity in the Biblical Narrative and Its Contribution to the Literary Formation" (Hebrew). Ph.D. diss., Bar Ilan University, 2006.

——. "'Dynamic Analogies' in the Book of Esther." *VT* 59 (2009): 394–414.

——. "'He Saw the Place from Afar' – The Binding of Isaac as Background for the
Covenant of the Basins and Other Stories" (Hebrew). *Megadim* 25 (1995/6): 79–90.

——. "'Today the Earth Was Conceived' – In Light of the 'Rebirth' of Noah and Jonah"
(Hebrew). Pages 41–69 in *B'Rosh Hashanah yikkateivun: Studies on Rosh Hashanah*.
Edited by Amnon Bazak. Alon Shevut, Israel: Tevunot, 2002/3.

Guillaume, Philippe. "Caution: Rhetorical Questions!" *BN* 103 (2000): 11–16.

——. "The End of Jonah Is the Beginning of Wisdom." *Bib* 87 (2006): 243–250.

——. "Rhetorical Reading Redundant." *JHS* 9.6 (2009). Online: http://www.jhsonline.org
/Articles/article_108.pdf.

Halevi, Yehudah. *The Kuzari: In Defense of the Despised Faith*. Newly translated and
annotated by N. Daniel Korobkin. Jerusalem: Feldheim, 2013.

Hallo, William W. "Jonah and the Uses of Parody." Pages 285–291 in *Thus Says the Lord:
Essays on the Former and Latter Prophets in Honor of Robert R. Wilson*. Edited by John J.
Ahn and Stephen L. Cook. LHBOTS 502. New York: T & T Clark, 2009.

Halpern, Baruch and Richard E. Friedman. "Composition and Paronomasia in the Book
of Jonah." *HAR* 4 (1980): 79–92.

Hamilton, Victor P. *The Book of Genesis: Chapters 1–17*. NICOT. Grand Rapids, MI: Eerdmans,
1990.

Handy, Lowell K. *Jonah's World: Social Science and the Reading of Prophetic Story*.
BibleWorld. London: Equinox, 2008.

Hauser, Alan J. "Jonah: In Pursuit of the Dove." *JBL* 104 (1985): 21–37.

——. "Linguistic and Thematic Links between Genesis 4:1–16 and Genesis 2–3." *JETS* 23
(1980): 294–305.

Hays, Richard B. *Echoes of Scripture in the Letters of Paul*. New Haven, CT: Yale University
Press, 1989.

Hepner, Gershon. *Legal Friction: Law, Narrative, and Identity Politics in Biblical Israel*.
Studies in Biblical Literature 78. New York: Peter Lang, 2010.

Hesse, Eric W. and Isaac M. Kikawada. "Jonah and Genesis 11–1." *AJBI* 10 (1984): 3–19.

Himmelfarb, Martha. "The Temple and the Garden of Eden in Ezekiel, the Book of the
Watchers, and the Wisdom of Ben Sira." Pages 63–78 in *Sacred Places and Profane Spaces:
Essays in the Geographics of Judaism, Christianity, and Islam*. Edited by Jamie S. Scott and
Paul Simpson-Housley. New York: Greenwood, 1991.

Holbert, John C. "'Deliverance Belongs to [Y-ahweh]!' Satire in the Book of Jonah." *JSOT*
21 (1981): 59–81.

Horwitz, William J. "Another Interpretation of Jonah 1:12." *VT* 23 (1973): 370–372.

Houk, Cornelius B. "Linguistic Patterns in Jonah." *JSOT* 77 (1998): 81–102.

Hunter, Alastair. "Jonah from the Whale: Exodus Motifs in Jonah 2." Pages 142–158 in *The
Elusive Prophet: The Prophet as a Historical Person, Literary Character and Anonymous
Artist*. Edited by Johannes C. de Moor. OTS 45. Leiden: Brill, 2001.

Jensen, Philip P. *Obadiah, Jonah, Micah: A Theological Commentary*. LHBOTS 496. New
York: T & T Clark, 2008.

Jeremias, Jörg. *Die Propheten Joel, Obadja, Jona, Micha*. ATD 24.3. Göttingen: Vandenhoeck & Ruprecht, 2007.

Joüon, Paul and T. Muraoka. *A Grammar of Biblical Hebrew*. StudBib 14. 2 vols. Rome: Pontifical Biblical Institute, 1996.

Kamp, Albert H. *Inner Worlds: A Cognitive Linguistic Approach to the Book of Jonah*. Translated by David Orton. BINS 68. Leiden: Brill, 2004.

Keel, Othmar. *The Symbolism of the Biblical World: Ancient Near Eastern Iconography and the Book of Psalms*. Translated by Timothy J. Hallett. New York: Seabury, 1978.

Keel, Yehuda. *The Book of Hosea* (Hebrew). *Da'at Mikra*. Jerusalem: Rabbi Kook Institute, 1990.

Keller, Carl-A. *Jonas*. CAT 11a. Geneva: Labor and Fides, 1982.

Kelly, Joseph R. "Intertextuality and Allusion in the Study of the Hebrew Bible." Ph.D. diss., Southern Baptist Theological Seminary, 2014.

——. "Joel, Jonah, and the [Y-HWH] Creed: Determining the Trajectory of the Literary Influence." *JBL* 132 (2013): 805–826.

Kim, Hyun C. P. "Jonah Read Intertextually." *JBL* 126 (2007): 497–528.

Kim, Yoo-ki. "The Function of היטב in Jonah 4 and Its Translations." *Bib* 90 (2009): 389–393.

Klapper, Aryeh. "'So Long' vs. 'Thanks for All the Fish': A New Reading of Sefer Yonah." Online: http://www.torahleadership.org/articles.html.

Klein, Neria. "The *shofar* of Isaac at Mount Sinai" (Hebrew). Online: http://www.etzion .org.il/dk/5770/1224maamar3.html.

Koch, Timothy R. "The Book of Jonah and a Reframing of Israelite Theology: A Reader-Response Approach." Ph.D. diss., Boston University, 2003.

Koller, Aaron. "לבוא and להיכנס: Synchronic and Diachronic Perspectives on the Semantics of לבוא in Ancient Hebrew" (Hebrew). *Leshonenu* 75 (2013): 149–164.

Lacocque, André and Pierre-Emmanuel Lacocque. *Jonah: A Psycho-Religious Approach to the Prophet*. SPOT. Columbia: University of South Carolina Press, 1990.

Landes, George M. "Jonah: A *Māšāl*?" Pages 137–158 in *Israelite Wisdom: Theological and Literary Essays in Honor of Samuel Terrien*. Edited by John G. Gammie et al. New York: Scholars Press, 1978.

——. "The Kerygma of the Book of Jonah: The Contextual Interpretation of the Jonah Psalm." *Int* 21 (1967): 3–31.

——. "Textual 'Information Gaps' and 'Dissonances' in the Interpretation of the Book of Jonah." Pages 273–293 in *Ki Baruch Hu: Ancient Near Eastern, Biblical, and Judaic Studies in Honor of Baruch A. Levine*. Edited by Robert Chazan, William W. Hallo, and Lawrence H. Schiffman. Winona Lake, IN: Eisenbrauns, 1999.

——. "The 'Three Days and Three Nights' Motif in Jonah 2:1." *JBL* 86 (1967): 446–450.

Lanfer, Peter T. *Remembering Eden: The Reception History of Genesis 3:22–24*. Oxford: Oxford University Press, 2012.

Lange, Armin and Matthias Weigold. *Biblical Quotations and Allusions in Second Temple Literature*. JAJSup 5. Göttingen: Vandenhoeck & Ruprecht, 2011.

Leonard, Jeffery M. "Identifying Inner-Biblical Allusions: Psalm 78 as a Test Case." *JBL* 127 (2008): 241–265.

Lessing, R. Reed. *Jonah*. Concordia Commentary. St. Louis: Concordia, 2007.

Levine, Etan. "Jonah as a Philosophical Book." *ZAW* 96 (1984): 235–245.

Lichtenstein, Aharon. "Criticism and *Kitvei ha-Kodesh*." Pages 15–32 in *Rav Shalom Banayikh: Essays Presented to Rabbi Shalom Carmy by Friends and Students in Celebration of Forty Years of Teaching*. Edited by Hayyim Angel and Yitzchak Blau. Jersey City, NJ: Ktav, 2012.

Lieberman, Chaim. *The Tent of Rachel* (Hebrew). New York: Empire Press, 1980.

Liebes, Yehuda. "Jonah as the Messiah Ben Joseph" (Hebrew). *Jerusalem Studies in Jewish Thought* 3 (1983/4): 269–311.

Lim, Sung U. "Jonah's Transformation and Transformation of 'Jonah' from the Bakhtinian Perspective of Authoring and Re-Authoring." *JSOT* 33 (2008): 245–256.

Limburg, James. *Jonah: A Commentary.* OTL. Louisville: Westminster/John Knox, 1993.

Love, Nathan P. "Translating Jonah 2.9: Looking for a Breath of Fresh Air." *BT* 64 (2013): 266–283.

Lubeck, R. J. "A Look at Jonah 3:2–4." *Trinity Journal* 9 (1988): 37–46.

Lundbom, Jack R. *Jeremiah: A New Translation with Introduction and Commentary.* AB 21B. New York: Doubleday, 2004.

Lux, Rüdiger. *Jona: Prophet zwischen 'Verweigerung' und 'Gehorsam': Ein erzälanalytische Studie.* FRLANT 162. Göttingen: Vandenhoeck & Ruprecht, 1994.

Magonet, Jonathan. *Form and Meaning: Studies in Literary Techniques in the Book of Jonah.* BBET 2. Frankfurt: Peter Lang, 1976.

Marcus, David. *From Balaam to Jonah: Anti-Prophetic Satire in the Hebrew Bible.* BJS 31. Atlanta: Scholars Press, 1995.

———. "Nineveh's 'Three Days' Walk' (Jonah 3:3): Another Interpretation." Pages 42–53 in *On the Way to Nineveh: Studies in Honor of George M. Landes.* Edited by Steven L. Cook and S. C. Winter. ASOR Books 4. Atlanta: Scholars Press, 1999.

Mathews, Kenneth A. *Genesis 1–11:26.* NAC 1A. Nashville: Broadman & Holman, 1996.

McKenzie, Steven L. "The Genre of Jonah." Pages 159–171 in *Seeing Signals, Reading Signs: The Art of Exegesis.* Edited by Mark A. O'Brien and Howard N. Wallace. JSOTSup 415. London: T & T Clark, 2004.

Meredith, Christian. "The Conundrum of חתר in Jonah 1:13." *VT* 61 (2014): 147–152.

Mettinger, Tryggve N. D. *The Eden Narrative: A Literary and Religio-Historical Study of Genesis 2–3.* Winona Lake, IN: Eisenbrauns, 2007.

Miles, John A., Jr. "Laughing at the Bible: Jonah as Parody." *JQR* 65 (1975): 168–181.

Miller, Geoffrey D. "Intertextuality in Old Testament Research." *CBR* 9 (2011): 283–309.

Moberly, R. W. L. "Preaching for a Response? Jonah's Message to the Ninevites Reconsidered." *VT* 53 (2003): 156–168.

Moi, Toril, ed. *The Kristeva Reader.* New York: Columbia University Press, 1986.

Muldoon, Catherine L. *In Defense of Divine Justice: An Intertextual Approach to the Book of Jonah.* CBQMS 47. Washington, DC: Catholic Biblical Association of America, 2010.

Muraoka, Takamitsu. "A Case of Diglossia in the Book of Jonah?" *VT* 62 (2012): 129–131.

Nel, Philip J. "The Symbolism and Function of Epic Space in Jonah." *JNSL* 25 (1999): 215–224.

Nielsen, Kirsten. *There Is Hope for a Tree: The Tree as Metaphor in Isaiah.* JSOTSup 65. Sheffield: JSOT Press, 1989.

Nitzan, Itamar. "Repentance: Between Jonah and Ezekiel" (Hebrew). *Alon Shevut* 161 (2001): 123–135.

Noble, Paul. "Esau, Tamar, and Joseph: Criteria for Identifying Inner-Biblical Allusions." *VT* 52 (2002): 219–252.

Nogalski, James D. *The Book of the Twelve: Hosea–Jonah.* SHBC 18.1. Macon, GA: Smyth & Helwys, 2011.

———. *Literary Precursors to the Book of the Twelve.* BZAW 217. Berlin: de Gruyter, 1993.

———. *Redactional Processes in the Book of the Twelve.* BZAW 218. Berlin: de Gruyter, 1993.

Paul, Shalom M. *Divrei Shalom: Collected Studies of Shalom M. Paul on the Bible and the Ancient Near East, 1967–2005*. CHANE 23. Leiden: Brill, 2005.

——. "Jonah 2:7: The Descent to the Netherworld and Its Mesopotamian Congeners." Pages 131–134 in *Puzzling out the Past: Studies in Northwest Semitic Languages and Literatures in Honor of Bruce Zuckerman*. Edited by Marilyn J. Lundberg, Steven Fine, and Wayne T. Pitard. Leiden: Brill, 2012.

Perry, T. A. "Changing God's Mind: Abraham versus Jonah." Pages 43–52 in *Universalism and Particularism at Sodom and Gomorrah: Essays in Memory of Ron Pirson*. Edited by Diana Lipton. Ancient Israel and Its Literature 11. Atlanta: SBL Press, 2012.

——. *The Honeymoon Is Over: Jonah's Argument with God*. Peabody, MA: Hendrickson, 2006.

Person, Raymond F., Jr. *In Conversation with Jonah: Conversational Analysis, Literary Criticism, and the Book of Jonah*. JSOTSup 220. Sheffield: Sheffield Academic Press, 1996.

——. "The Role of Nonhuman Characters in Jonah." Pages 85–90 in *Exploring Ecological Hermeneutics*. Edited by Norman C. Habel and Peter Trudinger. SBLSymS 46. Atlanta: SBL Press, 2008.

Postell, Seth D. *Adam as Israel: Genesis 1–3 as the Introduction to the Torah and Tanakh*. Cambridge: James Clarke, 2012.

Potgieter, J. Henk. "'David' in Consultation with the Prophets: The Intertextual Relationship of Psalm 31 with the Books of Jonah and Jeremiah." OTE 25 (2012): 115–126.

Pyper, Hugh S. "Swallowed by a Song: Jonah and the Jonah-Psalm through the Looking-Glass." Pages 337–358 in *Reflection and Refraction: Studies in Biblical Historiography in Honour of A. Graeme Auld*. Edited by Robert Rezetko, Timothy H. Lim, and W. Brian Aucker. VTSup 113. Leiden: Brill, 2007.

Riffaterre, Michael. *Semiotics of Poetry*. Advances in Semiotics. Bloomington: Indiana University Press, 1978.

——. "Syllepsis." *Critical Inquiry* 6 (1980): 625–638.

Roberts, J. J. M. "ṢĀPÔN in Job 26:7." *Bib* 56 (1975): 554–557.

Robinson, Bernard P. "Jonah's Qiqayon Plant." ZAW 97 (1985): 390–403.

Robson, James E. "Undercurrents in Jonah." *TynBul* 64 (2013): 189–215.

Rudolph, Wilhelm. *Joel–Amos–Obadja–Jona*. KAT 13.2. Gütersloh: Gerd Mohn, 1971.

Ryu, Chesung J. "Silence as Resistance: A Postcolonial Reading of the Silence of Jonah in Jonah 4.1–11." *JSOT* 34 (2009): 195–218.

Salters, R. B. *Jonah and Lamentations*. OTG. Sheffield: JSOT Press, 1994.

Sasson, Jack M. *Jonah: A New Translation with Introduction, Commentary, and Interpretation*. AB 24B. New York: Doubleday, 1990.

Schapiro, Moshe. *The Book of Yonah: "Journey of the Soul": An Allegorical Commentary Adapted from the Vilna Gaon's Aderes Eliyahu*. Artscroll Judaica Classics. Brooklyn, NY: Mesorah, 1997.

Schart, Aaron. "The Jonah-Narrative within the Book of the Twelve." Pages 109–128 in *Perspectives on the Formation of the Book of the Twelve: Methodological Foundations – Redactional Processes – Historical Insights*. Edited by Rainer Albertz, James D. Nogalski, and Jakob Wöhrle. BZAW 433. Berlin: de Gruyter, 2012.

Schellenberg, Annette. "An Anti-Prophet among the Prophets: On the Relationship of Jonah to Prophecy." *JSOT* 39 (2015): 353–371.

Schmidt, Ludwig. *"De Deo": Studien zur Literarkritik und Theologie des Buches Jona, des Gesprächs zwischen Abraham und [J-ahwe] in Gen 18:22ff. und von Hi 1.* BZAW 143. Berlin: de Gruyter, 1976.

Schoors, A. "The Particle כי." Pages 240–276 in *Remembering All the Way: Collection of Old Testament Studies.* Edited by Bertil Albrektson. OTS 21. Leiden: Brill, 1981.

Seltzer, Arthur J. "Jonah in the Belly of the Great Fish: The Birth of Messiah Ben Joseph." *JNSL* 25 (1999): 187–203.

Sharp, Carolyn. *Irony and Meaning in the Hebrew Bible.* ISBL. Bloomington: Indiana University Press, 2008.

Shemesh, Yael. "'And Many Beasts' (Jonah 4:11): The Function and Status of Animals in the Book of Jonah." *JHS* 10.6 (2010). Online: http://www.jhsonline.org/Articles/article_134.pdf.

Sherwood, Yvonne. *A Biblical Text and Its Afterlives: The Survival of Jonah in Western Culture.* Cambridge: Cambridge University Press, 2000.

Shipp, R. Mark. *Of Dead Kings and Dirges: Myth and Meaning in Isaiah 14:4b–21.* Academia Biblica 11. Atlanta: SBL Press, 2002.

Simon, Uriel. *Jonah: The Traditional Hebrew Text with the New JPS Translation.* JPS Bible Commentary. Philadelphia: Jewish Publication Society, 1999.

Simundson, Daniel J. *Hosea, Joel, Amos, Obadiah, Jonah, Micah.* AOTC. Nashville: Abingdon, 2005.

Sommer, Benjamin D. "Dating Pentateuchal Texts and the Perils of Pseudo-Historicism." Pages 85–108 in *The Pentateuch: International Perspectives on Current Research.* Edited by Thomas B. Dozeman, Konrad Schmid, and Baruch J. Schwartz. FAT 78. Tübingen: Mohr Siebeck, 2011.

———. "Exegesis, Allusion and Intertextuality in the Hebrew Bible: A Response to Lyle Eslinger." *VT* 56 (1996): 479–489.

———. "Is It Good for the Jews? Ambiguity and the Rhetoric of Turning in Isaiah." Pages 321–345 in *Birkat Shalom: Studies in the Bible, Ancient Near Eastern Literature, and Postbiblical Judaism Presented to Shalom M. Paul on the Occasion of His Seventieth Birthday.* Edited by Chaim Cohen et al. Winona Lake, IN: Eisenbrauns, 2008.

———. *A Prophet Reads Scripture: Allusions in Isaiah 40–66.* Contraversions. Stanford, CA: Stanford University Press, 1998.

———. "Reflecting on Moses: The Redaction of Numbers 11." *JBL* 118 (1999): 601–624.

Sternberg, Meir. *Hebrews between Cultures: Group Portraits and National Literature.* ISBL. Bloomington: Indiana University Press, 1998.

———. *The Poetics of Biblical Narrative: Ideological Literature and the Drama of Reading.* ISBL. Bloomington: Indiana University Press, 1987.

Stordalen, T. *Echoes of Eden: Genesis 2–3 and Symbolism of the Eden Garden in Biblical Hebrew Literature.* BBET 25. Leuven, Belgium: Peeters, 2000.

Strawn, Brent A. "On Vomiting: Leviticus, Jonah, Ea(a)rth." *CBQ* 74 (2012): 445–464.

Strazicich, John. *Joel's Use of Scripture and the Scripture's Use of Joel: Appropriation and Resignification in Second Temple Judaism and Early Christianity.* BINS 82. Leiden: Brill, 2007.

Sweeney, Marvin A. *The Twelve Prophets.* Berit Olam. 2 vols. Collegeville, MN: Liturgical Press, 2000.

Timmer, Daniel C. "The Intertextual Israelite Jonah *face à l'empire*: The Post-Colonial Significance of the Book's Cotexts and Purported Neo-Assyrian Context." *JHS* 9.9 (2009). Online: http://www.jhsonline.org/Articles/article_111.pdf.

Trépanier, Benoit. "The Story of Jonas." CBQ 13 (1951): 8–16.

Trible, Phyllis L. *Rhetorical Criticism: Context, Method, and the Book of Jonah*. GBS, OTG. Minneapolis: Augsburg Fortress, 1994.

——. "Studies in the Book of Jonah." Ph.D. diss., Columbia University, 1963.

Tucker, W. Dennis, Jr. *Jonah: A Handbook on the Hebrew Text*. Baylor Handbook on the Hebrew Bible Series. Waco, TX: Baylor University Press, 2006.

Tull, Patricia K. "Intertextuality and the Hebrew Scriptures." *CurBS* 8 (2000): 59–90.

Van Heerden, Willie S. "Humour and the Interpretation of the Book of Jonah." OTE 5 (1992): 389–401.

Vanoni, Gottfried. *Das Buch Jona: Literar- und formkritische Untersuchung*. ATSAT 7. St. Ottilien: EOS, 1978.

——. "Elija, Jona und das Dodekapropheton: Grade der Intertextualität." Pages 113–121 in *Wort [J-HWHs], das geschah . . . " (Hos 1,1): Studien zum Zwölfprophetenbuch*. Herders Biblische Studien 35. Freiburg: Herder, 2002.

Van Wolde, Ellen. "Texts in Dialogue with Texts: Intertextuality in the Ruth and Tamar Narratives." *BibInt* 5 (1997): 1–28.

——. "Trendy Intertextuality." Pages 43–49 in *Intertextuality in Biblical Writings: Essays in Honour of Bas van Iersel*. Edited by Spike Draisma. Kampen: J. H. Kok, 1989.

Weber, Beat. *Jona: Der widerspenstige Prophet und der gnädige Gott*. Biblische Gestalten 27. Leipzig: Evangelische Verlagsanstalt, 2012.

Weimar, Peter. *Eine Geschichte voller Überraschungen: Annäherungen an die Jonaerzählung*. SBS 217. Stuttgart: Katholisches Bibelwerk, 2009.

Wenham, Gordon J. *Genesis 1–15*. WBC 1. Waco, TX: Word Books, 1987.

Wildberger, Hans. *Isaiah 13–27*. CC. Minneapolis: Augsburg Fortress, 1977.

Wilson, Ian D. "Tyre, a Ship: The Metaphorical World of Ezekiel 27 in Ancient Judah." ZAW 125 (2013): 249–262.

Witzenrath, Hagia. *Das Buch Jona: Eine literature-wissenchaftliche Untersuchung*. ATSAT 6. St. Ottilien: EOS, 1978.

Wöhrle, Jakob. "A Prophetic Reflection on Divine Forgiveness: The Integration of the Book of Jonah into the Book of the Twelve." JHS 9.7 (2009). Online: http://www .jhsonline.org/Articles/article_109.pdf.

Wolff, Hans W. *Obadiah and Jonah: A Commentary*. Translated by Margaret Kohl. CC. Minneapolis: Augsburg, 1986.

——. *Studien zum Jonabuch: Mit einem Anhang von Jörg Jeremias: Das Jonabuch in der Forschung seit Hans Walter Wolff*. Neukirchen-Vluyn: Neukirchener, 2003.

Wright, Christopher J. H. "God, Names of." Pages 504–509 in vol. 2 of *International Standard Bible Encyclopedia*. Edited by G. W. Bromiley. 4 vols. Grand Rapids, MI: Eerdmans, 1979–1988.

Zakovitch, Yair. "Through the Looking Glass: Reflections/Inversions of Genesis Stories in the Bible." *BibInt* 1 (1993): 139–152.

Zlotowitz, Meir. *The Twelve Prophets: Yonah/Jonah: A New Translation with a Commentary Anthologized from Midrashic and Rabbinic Sources*. Artscroll Tanach Series. Brooklyn, NY: Mesorah, 1978.

YITZHAK BERGER

is Associate Professor and Head of the Hebrew Division at Hunter College of the City University of New York. He received his Ph.D. from Yeshiva University. His published work focuses on the literary study of the Bible and on medieval biblical interpretation.